NATIVE AMERICAN HERBALIST

Discover the Oldest Natural Remedies and Herbal Healing Recipes to Improve Your Health with Inexpensive and Easy-to-find Herbs.

Felicia Loparon

TABLE OF CONTENTS

NATIVE AMERICAN HERBALISM ENCYCLOPEDIA

Introduction

Naturopathic medicine, the sister profession of Traditional Chinese Medicine, is a form of holistic healing that goes one step further by also including herbs from the native tradition. This book will talk about naturopathic medicine's history in Native American herbalism and how it has shaped the practice. We'll also explain how you can use plants in your herbal remedies alongside other natural healing modalities to promote a stronger, healthier body and mind. Native American traditional medicines have been used for millennia according to passed down oral traditions among tribes and families. These medicines were used to cure illnesses like aches and pains, colds, flu, skin ailments, and many more. As society has become more industrialized and health care has become less accessible, many people have found it difficult to treat themselves using native medicines over the ever-growing pharmaceutical industry. Not only that but these medicines were passed down orally, which made it difficult for researchers to access them.

This awareness of Native American herbalism is essential for understanding naturopathic medicine today. We'll be looking at how this knowledge is used by naturopaths today to create effective natural remedies for modern-day ailments.

Naturopathic medicine is a relatively new profession that didn't exist until the late 19th century. In the beginning, most medical practitioners used a more comprehensive approach to treating patients based on modern-day science and technology. However, as society became more industrialized and medicine became more expensive, many people left medicine because of its rising costs. That prompted an alternative approach that was less invasive and more affordable to treat patients at home. Today, this alternative treatment model of naturopathy is called 'holistic,' which integrates new-age healing techniques like herbs and acupuncture alongside traditional Chinese and Ayurvedic healing methods.

The rise of naturopathic medicine saw the integration of herbal medicine methods. They have become almost like conventional medicine today, where prescription drugs aren't used as often. The fact that herbs are very effective at curing common illnesses, precisely the types of ailments treated with pharmaceuticals, makes herbs a popular choice for naturopathic patients. It's a win-win situation where the patient gets a more holistic approach to treatment with fewer side effects and no drug dependency. In addition, the practitioner gains experience by treating patients with various conditions.

Naturopathic medicine wasn't born as a profession. The use of herbs in naturopathy can be traced back to Europe in the early 1900s when it became popular among alternative healthcare practitioners. The practice was eventually adopted by American naturopathic schools, especially after passing the NPLEX licensing exam in 1971. Until the 1980s, the profession took off in America, with several naturopathic schools offering licensure exams to students.

Graduates are now registered with different state boards to practice naturopathic medicine in either conventional treatment or as part of a holistic approach.

The partnership between native Americans and native doctors is an exciting story that has been around for thousands of years.

Origin of Native American Herbalism

What Is Herbalism?

Native Americans have been around since the beginning of time, and they still exist today. They are a group of people that identify themselves with a specific tribe, and an individual must be born into the tribe to become one. This type of society is different from others because it was developed by people instead of by someone else. They were led by spiritual leaders such as shamans, who used plants and other natural materials to treat diseases and cure ailments. They could cure and treat illnesses because they had a connection with the earth and natural materials. In addition, they could communicate with these natural items, using this for their medicinal purposes. The Native American people believe that the earth is a sacred place devoted to their creator, and it is where they live, hunt, and protect. They believe that they must take care of the earth because the creator created it for them to use as they please. The Native Americans' lifestyle was based on how the earth was formed; everything that happened in nature was affected by the environment.

Native Americans' medicine is usually made up of plants, roots, bushes, and other natural materials like tree bark. Before they start making their medicine, they pray to their creator. The Native American people believe that the plants were given to them by the creator, who wanted them to use them for medicinal purposes. They believe that plants are beneficial in treating diseases, so they use them for that purpose. To make their medicine, they gather whatever plants are available and all the other items they need before they start using them. The Native American people do this to make their medicine well organized. This way, when it comes time for them to use these natural materials in making their medicine, at least one material will already be prepared. The Native Americans typically use the plants to prepare their remedies, but if they cannot harvest something, the medicines are also made up of substances obtained from animals. This way, it can treat illnesses and diseases just like plants can. The natives themselves put together the Native American plants for medicinal purposes. The medicine is usually made up of two different plants; they would use one plant to cure an ailment and one plant to prevent an ailment. Either type can be used depending on what disease or illness is being treated or controlled under any given conditions. The treatment for ailments usually consists of drinking liquid with its medicine. Sometimes, the treatment is meant to be inhaled. The most common diseases cured by the medicine are infections like colds, sore throats, fevers, and headaches. They would drink this medicine to cure their ailments, and they believed if they didn't use it immediately when they got sick, it would result in something worse than their original condition.

The Indigenous People of North America

The relationship between indigenous people of North America and the plants has been viewed in many different ways over time, but its importance is largely unappreciated. Many scholars argue that this relationship is rooted in the fact that Native Americans had to rely on the plants for survival. However, some say that this dependence had more to do with sharing their culture than food or medicine.

This book will explore how these two groups relate to one another through their interactions. I will discuss how the plants have influenced these indigenous people, whose interactions have shaped their culture. I will also discuss how their interactions with the plants are tied to their spirituality and belief systems. However, no matter how meaningful this relationship is to these indigenous people, it has not been reflected in the wider American society until recently.

Both indigenous people of North America and plants are considered sacred. That has inspired many to see the two groups as one in terms of spirituality and religion. One example of this would be that Native Americans believe that plants are alive with spirit, thereby making them sacred. That is because anything that can live can be considered sacred if it has spirit. Therefore, that is what makes plants sacred. This same concept applies to plants since they are living organisms with spirit. Consequently, plants can be considered sacred because of this. Therefore, plants are seen as more than just food or medicine by Native Americans, making them an integral part of their spirituality and religion.

Many scholars argue that this bond between plants and Native Americans is rooted in the fact that Native Americans had to rely on the plants for survival. However, as discussed before, some say that this dependence had more to do with sharing their culture than purely food or medicine. The idea that plants and these indigenous people shaped one another is not a new concept. Many believe that plants are necessary as food and medicine to survive. That is why they see the bond between the two as important. This bond becomes more important when considering its ties to survival.

The Original Native Americans Beliefs and Traditions for Using Herbs

Ceremony plays a vital role in the well-being of Native American people and healing. The healing process often involves not only the patient and the healer but also the patient's family and the entire community. Participants can support the patient by caring for their physical body with a place to stay while recovering from an illness or with food. It could mean participation in songs, prayer, music, and dance to lend their healing energy to the patient.

Ceremonies generally include a feast to feed the friends, relatives, and healers who have come to help the person. Healing rites strengthen everyone attending by linking them to their origins and reaffirming their commitment to tradition. Feeling connected to a support network of family, friends, and community helps prevent illness and speed recovery. When people have a ceremony done for them, it relaxes their body, relaxes their mind, and takes them into another world for a while as their physical body undergoes healing.

Since Native American culture sees the body and spirit as intertwined, many healing prescriptions include medicine for the body and a ceremony to help re-align the afflicted person's spirit. Native American healers use a variety of ceremonies when treating their patients.

Sweat Lodge

The sweat lodge is a cleansing, and regenerative experience likened to a rebirth, often compared with the womb of Mother Earth. The lodge honors the process of transformation and healing and is a widely accepted way of purifying people undergoing transformation. Attending a sweat lodge for healing is part of the detoxification process when curing an illness. It can be helpful when healing both physical and emotional disorders. In addition, a sweat lodge is the opportunity to pray, speak, and ask for forgiveness from the Creator and other people attending the club.

The cleansing heat of the sweat lodge increases the body temperature, which helps to increase the enzymatic activity in the body. This increased enzymatic activity helps the body destroy viruses and bacteria while stimulating immune function. As the body temperature rises, the endocrine glandular function is stimulated, cleansing and improving the body functions.

Sweating opens clogged pores, which allows the skin to detoxify by eliminating internal toxins, heavy metals, and metabolic by-products. The heat dilates the blood vessels and capillaries, stimulating increased blood flow to the skin and helping the organs to flush any toxins. Removing toxins and other waste products helps to improve metabolic function, circulation, digestion, and absorption of nutrients.

The moist air inside the lodge helps to improve lung function, dilating clogged respiratory passages and helping minor respiratory problems and colds. In addition, the steam from pouring water on the hot rocks releases negative ions. Positive ions are associated with tension and fatigue, allergies, rheumatism, arthritis, insomnia, and asthma. Increasing the negative ions in the air helps to combat these issues.

Sweat lodges are constructed using materials found in the local environment. Some lodges are underground and accessed by a ladder into a space hollowed out from the ground. In the north, the communities will commonly construct their sweat lodges from ice bricks, similar to an igloo in the winter. The most common kind of lodge is a low, domed hut made from willow branches or another tree with slender branches or saplings that are flexible. Traditionally, the sweat lodge is circular, therefore, sacred in Native American culture. The circle symbolizes the interconnectedness of all living things and the creator and the connection between life and death.

Before building the sweat lodge, the medicine man will choose a location. Sometimes a community will have a permanent space used for the sweat lodge. If possible, build the lodge near a stream, lake, river, or ocean. This way, there will be a convenient water source for cooling the body after being in the lodge.

Sweat lodges hold 10-15 people. First, the medicine man will draw a large circle, about 10 feet in diameter, on the ground, and the poles or saplings will be fastened around this circle. The saplings need to be long enough so that when they are bent towards the center of the lodge and tied, the roof of the lodge will be about 2-4 feet high, and people can sit comfortably inside. A pit at the very center of the structure, about two feet deep and 2-3 feet wide, is the space for placing the heated rocks.

Since the cardinal directions play an essential role in much of Native American spirituality, usually the lodge door faces a particular direction, often east, but this may change depending on the ceremony. The placement of a fire outside the lodge and seating within the lodge is also oriented to connect the participants with the spirit world.

Blankets, animal skins, or canvas sheets cover the lodge frame so that the inside will be completely dark, even during the day.

Outside the sweat lodge door, another pit will hold fire for heating the rocks before bringing them inside. An offering is made, usually tobacco, to the fire once it is lit. One person will be the guardian of the fire and ensure that the fire stays lit and rocks are hot and ready for passing into the sweat lodge when needed. The door to the lodge should be kept closed as much as possible since the heat and the dark are essential. There is no fire inside the lodge since the smoke coming off a fire in a small space would not be desirable for the participants' health, and the fire inside the lodge would also create light, which is not desirable in this ceremony.

Vision Quest

The vision quest is a healing ritual where the individual removes themselves from their daily activities and enters a space where they can focus on spiritual pursuits and internal self-reflection. It is often a journey taken alone to experience remarkable personal growth. The quest begins with a purification ceremony, and then the person enters a meditative state or goes on a physical journey to gain insight into their life.

In one version of a vision quest, the medicine man will select an area and mark out a circle of sacred space. The quester will stay in the same holy circle throughout their vision quest. Another version of a vision quest is to have the quester go out into the woods or desert and fend for themself for a predetermined amount of time.

Either way, the vision quest is a period of social isolation. The quester will be isolated for a night, a few days, or a week. The idea is to remove outside stimulation and allow the person to focus on internal or spiritual elements. Often, the quester will be required to refrain from eating during the quest or will only be permitted to eat or drink food they can obtain from their immediate environment. The deprivation of food and water can also bring on a heightened awareness where the person is more open to receiving messages from the spirits. Often, this type of ceremony is a coming-of-age ceremony, but those suffering from an ailment and need guidance or help from the Great Spirit can also use it.

People seeking their path and purpose in life often do the vision quest, and in many traditions, it is a coming-of-age ceremony for young men who must prove that they can stand on their own without help from their elders.

In most traditions, like a sweat lodge, a medicine man who has meditated on the spot to ensure the suitable ceremony space generally chooses a quest site. If the quester is to stay in one place for the duration of the vision quest, then the area will be marked out using the stones and colors of a medicine wheel. The area is smudged, and offerings are given to the site while prayers are said. The person will remain inside the circle for the duration of the quest and bring enough firewood to last them for the entire time. The person on the vision quest will get a drum into the circle or have some other form of raising the alarm if they need help urgently.

While the person is inside the vision quest circle, they will spend their time praying and conversing with the Great Spirit and their spirit guides while meditating on the question that they need an answer to or asking for help with a specific problem or ailment.

Smudging Ceremony

Smudging is a way to 'wash' oneself and purify people, ceremonial grounds, homes, sacred objects, or send messages to the Great Spirit. Various mixtures of herbs and grasses are used for this ceremony, but sage, cedar, juniper, lavender, wormwood, and sweetgrass are the most common. The mixture used will depend on the specific healing process or ceremony requirement.

The act of smudging demarcates the ceremonial time, marking that from this time forward, everything is sacred. In addition, smudging clears negative influences and restores balance.

- **Cedar**: Attracts good spirits and eliminates negative energy. It also enhances courage in difficult times.

- **Juniper**: Fights bad magic and negative influences.

- **Lavender**: Used when the ceremony requires participants to relax or sleep.

- **Mugwort**: Brings clarity and develops or deepens psychic abilities.

- **Rosemary**: A powerful cleanser for the home and the aura.

- **Sage**: Used to clear negative energy from a place or a person.

- **Sweetgrass**: It is used to symbolize the hair of Mother Earth and is often braided. It welcomes the good spirits and good energies to an area.

When smudging, place the dried herb in a bowl, a large shell, or another container and ignite it. Alternatively, create a smudge stick by bundling herbs together with string and burning one end. The flame is extinguished, allowing the herbs to smolder, and then the smoke rises and is fanned with a hand or a feather. The medicine man will say prayers while the smoke is wafting. Finally, the participants can spend the time silently calling on the Great Spirit to accompany them in the upcoming ceremony.

Blessing Way

The Blessing Way is traditionally Navajo. The aim of the blessing way is to restore harmony, balance, or equilibrium to an individual, family, clan, community, nation, or the universe in general. The blessing way ceremony is a chant, song, or dance, and the ceremony traditionally lasts for two days but is often part of a more extended ceremony or rite.
Most Navajo people will experience all or part of the blessing way ceremony four times throughout their lives. It is performed on pregnant women to prevent pregnancy complications, as part of a girl's puberty rites, at a marriage, and when preparing to have a child. The ceremony helps to restore a person's balance. The blessing way promotes spiritual, psychological, physical, and emotional harmony. It reminds people that goodness surrounds them, and goodness is accessible to them when they have their lives in balance.
The purpose of the blessing way is not to cure illness but to invoke positive blessings and avert misfortune during times of change. Another use of the blessing way is to bless and protect a home or a community. It is a highly spiritual, sacred, and private event.

The Native American Spiritual Healing Methods and Rituals

From the viewpoint of Native American people, physical, emotional, or spiritual trauma can lead to various mental and emotional distresses, loss of soul, or loss of spiritual power, which leads to disease. Therefore, the healer must use ritual and other healing methods to return the soul and strength to the patient. In these cases, the patient receives cleansing and healing to restart their lives traditionally.

Healers and medicine men have several procedures available to them for diagnosing issues. The method of diagnosis varies from healer to healer. Generally, it will start with discussing the patient about their symptoms and personal and family history. The healer will also use a variety of non-verbal cues that they learn through years of practice, like posture and medical divination.

The energy of the Great Spirit and the medicine man work through and with the energy of the crystal or pendulum to help with the patient's diagnosis.

When diagnosing, medicine men use their senses and intuition to assess a patient before choosing a remedy or therapy. Over years and practice, they can often assess the patient's needs very quickly by watching for signs unknowingly transmitted by the person, including how the patient sits, eye contact, skin feeling, and breathing quality. In addition, the body relays various signals when it is unwell, which can help guide the medicine man towards the correct treatment.

Dowsing

Dowsing is a form of diagnosis used to detect physical and spiritual imbalance. Many Native Americans dowse using the feather from the wing of a predator bird, ideally an eagle. Federal rulings in the United States allow Native Americans to wear, give, or loan eagle feathers for religious and cultural purposes even though the bird is a protected species. Check the regulations in your area. Hawk feathers are also used, and hawks are just one step below eagles in the hierarchy of animals.

One end of the feather is dressed with leather bands and tassels for dowsing to give it the correct balance. The healer balances the dowsing feather gently on his forefinger parallel to the patient's body. The feather slowly passes along the body's meridian lines, up the legs, up the arms, up the torso, and over the head. The feather will remain balanced where there is no issue. If there is an imbalance in the body, then the feather will waver on the finger of the medicine man and will dip down towards the body in the area where the imbalance lies.

The imbalance may indicate tissue damage such as bruising or an internal problem. In such cases, dowsing can do no more than indicate the problem area and give the medicine man an idea of where to start investigating the background issue.

Drumming

Drumming is a common tool used in shamanic work or ceremony since the rhythm of the drum can cause a sense of altered consciousness to enter the spirit world. In Native American healing, the drum's resonance is similarly used for its resonance to how dowsing is used. The healer beats as it passes along the skeletal lines of the body. The medicine man listens to the drum's vibration, and experienced healers can hear the difference in tone as different parts of the body are passed, indicating areas that should be explored further.

Drumming can also help to rebalance internal areas by providing resonance, which stimulates organ activity similar to the cupping movement used in massage in Western complementary therapy.

Pendulum

Using a pendulum is another way to help the healer determine which area(s) of the body needs more attention. A healer will create a pendulum by attaching an object, sometimes a metal object that belongs to the patient or a crystal, on a thread or rope and moving slowly along the patient's body. An experienced healer will be able to determine which areas require further investigation based on how the pendulum moves.

Another way of using a pendulum is to ask yes/no questions. The pendulum will be able to divine the answer and will, for example, swing back and forth for yes or swing in a circle for no. This type of divination helps to determine the origin of the patient's problem and determines whether a specific remedy will work for the patient or not.

Crystals

Healers use crystals for their healing properties. Before using crystals, the healer will purify them because crystals can hold energies they meet. Dowsing with an eagle feather, as described above, can be used to determine if a crystal needs to be purified. When passing an eagle feather over the crystal, if it rises, the crystal is clean and can be used; if it dips, then the crystal contains negative energy and must be purified. The preferred method of purifying crystals is to smudge them with sage, place them in spring water, and finally dry them under the light of a full moon.

One of the most honored crystals in many Native American cultures in the southwest regions of the United States is turquoise, which possesses hidden truth and causes those holding it to speak the truth.

Dream Analysis

Diagnosis of a patient often includes the analysis of their dreams. Dreams can provide people with insight into their issues or even future visions.

In Native American cultures, dreams are highly regarded. When people are asleep, they can speak directly with the Great Spirit or with their ancestors without daily life distractions. The medicine man will often ask the patient what they have seen in their dreams while feeling unwell, or sometimes he will ask the Great Spirit to come to him in his dreams regarding an ailment with which they are helping a patient.

Ignoring dreams were said to be madness and destined to result in disaster since it went against the gods' wishes.

Some people in the community are trained to interpret dreams and provide that service to the community. An important part of dream analysis is dream sharing, where a person tells others about their dream, and the dream interpreter explains all of the elements of the dream so that all understand the deeper meaning of the dream. Many nations regard dreams very highly, including the Iroquois. The dreams would guide all parts of life, from hunting to marriage and even battle. If one of the clan members has a goal about failure on the night before a battle, then the entire army will forfeit the battle and not fight because they will be destined to lose the fight.

There is a story about Chief Completer of the Seneca Iroquois. One night, he had a dream that he could not interpret. He told others about his dream, and they interpreted it as meaning that he needed to change his name and give up his chieftainship. He immediately gave up his chieftainship and never regretted the decision since the Great Spirit mandated it.

Some dream rituals involve fasting for up to 30 days in the hope of having a very powerful dream during a festival. The Iroquois people would wear wooden masks during a ceremony to invoke the dream world.

How Can We Implement Their Valuable Knowledge in Our Modern Lives to Enhance Our Everyday Wellbeing?

Since ancient times herbalism has been an integral part of the medicinal world for curing diseases, including mild fever, cold, cough, and flu, to severe infections and allergies. Native Americans still believe in these traditional herbal tactics, but most of the population now incorporates modern medicines in their conventional health treatment mechanisms. Thus, their healing beliefs and health practices are diverting their way. But the fact is that herbal treatment has always successfully secured a unique place in the medicinal world with astonishing outcomes. For this reason, the importance of herbalism is inevitable. Modern medicines are based on individualistic and mechanistic approaches, which are very helpful in fast recovery from mild to chronic illness. Still, it is a general trend that people are more inclined toward herbal treatment, and the popularity of these natural remedies is increasing with each passing day. Because of the positive record of encouraging and healthy benefits of herbal products, the general public trusts more natural treatment than chemically synthesized allopathic formulas. Much research and progress have been made in herbalism in the past few decades. Several research studies and clinical trials have proved herbal remedies' positive and healthy impact. Many websites refer to different manufacturers' available Native American terms for their herbal remedies.

The Native Americans are now integrating herbal healing circles into modern practices prevalent in community centers. The basic herbal treatment rules are the same; however, the discussion subjects have been changed to current issues. A historian in California traveled to learn about the NA - Native American tribes and composed a considerable account. Although most Native American tribes have moved to urban areas, they still believe in their traditional healing system. They consider natural herbal remedies the best alternative to modern health treatment systems and are very concerned about their cultural heritage of herbal treatments and identity. But with the changing demands of time, health-related issues are also varying. For example, diabetes and such chronic diseases were non-existent among the Native Americans around 1000 years ago; but now, such diseases are rapidly spreading.

This rapidly increasing diabetes incidence may be due to the modern way of work, less physical activity, and consumption of highly processed food. Many research studies have shown that if Native American tribes return to their traditional herbal diet like fruits, wild grains, and root vegetables, the adverse effects of various metabolic disorders can be reversed. But there is a difficulty: different tribes have varying beliefs about such diseases. For example, people of the Navajo tribe believe that diabetes is caused by disharmony and other influences, like white people. On the other hand, the people of northern Utes take diabetes as an entity taking possession of the people compelling them to do evil things. However, ancient native tribes in America believed illness was brought by deviance from the traditional ways.

But it will be correct to say that herbalism has been a staunch part of the medical world. Herbal medicines are composed of active ingredients, many of which are still unknown. Still, herbal physicians believe that these active agents will be more effective using the plants instead of using isolated versions of these active compounds. According to them, the effect of using the whole plant is more significant than their parts. However, critical to these herbal treatments argue that sometimes it becomes challenging to prescribe the measured dose of any specific ingredient.

Herbal medicines play an essential role in maintaining the human body's natural balance. Different herbs react differently to body systems. Very commonly, some herbs can be prescribed to treat common ailments such as cough, cold, or flu. However, some available herbs require caution because their dose above the optimal amount may cause undesirable side effects, showing that herbalism is a separate medical discipline. We should be an expert on herbalism before prescribing any medicine to the patient, as the concept of taking the herbal medicines completely safe is not correct.

However, to emphasize the importance of herbal medicines, a few examples are quoted here. For example, the Echinacea herb stimulates the immune system, helpful in resisting various infections, and treats ailments like fever, herpes, and boils. The Dong Quai herbs are used to cure premenstrual tensions, period pain, and symptoms of menopause. It also helps lower high blood pressure. Garlic is an abundant plant to deal with high cholesterol levels, thus protecting from heart diseases and an excellent antioxidant. It is also very beneficial for dealing with several respiratory infections, colds, fever, and coughs. Ginger helps treat nausea and motion sickness. Ginkgo Biloba herb helps maintain the circulatory system of the body and tinnitus. Ginseng herb is used to treat fatigue, high blood pressure, and high cholesterol. Hypericum herb is an excellent antidepressant. This herb is used by various pharmaceutical companies in their anti-depression pills; it is also handy to deal with insomnia and anxiety. But where herbal medicines have many benefits, some adverse effects are also associated with their excessive use. Therefore, we should not use any medicine without proper prescription and instruction by our physicians. Always purchase the medicines from a pharmacist with a good market reputation and see the composition on the label wrap of herbal products. Pay attention to the dosage and consult your doctor if any irritating reaction is felt.

Choosing Herbs as a Treatment

Native American medicine is a complete framework that balances every sphere of our lives, including lifestyle and social interactions with our inner world. Native medicine assumes that the roots of every imbalance lie in the divine realm. In the course of every recovery procedure, spiritual approaches are vital. Clinical systems are clearly and uniquely tailored for the patient, including fees and rates. As part of the healing method, they require the process of fee negotiation. The Healing Elder seems to have the most healing strength, and the elder practitioner loses his prestige as a powerful healer when treatment fails. The person who needs healing makes a proposition to the medicine man and waits to see if it is approved. Face-to-face, they rarely negotiate. The customer leaves the bid outside the healer's door, and if it remains there till the morning, it means that it has not been approved, and we can go somewhere else. Once they understand, therapy will, for example, start with a behavioral prescription, a pledge, a selfless act, genuine repentance, or scaling a holy mountain. Techniques include self-inquiry and discovery to ascertain whether there is a need for a dietary improvement, prayer, herbs, massage, a sweat lodge ritual, or a vision quest.

What Are Herbs?

Herbs are plants that can be used for their medicinal qualities. They're often found in gardens alongside vegetables, spices, and other fruits like strawberries, peaches, and apples.

Many people grow herbs because they enjoy their taste or scent or want to learn more about herbalism—the art of using plants for wellness. Some people use them to help cook or create things like soaps and candles. And many still use them today in the traditions of folk medicine.

Herbs can grow from seeds, rhizomes, tubers, bulbs, roots, and cuttings. The flowers of some herbs are edible, while others have a bitter taste. Herbal remedies that include aerial parts of the plant, such as leaves and flowers, are called 'infusions,' while those that also use hard parts of the plant are called 'decoctions.' Herbal oils can be made from leaves and flowers.

In India and countries where "Ayurveda" is followed, herbs are used for both cooking and medicines to cure illnesses.

Herbs are most often defined as plants with culinary, medical, and aromatic properties. These plants may be harvested to be used fresh or dried and stored for later use. Most originate from the Mediterranean region, Europe, and Asia. There are two groups of herbs, annuals and perennials. Annual herbs grow for one season only before dying off; perennial herbs live another year after the first season's growth is complete.

However, not all edible plants are classified as 'herbs.' For example, garlic is a root rather than an herb despite its culinary uses.

The botanical classification can be determined by looking at its leaves, stem, roots, seeds, flowers, or fruit. Herbs are usually classified into three main groups based on these tissue parts: the roots (also called the rhizome), stems (also called the xylem), and leaves (also called the bracts).

Herbaceous plants are defined as those which have stems to support flowers or fruits. They are mainly found in forests and grasslands. The characteristics of herbaceous plants include having no permanent woody parts except for woody buds at their bases. Herbs also tend to have vascular bundles that grow to support the stem throughout the plant's life.

The stem is the main organ in which leaves are produced. The leaves are also referred to as bracts in the case of herbs that have them. These bracts are usually simple in shape, do not have any veins or stipules, and often have blades with smooth edges. The cells of herbaceous plants are generally rectangular or polygonal.

Herbaceous plants go through the process of sexual and asexual reproduction. Asexual reproduction refers to plants producing offspring by themselves, while sexual reproduction refers to plants producing offspring only when another plant has pollinated them.

The roots of herbaceous plants serve as anchors to attach themselves to the ground. They are also responsible for anchoring the leaves in place while the stem supports the flowers produced on top of them. Herbaceous plants generally have a single taproot with numerous lateral roots attached. Their root systems include corms, bulbils, rhizomes, and tubers.

Plants grown for medicinal or aromatic uses tend to have very different characteristics from those used for culinary uses.

Medicinal herbs tend to have taproots no deeper than 10 inches. In contrast, culinary herbs have deeper taproots that can grow as deep as 30 inches below the soil surface. In addition, medicinal herbs usually grow from a single root system with no noticeable secondary roots. That makes it easy for the herb to be removed from the ground during harvest. On the other hand, culinary herbs tend to have a larger and more complex root system composed of secondary roots and several minor roots growing off these secondary roots.

Several different floral structures have been identified as being characteristic of culinary herbs. These include:

The seeds of herbaceous plants are also the basis for asexual reproduction. The seeds consist of a large number of cells surrounding an ovary. The ovary is often paired with a parietal placenta composed of several layers that may contain endosperm, chalaza, and an embryo. The seeds are not viable for germination in culinary herbs unless adequately dried and stored at the proper moisture levels required for survival in nature. That makes it necessary to harvest these plants at their flowering stage rather than waiting until they have produced seeds to make them harvestable.

Herbs are typically defined in two ways: either by using characteristics such as taste and odor or by looking at the tissue parts in the plant. Plants that look like herbs but do not taste or smell like them can still be considered herbs because they share other characteristics, such as their growth pattern and reproduction process. That is especially true when comparing different types of plants. In addition, some plants that are generally considered non-herbs may become herbs based on how they're used to produce food, medicine, or aromas. For example, garlic is viewed as a root and not an herb because of its lack of tastiness and odor. However, garlic can still be defined as an herb because it produces aromatic compounds in food.

Herbs are generally defined according to their botanical characteristics in food, medicine, or perfume. The botany of these plants allows us to classify them based on their growth patterns, aromas and uses.

Although we often use the terms "herbs" and "plants" interchangeably as they have medicinal and culinary uses in most cases, they are in themselves very different. Whereas herbs are usually considered to be perennials, plants are annuals. Plants also have a vascular system, while herbs possess none. Plants contain seeds, while herbs do not.

Herbs are often used to make beverages, condiments (especially vinegar or oils), perfumes, and spices. Medicinal herbs are used as remedies to treat various illnesses to be applied externally or taken internally and prepared from herbs that have been dried or extracted. Herbal preparations are then mixed with other ingredients to create the desired remedy for particular illnesses, injuries, conditions, etc. The primary purpose of herbal remedies is generally to relieve certain types of pain and block the effects of other body processes that cause illness. Herbs are known to provide benefits that conventional medicines can't.

Herbs are also used to flavor food and beverages. Culinary herbs generally produce their oils and aromas when heated. These oils and aromas add flavor to the food while the heat releases them into the air. Herbs used for culinary tastes include rosemary, sage, oregano, parsley, bay leaf, rose petals, lavender, mints, thyme, chives, garlic, or onion, among many others.

Where Can We Find Herbs?

Herbs are one of the most multipurpose ingredients in cooking. Most have a natural cleansing and revitalizing effect on the digestive system, making them great for people looking to eat healthier without sacrificing flavor. They also come in handy for disease prevention and treatment and are easy to grow in the home. Here are some tips for growing herbs.

There are two different ways to start herb gardens. The first is to plant seeds directly in the garden or window sill in early spring (before the ground thaws). This method can get crowded quickly and can be difficult if you have a lot of plants or if you don't have a green thumb or time to grow your plants from seeds or seedlings. The second way is by starting roots from seedlings, which takes a little more planning and work but has much less competition for resources and room. Also, you can start with a limited number of plants in the early stages.

Some herbs like to be spread by runners, and some (like parsley) prefer to sprawl. Try both ways and find the one that works best for your situation.

Choose plants that are well adapted to your area. You can also avoid invasive species and just grow native species that tolerate your climate. This way, you won't have to worry about future non-native species import because gardeners will grow them natively.

Most of the herbs you will use are worth growing yourself. Although proper wildcrafting is the best choice, it takes time.

Here are 11 plants you might consider growing yourself. They are relatively easy to grow, especially from plants rather than seeds; they are all quite common and inexpensive.

1. **Garlic**: infection fighter, stimulant

2. **Rosemary**: cancer-fighting antioxidants, stimulant

3. **Basil**: antioxidants, infection fighter

4. **Mint**: stimulant, digestive

5. **Lemon balm**: relaxing tonic for mild depression, irritability, anxiety

6. **Fennel**: anti-inflammatory, analgesic, appetite stimulant, anti-flatulent

7. **Lovage**: respiratory and digestive tonic, anti-bronchitis

8. **Oregano**: antiseptic, anti-flatulent, stimulate bile and stomach acid, anti-asthmatic

9. **Cilantro (coriander)**: to treat flatulence, bloating, and cramps; breath sweetener

10. **Horseradish**: promote perspiring, stimulant

11. **Thyme**: tea for preventing altitude sickness, antiseptic, inhalant (anti-asthmatic), stimulant

Common Ailments We Can Treat with Herbal Remedies

With proper guidance, minor ailments can be dealt with easily using herbal remedies instead of being exposed to harsh medicine right away.

Allergies

Allergies are immunological reactions to a common material, including cat dander, pollen, and abnormal dust. Food, beverages, and the environment contain allergens, making it impossible to avoid them entirely. Herbal therapies are much milder than conventional treatments, which inhibit your body's immunological reaction to allergens that harm you.

Feverfew-Peppermint Tincture

During an allergic attack, feverfew or peppermint clear up the airways. If you can't have feverfew, prepare this tincture using just peppermint. The tincture will last up to 7 years in a cold, dark location.

Ingredients:

- 6 ounces dry peppermint

- 2 ounces dry feverfew

- 2 cups vodka, 80 proof, unflavored

Directions:

1. Combine the feverfew or peppermint in a sterilized pint jar and top up the jar with vodka.

2. Close the jar tightly and shake it properly. During 6 to 8 weeks, keep it in a cold, dark cabinet or shake it many times a week.

3. Soak a sheet of cheesecloth in water and lay it over the funnel's mouth. Pour the tincture into another sterilized pint jar using the funnel. Remove the moisture from the herbs by wringing them out. Transfer the completed medicine to dark-colored glass bottles after discarding the wasted herbs.

4. When allergy symptoms flare up, use five drops orally. If the flavor is too intense for you, combine it with some water or juice to consume it.

Caution:

If you are sensitive to ragweed, do not take feverfew. Avoid during pregnancy and breastfeeding.

Garlic-Ginkgo Syrup

Ginkgo Biloba is a potent antihistamine with over a dozen anti-inflammatory components, while garlic helps to strengthen your immune system. If possible, use local honey since it may aid in the development of tolerance to allergies prevalent in your region. When refrigerated, this syrup will last up to 6 months.

Ingredients:

- 2 ounces chopped fresh and freeze-dried garlic

- 2 ounces crushed or chopped Ginkgo Biloba

- 2 cups water

- 1 cup honey from the area

Directions:

1. Combine the garlic, Ginkgo Biloba, and water in a saucepan. Decrease the fluid by half by bringing it to a low simmer and partly covering it with a lid.

2. Pour the saucepan mixture into a glass measuring cup and put the contents back into the saucepan through a wet piece of cheesecloth, squeezing the cheesecloth until there is no more liquid. Note how many ounces of liquid you have because you will need at least half of this amount of the honey to stir in to preserve well.

3. Stir in the honey and reheat at low temperature, stirring continuously, until the heat hits 105°F to 110°F.

4. Transfer the liquid to a sterile jar or container and keep it refrigerated.

5. Take one tablespoon three times each day orally until your allergy signs disappear.

Caution:

- Don't take it if you're using a monoamine oxidase inhibitor (MAOI) for depression. Ginkgo Biloba may make blood thinners work better, so consult your doctor before taking it.

- Don't use if pregnant or breastfeeding.

Asthma

Inflammation in the airways across the lungs and restricted bronchial tubes characterize this chronic illness. Asthma episodes may be scary. Some individuals suffer panic attacks when breathing becomes difficult.

Ginkgo-Thyme Tea

Ginkgo Biloba or thyme expands your lungs and calms your chest muscles, allowing you to breathe more easily. Whether you don't like the taste of this tea, you may enhance it by adding a teaspoon of honey and powdered peppermint to the mix.

Ingredients:

- 1 cup hot water

- 1 teaspoon Ginkgo Biloba powder

- 1 teaspoon dried thyme

Directions:

1. Fill a big cup halfway with boiling water, add dried herbs and cover the cup. Let the tea to steep for 10 minutes.

2. Take a deep breath and gently sip the tea while inhaling the heat. This therapy can be repeated up to four times a day.

3. Don't take it if you're using a monoamine oxidase inhibitor (MAOI) for anxiety. Ginkgo Biloba may make blood thinners work better; consult your doctor before taking it.

Peppermint-Rosemary Vapor Treatment

Rosemary leaves contain vital histamine-blocking oil, while peppermint helps expand your airways and improve breathing. Instead of fresh herbs, you can also use two drops of peppermint essential oil and four drops of rosemary essential oil for this therapy.

Ingredients:

- 4 cups scalding warm water (not boiling)

- 1/2 cup fresh peppermint leaves, crumbled

- 1/2 cup fresh rosemary leaves, freshly chopped

Directions:

1. Combine herbs and warm water in a large, deep mixing bowl. Put the bowl on a table and comfortably sit in front of it.

2. Protect your head and also the bowl with a large cloth. Inhale the fumes released by the plants. As required, get some fresh air and shut your eyes if the fumes are too intense. Carry out the procedure until the water has cooled down.

3. If asthma symptoms occur, repeat as required. This therapy is mild enough that you may use it as frequently as you like.

Caution:

- If you have epilepsy, avoid using rosemary. While certain soothing oils, such as jasmine, chamomile, ylang-ylang, and lavender, have been found to help prevent seizures, other aromatic oils, such as rosemary, sage, fennel, eucalyptus, camphor, hyssop, and spike lavender, have been known to cause seizures.

Chest Congestion

When you're experiencing breathing difficulties, plants may help relax your lungs or help you feel more at peace while you figure out what's causing your congestion.

Hyssop-Sage Infusion

Hyssop is a potent antiviral as well as a good expectorant. In addition, Sage provides its antibacterial properties, which aid in quicker healing. Some individuals like the solid herbal flavor of this mix; others discover that they need to include a little honey to help it go down smoother.

Ingredients:

- 4 cup heated water

- 4 tablespoons hyssop, dried

- 4 tsp. sage (dried)

Directions:

1. Mix the warm water and dry herbs in a teapot. Allow the infusion to steep for 10 minutes after covering the pot.

2. Take a deep breath and gently sip a cup of the infusion while inhaling the steam. The remainder may be reheated or refrigerated and sipped throughout the day.

Cold

Coughing, a sore throat, and sneezing are just some of the symptoms of a typical cold. Begin therapy as early as symptoms develop to shorten the length of your cold.

Thyme Tea

Thyme is an antitussive and cough suppressor that relieves coughing fast. It also serves as an expectorant, which helps to remove congestion from the lungs. It also helps alleviate the discomfort of a sore throat and the body aches that come with a cold. Add some honey to the tea if you want a sweeter taste.

Ingredients:

- 1 cup of boiling water

- 2 tsp. thyme (dried)

Directions:

1. Fill a big cup halfway with boiling water.

2. Include the thyme, lid the cup, and set aside for 10 minutes to steep.

3. Take a deep breath and gently sip the tea while absorbing the steam. Repetition is allowed up to six times per day.

Herbal Cold Syrup with Comfrey, Mullein, and Raspberry Leaf

Coughs or sore throats are relieved by comfrey, while fever, body pains, and lung irritation are relieved by mullein, thyme, or raspberry leaf. Don't worry if you're missing one and two of the herbs in this recipe; they're all healthy and can help you get rid of your cold symptoms. When refrigerated, this syrup may last up to 6 months.

Ingredients:

- 1/2 oz. comfrey, dry

- 1/2 oz. mullein, dry

- 1/2 oz. raspberry leaf, dried

- 1/2 oz. dried thyme

- 2 cup water

- 1-quart honey

Directions:

1. Combine the herbs and water in a saucepan. Decrease the liquid by half by bringing it to a low simmer and partly covering it with a lid.

2. Pour the saucepan mixture into a glass measuring cup, and transfer the liquid back into the saucepan through a wet piece of cheesecloth, squeezing the cheesecloth unless there is no more liquid.

3. Pour in the honey, then reheat on low flame, stirring continuously, until the heat hits 105°F to 110°F.

4. Transfer the liquid to a sterile container or jar and keep it refrigerated.

5. Take one tablespoon 3-4 times a day, orally, unless your symptoms go away. Children under the age of 12 must require approximately one teaspoon twice or three times each day. Don't give to children under one year old. Consult with your health practitioner before giving any herbal creations to children.

Caution:

- Fresh raspberry leaves may induce nausea, so never use them if they aren't thoroughly dried.

Colic

Colic is a distressing disease that affects babies between two weeks and four months old. The most frequent symptoms are long bursts of weeping and insomnia. Because there are numerous reasons for colic, herbal treatments cannot prevent it; nevertheless, they may help to relieve the discomfort.

Chamomile Infusion

Spiro ether, a powerful antispasmodic component of chamomile, relaxes tight, painful muscles and helps alleviate colic discomfort. Its capacity to relieve tension and anxiety may also assist your kid in getting the rest they need. If you're nursing, you may discover that chamomile tea helps to alleviate your baby's discomfort.

Ingredients:

- 1 tsp. chamomile (dried)

- 1 cup hot water

Directions:

1. Mix the chamomile and hot water in a teapot. Allow the tea to steep for 10 minutes after covering the pot. Let the infusion cool to a lukewarm temperature.

2. Pour two teaspoons into a sterilized bottle and give it to your baby to drink. When colic symptoms develop, repeat once or twice a day.

Caution:

- If you're using prescription blood thinners, avoid chamomile.

Constipation

Constipation is characterized by abdominal discomfort and difficult bowel motions. Herbs are much less rigid on your system than harsh pharmaceutical laxatives and offer excellent relief. Increase your fiber intake, drink lots of water, and increase your physical activity to help things go along quicker.

Aloe Vera Juice

Aloe Vera juice aids digestion and cleanses the gastrointestinal system. Because of this, it's ideal for treating persistent constipation. Aloe juice must be drunk within three days after making it.

Ingredients:

- 1 fresh 3-4-inch aloe leaf from the plant's inside

- 3 cups fresh liquid, coconut water, and water

Directions:

1. Grab the aloe leaf upside down on the sink, allowing the resin to drain away from the wound. Split the leaf in half lengthwise after the glue has stopped pouring, then gently take out the gel from the interior.

2. Place the gel in a blender, then pour the liquid over it. Blend until smooth, then chill before serving. Drink 1 cup each day and keep the leftovers in a securely sealed container or jar in the refrigerator.

Caution:

- If you're pregnant or nursing, avoid taking aloe.

Dandelion-Chickweed Syrup

Dandelion or chickweed are both mild laxatives that relieve constipation without unpleasant medications. You may find both of these plants in your garden; just make sure they haven't been polluted with herbicides or chemical fertilizers. When refrigerated, this syrup may last up to 6 months.

Ingredients:

- 1 oz. chopped dandelion root

- 1 oz. chickweed, fresh or dried

- 2 cup water

- 1-quart honey

Directions:

1. Mix the dandelion root, chickweed, and water in a saucepan. Decrease the liquid by half by bringing it to a low simmer and partly covering it with a lid.

2. Pour the saucepan mixture into a glass measuring cup, and put the liquid back into the saucepan through a wet sheet of cheesecloth, squeezing it until there is no longer liquid.

3. Stir in the honey or reheat on low flame, stirring continuously, until the heat hits 105°F to 110°F.

4. Transfer the syrup to a sterile container or jar, let it cool down, and keep it refrigerated.

6. Orally use one tablespoon 3 - 4 times a day until your symptoms disappear. Children under the age of 12 must take one teaspoon twice or three times each day. Don't give to children under one year old. Consult with your health practitioner before giving any herbal creations to children.

Diarrhea

Diarrhea is often induced by food indiscretion, although it may also develop due to a disease. It's usually accompanied by mild stomach discomfort, and it goes away after the offending material has been removed. Because diarrhea may induce dehydration, be sure to drink enough water. If your diarrhea is persistent or regular, and if blood and mucus are present, get medical help.

Catnip–Raspberry Leaf Decoction

Mild astringents like catnip or raspberry leaf may help halt diarrhea. That is an excellent treatment to try if stomach cramps accompany your diarrhea since raspberry leaves can assist smooth muscle tissue in relaxing. If refrigerated in a securely sealed container, this decoction can keep for up to 2 days. Add some honey to the tea if you want a sweeter taste.

Ingredients:

- 8 quarts water

- 2 tbsp. catnip (dry)

- 2 tbsp. raspberry leaf (dry)

Directions:

1. Put the herbs and water in a saucepan over high heat to start boiling, then lower the heat.

2. Simmer the herbs until the liquid reduces by half. Let the mixture cool to the point where it is safe to consume.

3. Serve a cup hot or chill it in a glass jar in the refrigerator.

Caution:

- Fresh raspberry leaves may induce nausea, so never use them if they aren't thoroughly dried. Catnip may cause a lot of relaxation; don't drive or operate equipment until you've figured out how it impacts you.

When Else We Can Choose Herbs?

Common Nonemergency Situations

Native Americans have been using herbs for over 10,000 years. From the moment they set foot on this continent until today, they have used plants to treat their ills. Plants are used to decorate objects and clothing and make teas, medicine, and ointments for ceremonial purposes. They also made sure not to destroy natural areas by clearing land to use all of its resources sustainably. Some of these practices are still being done today in Native communities throughout America.
The use of herbs is similar to modern medicine. Herbs can help treat different common illnesses that many people experience. These include treating colds, stomach problems, muscle pain, and venereal diseases. The history of using plants in this manner is reflected in the languages spoken on the continent during the domination by Europeans. Using plants was important because it allowed them to be more productive on their lands.

The plants chosen by Native Americans were both medicinal and ceremonial. Many different plants were used for medicinal purposes because of their healing abilities. Famous Native American herbs included the following:

Bilberry

The plant was used to relieve colds, coughs, and sore throats, and it also helped treat eye diseases such as swollen eyes and irritated eyes. In addition, the root, leaves, and flowers were used in various ways when creating remedies.

Cattail

This plant provided relief from stomach problems such as diarrhea and abdominal pain. The seeds of the plant that resemble a mouse's tail were also helpful in treating backaches and muscle pain after a fall or injury. The roots were used to make poultices for treating headaches.

Chestnut

This herb was used for problems related to the urinary system. The powdered nuts were effective in solving prostate problems, and they also effectively brought about minor healing of sores on the skin.

Horse Chestnut

The seeds of this plant helped treat peptic ulcers and inflammatory conditions of the urinary tract.

It is also helpful in relieving varicose veins, hemorrhoids, and leg cramps associated with diarrhea or diarrhea.

Poke

The fresh plant and its dried seeds treated various ailments such as stomach pain and vomiting. The roots may also be used to make ointments and poultices for treating indolent ulcers. The leaves can be made into a salve or poultice to treat skin problems such as burns and boils.

Rock Rose

This plant is effective against parasites such as intestinal worms and pinworms, and it may also be used to reduce blood pressure and relieve headaches. Crushed flowers can be used to neutralize acids in the body. Natives applied crushed flowers to wounds and sores on the skin before exposing them to heat, i.e., a heated stone or fire.

Sassafras

The roots and bark of this tree provide a soothing effect on the stomach. It was also used to treat backaches, headaches, toothaches, and fevers. The seeds were often chewed to improve dental health.

Yarrow

This herb was used to treat muscle pain and relieve headaches, fevers, and rashes. It was also sometimes referred to as "soldier's woundwort." Poultice from the leaves was used to treat sprains accompanied by swelling or bleeding. Yarrow is possibly one of the most widely used herbs among Native Americans due to its effectiveness against various ailments.

Prevention

The herb most commonly used for this purpose is ginseng.
Some people use this herb as a preventative measure because they have been proven to work. These include the ability to transfer nutrients easily and fight infections effectively. In addition, most plants used for prevention do not create drug interactions or reactions with other medications or supplements. But if you are on medications or supplements, always consult with your health practitioner before using the herbs.
The other benefit of using Native American plants as preventatives is that it is widely available and should not cause complications if taken orally in an appropriate dose.

Experimental Treatments

Native American herbs can be used in many ways as experimental treatments, like an antibiotic or nutritional supplements.

The advantages and disadvantages of using herbs for this purpose can vary depending on the type of herb and how it is used. A common problem with using these herbs as a treatment is that sometimes they may cause complications with other medicines. Another disadvantage of using Native American herbs as experimental treatments is that they are not always as effective as other options, such as antibiotics. However, some people still prefer to use Native American remedies because they do not cause drug interactions or reactions.

Native American herbs in emergencies are considered part of complementary, alternative, integrative, or holistic medicine. However, this does not mean that these herbs can replace an emergency treatment. Alternative medicine is used in emergencies because it can sometimes help reduce symptoms.

The nutrients found in Native American herbs make them an effective supplement. For example, the nutrients found in ginseng include vitamins B1 (thiamin), B2 (riboflavin), and C (ascorbic acid). In addition, Native American plants contain many types of minerals, such as calcium, copper, and zinc.

Some of the benefits of using herbs as nutritional supplements are that they do not cause complications with other prescription medications.

Secondary Therapeutic Agents

In cases where there is a second therapeutic agent, such as antibiotics, Native American herbs can be used as a secondary treatment. For example, if you need antibiotic therapy, it has adverse effects or complications or requires a higher dose than initially described. In these cases, herbs can help treat this unfortunate circumstance.

By adjusting the proper dosage according to your weight, you make sure you receive the correct amount of herbs and not too many or too few. Native American herbs will work best with other treatments such as prescription medications and alternative therapies.

Most Native American herbs can be used therapeutically, especially if you can tolerate the medicinal effects that these plants may produce. However, you must not use any of these remedies if you do not need them due to adverse effects or drug interactions. A common problem with using these remedies is overused or misused. For example, if ginseng is given too much, it can cause adverse reactions.

You must first consult with your practitioner and certified herbalist about using herbal therapy alongside your prescribed treatment.

How to Begin?

To begin using Native American herbs as a treatment, you first need to talk with your doctor about what kind of herb will work best for treating your ailment or illness. You should also make sure that you are aware of any contraindications before beginning the treatment process.

To select the proper Native American herbal remedy, you should consult with someone familiar with these types of herbs. Once you find out that there are no contraindications to the use of the herb, you should find out how much of this medicine you can take.

Depending on the type of herb, it may be possible for you to grind it into powder or rub it into your skin. This facilitates the body's absorption of nutrients and ensures the effective transfer of all healing properties.

If you are in a dire emergency where your life is in danger, you must seek professional medical advice.

Herbalism Safety

Several plants have been used for natural remedies, including herbs. When these plants are used properly, they can provide a range of benefits, including repairing the heart, helping to prevent cancer, and even regulating hormones. However, not all herbs are safe, and some can be pretty dangerous. That is why it is vital to use them responsibly and wisely.

Here are a few safety tips to consider when using any Native American herbs.

Know Your Plants

Hundreds of herbs exist out there, which have unique benefits and effects on the body. Some look very similar to others, but they can vary quite a bit in their appearance and impact on the body. That is why it is crucial to learn about them first. If you are using herbs for healing purposes, you should know what they look like to avoid getting confused with another herb at the store. I recommend taking a picture of a herb with your cell phone and buying a book on them to look up and compare any unfamiliar plants when necessary.

Abuse of Native American Herbs

The usage of herbs for personal benefit or as a means of "self-treating" is unfortunately very prevalent among those who do not know better. Thankfully, most of these people are quickly caught because many customs and laws come from indigenous cultures across the country.

If you believe in Native American herbal remedies but want to know more about what these people were doing, it may be time to read a book or two on the subject. It is incredible how much information is readily available if you look at it. When reading any book on this type of topic, the first thing that you should realize is that these types of herbs are hazardous when used incorrectly or improperly, and misusing them may result in severe health hazards, including death.

How you consume these herbs is very important, and it should be done in ways that are natural to the people who are using them. If you happen to find some of these old recipes, check the ingredients to ensure that they are safe. Most of these herbs have been studied for hundreds of years, and a great majority of them are entirely safe when used correctly.

Before starting any type of research project, the first activity you should do is look around your house. You should find pages from books, magazines, or medical journals.

You can easily find much information related to this topic when they are kept in an old book or magazine somewhere in your home.

If you happen to come across old magazines or medical journals, it is probably best to keep them for your reference. You will be able to quickly refer to them while attempting to accomplish other tasks in the future.

When looking for information relating to Native American herbal remedies, you should always be careful of what material you use because there are so many different "facts" out there; it can be hard to tell what is right and what is not. Next time you are looking for information on these types of herbs, do your homework beforehand because this will improve your grades immensely and help keep your body safe when working with any kind of herb from this culture.

However, if you have had a severe injury or been diagnosed with a disease that you cannot get rid of with modern medicine, it may be worth considering trying these remedies. After all, they have helped people in the past. Why not go with it?

Disclaimer:

Information in this book is not a replacement for professional medical advice and treatment, and information in this book is for educational and informational purposes. The author and publisher do not accept any loss, harm, or damage from using or misusing this book or your failure to seek proper medical advice.

Understanding Your Body Systems

Many people living in Western society don't know how their body system is supposed to function. It has been said that most adults still take medicine instead of administering their treatment, which continues to be a trend. Knowing your body and its systems can help you feel better and live longer and can also help your friends and family.

Below are some basic facts about the human body. I hope this is helpful for you all to know even if you do not want to be a 'doctor'...knowing your body is the best start to learning about natural medicine.

The human body has two parts: The external and internal organs and systems:

- **External:** Skin, Nails, Hair

- **Internal (Organs and Complexities):** Heart/Pump System, Digestive System, Circulatory System, Muscular System.

The skin is made mostly of dead cells and dead keratinized cells (skin cells). It is the largest human body organ and has millions of sweat glands under its surface. The skin secretions include sebum (oil), water, air, and salts. There are also receptor cells for temperature, touch, pain, etc. It is the only human body organ that is not directly connected to all other organs. An average healthy person can think of their body as an apple. The skin is like the apple's peel; it protects the internal organs and tissues inside of you. Typically, the muscles are not considered part of the 'apple' unless you are doing some exercise (we will discuss this later). The vagina and penis are also not considered a part of the 'apple.'

The liver is a large, spongy organ in the middle of the abdomen, and it consists of hundreds of microscopic, bean-shaped nodules called hepatic lobules. The liver filters, cleanses, and repairs the blood, and it also helps absorb vitamins and minerals from food.

The brain is about 2 1/2 pounds (1 kg) in weight and is located toward the middle back of the head. The brain provides movement to all parts of your body, controls memory, and is a vital part of your nerve system. You use your brain for perception (seeing), thought (thinking), and emotion (feeling).

The Nervous System

The nervous system is the set of physical structures that controls the body's functions, and this is vital for all living entities, especially plants and animals. Physical body: The physical body determines how well an organism receives or gives out information through its senses, motor abilities, and biological functions (e.g., food digestion). For example, the physical body allows for sensory information received by the eyes, while the feet allow for sensory information to be received by touch. Native American herbalists rely on their sense of touch to gather knowledge, and they must be sensitive enough if they encounter something new (e.g., plants).

How Continuous Stress and Anxiety Can Harm Our Body and Health?

Continuous stress and anxiety can lead to the development of many physical ailments due to their effects on the nervous system. The brain's rational process, which is required for people to make good decisions, becomes significantly impaired when someone experiences chronic or habitual stress. This impairment can manifest in fear-based behaviors without the person even recognizing it. For example, someone may be subconsciously angry with their partner after having experienced stressful events with them before. That person might then not be able to take responsibility for their actions because they were overwhelmed by fear and anger. The person might then experience more stress due to the anger and fear of the partner and, consequently, continue on this vicious cycle.

The nervous system of Native American herbalists relies on herbs and certain medicines that they use for medicinal purposes. Native American herbalists use moss, tobacco, and even ingested animal by-products to achieve their health objectives. One common ingredient used by many Native American herbalists is tobacco. Tobacco has been known to aid in concocting various teas and mixtures for medical treatment. Some of these treatments were designed to help aid the digestion process after a tough day's work in the field. However, tobacco was also used to soothe and relieve pain and discomfort. It may be because tobacco has been researched to contain high levels of chemicals such as nicotine, pyridines, and pyrazines. These chemicals are known to induce sedation and promote alertness.

Native American herbalists' physical bodies can help explain why some individuals may still experience stress or anxiety despite regularly exercising and maintaining a healthy diet. For instance, some people believe that exercise is a panacea for stress relief; however, research shows that this is not always the case.

How Can We Protect Our Nervous System and Release Everyday Stress and Anxiety?

Many people do not have this type of access to the natural world, which has led to their cognitive processes being impaired by chronic or habitual stress.

Native American herbalists can use herbs and medicines for medicinal purposes to help them with the rehabilitation process after experiencing stressful events in life. Combining the physical body, motion, and herbs provide additional protection against daily stress. People can prevent the effects of stress on the brain's rational process, which is necessary for rational decision-making.

Aerobic exercise is a proven way that people can improve their mental health through exercise. This type of workout includes exercises that increase heart rate and breathing rate to help burn calories and improve cardiovascular functions. Sedentary behaviors are associated with increased mortality rates, increased risk of stroke, diabetes, obesity, and low back pain. Exercise also improves cognitive functions such as reaction times and memory. Other physical activities such as yoga or tai chi may also be good options for improving mental health.

Another way that people can avoid experiencing chronic or habitual stress is through cognitive reframing. According to Vohs and Baumeister, people who interact with more "friendly" individuals experience less anxiety and enjoy a happier life. This can be applied in daily life by being friendly to others and staying open to new social interactions. The social cognitive theory also says that being proactive increases a person's self-control, which is a strong inhibitor of many of the effects of stress on the body. More proactive people tend to have better family relationships, have higher job satisfaction, and have fewer perceived problems in general.

Which Native American Herbs Are Good for The Nervous System?

If you are looking for help with calming your nerves, soothing anxiety, or just treating some minor symptoms of the common cold, the following list of herbs may provide an answer.

Native Americans have used some herbs for centuries to treat various medical conditions. These traditional healers were the first to recognize and use plants as medicines. Today there is a resurgence in using herbal remedies from all over the world to treat chronic diseases such as depression and epilepsy. The following herbs have been adapted for this purpose:

Catnip

Catnip has been used for centuries to calm upset stomachs and relieve respiratory irritations while reducing fever symptoms. It has a calming effect on people, similar to chamomile tea. These herbs are in the mint family and can grow in fields, meadows, and open forests. Catnip is great for soothing nervous tension, stomach problems, and menstrual cramps.

Skullcap

It is an herb that grows well in damp soil conditions. This Native American herb helps relieve stress, anxiety, and nervous tension. Research has been done to show its calming effects on the nervous system. It can help reduce feelings of depression or agitation while increasing your response to outside stimuli.

Use it in teas, capsules, or even as a beneficial ingredient for a relaxing bath.

Valerian Root

Valerian root comes from a flower that has been used for centuries to treat nervous disorders. Some have found it helpful in stress reduction, anxiety, and insomnia. It also has a calming effect on the digestive system, which can be helpful to those with stomach problems or irritable bowel syndrome.

Lemon Balm

Lemon balm is a common herb that Native Americans have used for years due to its mild sedative properties. It can help reduce nervous tension, stress, and even irritability while promoting a sense of well-being. Lemon balm tea is popular in Europe, where it helps to treat depression and chronic coughs while boosting energy levels and concentration.

Sage

Sage has helped treat sore throats, nervous disorders, upset stomachs, and pain for centuries. Native Americans would chew on sage leaves when they had a sore throat. It's also considered an antiseptic, antispasmodic, and anti-inflammatory herb. Sage can be consumed by drinking several cups of sage tea or in capsule form.

Gingko Biloba

Gingko Biloba is an herbal remedy that helps with circulation problems in the brain. It works by increasing blood flow through the brain, promoting mental alertness and clearer thinking. You add it to your favorite drink or take it in capsules.

Licorice Root

Licorice root is an herb with a pungent taste when used in tea or capsules. It is high in antioxidants and promotes good health when your body works best. Licorice root is anti-inflammatory, diuretic and antiemetic. It helps treat ulcers, diabetes, and coughs.

Cayenne

It is a great herb to help with stomach problems, ulcers, and even bronchitis. Cayenne is the key ingredient in the famous hot sauce Tabasco. This herb is used to stop bleeding, induce sweating, reduce congestion of mucus membranes and increase circulation to sore or swollen areas of the body.

Ginger Root

Ginger has been used for centuries as a natural remedy for nausea or gastrointestinal discomfort due to its mild sedation ability. Ginger root aids in digestion and has anti-inflammatory properties, and it is also used to relieve pain, reduce fever and reduce inflammation.

Mullein Leaves (also known as "MULLEIN")

This herb is also known as the herb of St. John's Wort. You can find it growing throughout the United States and Canada. Its compound is called alpha-bisabolol, which helps promote a sense of well-being, and clarity of thought and reduces stress. Mullein tea is an excellent cold remedy for those suffering from the common cold or other respiratory problems such as asthma, bronchitis, or who have a sore throat from laryngitis.

Calendula (also known as "CALENDULA" or "POT MARIGOLD")

This herb contains many healing properties, including anti-inflammatory and anti-bacterial properties. It is also used to treat irritable bowel syndrome.

Aloe Vera

Aloe Vera is an herb that has long been used to help with skin problems and digestive upsets and relieve stress on the body. The leaves of this plant are also known for their healing abilities on open wounds. The digestive benefits of aloe Vera can help with indigestion, ulcers, and even diarrhea.

Burdock Root

Burdock root has been used on the European continent for hundreds of years as a mild laxative. Burdock root also has a strong anti-bacterial component to it, which can be helpful during times of infection or illness. It is a great herb to eat daily as well.

Wheatgrass

Wheatgrass is a very popular herb in the U.S. and, for centuries, helped with heartburn because it has proven to be safe and effective in helping keep the digestive system in good working order. Wheatgrass also promotes healthy blood and helps improve circulation, which can be helpful if you suffer from poor circulation or arthritis.

Devil's Club

Devil's club is a medicinal herb that grows in Europe and North America. It has been used for centuries as an antiseptic and anti-inflammatory. It can also help treat pain, sore muscles, and other aches and pains.

Tulsi (also known as "TULSI" or "CURRY LEAF")

This herb contains many healing properties, including anti-inflammatory and anti-bacterial properties. It is also used to treat irritable bowel syndrome.

Goldenseal

Goldenseal is a medicine that Native Americans have used for generations. Traditionally, it was applied to wounds to promote healing, stop bleeding and destroy bacteria and fungi because it is effective as an antibacterial and antifungal agent.

The Respiratory System

The Function of the Respiratory System

The lungs and the respiratory system work to extract oxygen from the air we breathe and remove waste products such as carbon dioxide. This inhalation and expiration of air allow us to talk, sleep, exercise, make love, and do other activities. The respiratory system stems from the pharynx (throat) and windpipe (trachea) to the lungs. The air passage that begins in the lungs is called bronchi, then directly into the windpipe. The air is warmed and humidified by deaminating and diffusion (expansion and contraction of the lungs).

Why Protect Your Lungs?

The lungs are a hollow organ found in all vertebrates and located in your chest next to your heart and protected by the ribs.
It is vital because it gives us oxygen, and this helps our heart function correctly because it gets oxygen from outside to inside our body tissues.
The lungs fill with air and then release this air, and this helps us get oxygen into our bloodstream to oxygenate our cells and remove carbon dioxide from them.

How Can Native American Herbs Help You Prevent Illness and Lungs Damage and Strengthen Your Lungs?

Native American herbs have long been known for their therapeutic properties and are traditionally associated with health and healing. Native Americans used these plants to prevent, heal, and cure various diseases. They will most likely present you with a general list of the plants available in different regions, or you can do an Internet search for herbal remedies.
A study explained the usefulness of Native American herbs, which have been known for their high sulfur content and can help to remove excess sulfur from the body naturally. They have been used for this purpose because it helps fight infection, asthma, and other respiratory problems. However, scientific studies had not verified this until recently, when scientific observations were made about the effectiveness of these herbs in protecting the respiratory tract and preventing free radical damage.

Which Native American Herbs Are Good for The Respiratory System?

Maybe you have been thinking of making a change for the better. Whether it is diet, exercise, or a healthier lifestyle in general, you want to take better care of yourself and your body. And herbal remedies can help you to do this.

Native American herbs are some of the most effective herbal remedies because they can address specific health issues without any side effects. This chapter will briefly discuss the Native American herbal remedies that are good for the respiratory system. The respiratory system is where the process of breathing happens. It consists of the nose, pharynx, larynx, trachea, bronchi, and lungs. This system filters out unwanted substances from the air we breathe and sends them back out. Allergic reactions or viral infections can irritate this system, leading to more severe illnesses like pneumonia. Native American herbs are used for respiratory problems because they are believed to help heal this vital part of your body.

Burdock root

It was a home remedy for many years to treat respiratory issues. It mainly aids in decongesting the lungs, which is helpful for asthma and sore throats.

Because it is also a diuretic, it helps your body urinate more often, and it helps the body remove excess fluids you don't need while balancing the amount of water you drink.

Pine needles

They are another favorite herb. It is often used to help you get a better night's sleep because it can relieve tension in your muscles.

If you have problems breathing when you sleep, this herb can also help reduce the irritation in your breathing passages so that they are easier to open, making it less complicated for air to pass through them.

Valerian

Valerian can relax muscles and nerves, and it can also help you sleep better at night if used as tea. Likewise, it will help you calm down, relax, and rest more soundly.

Slippery elm bark

The following herbal remedy is a little different from the others. It has been used for centuries to get rid of excess mucus from the respiratory system. You can purchase it from most health stores or pharmacies. This useful herb works by stimulating the mucous membranes of your body, allowing them to work without having to fight the excessive mucus that can be found in the body's passages.

Agastache

It is used to treat irritation in nasal passages. It is believed to help reduce congestion and open the nasal passages.

Chewing on Agastache leaves or drinking tea made from it can help with these respiratory problems.

Because of its ability to treat coughs, colds, and sore throats, Agastache can be used in place of conventional cold medicines. However, because there is no research on this herb, it should not be taken if you are pregnant or breastfeeding. Side effects may cause headaches, nausea, dizziness, and vomiting. Agastache may interact with other medications, so you must consult your doctor before taking this herb.

The roots of this herb are powdered and used as tea to treat sore throats and coughs. Add some honey to the tea to relieve a sore throat.

The leaves can also be chewed to soothe the mouth and reduce pain.

Cat's claw

It is used for treating infections inside the throat and upper respiratory system. It can also help heal wounds, broken bones, and cracked skin. The small brownish-red berries of Cat's claw look like they have claws on them, which is why this plant has been referred to as "cat's claw."

This herb does come with side effects. It may lower your immune system or cause kidney stones. People taking warfarin or diabetes medications should avoid using this herb. It may also interact with medications like anti-depressants, diuretics, and antibiotics.

Avoid this herb if you are pregnant or breastfeeding, as it can cause complications in your baby's development.

First, consult with your doctor before taking Cat's claw, as there is not enough information on how safe it is to take it during pregnancy, breastfeeding, if you suffer from a bleeding disorder, autoimmune disease, or are taking medication for any health problems.

Hawthorne

Hawthorne is used for treating respiratory issues. It can help treat coughs, colds, sore throats, and asthma. Hawthorne also has many other uses, including treating wounds, sores, or burns. The leaves are made into a tea that can be taken to soothe sinuses and reduce irritation.

Some people have reported side effects when taking Hawthorne, and the most common include nausea, vomiting, stomach pain, diarrhea, or bloating after prolonged use of this herb. Although insufficient research has been done on this herb, it should always be taken along with a doctor's recommendation, especially if you are pregnant or breastfeeding, as it can harm your baby's development.

Cayenne

Cayenne increases the body's blood flow and heart rate, which can help move phlegm that causes difficulty breathing. It can also be a pain reliever for sore throats, coughs, and congestion. The powdered root of this herb is made into a tea, or it can be mixed with honey and taken on a spoon to relieve coughs and sore throats.

Cayenne should not be used by those with bleeding disorders, those taking medications for diabetes, or high blood pressure. It may cause your condition to worsen because the herb will counteract those medications.

Ginger

This plant helps reduce inflammation in the respiratory system. It can reduce inflammation in the upper respiratory system, including the nose, sinuses, and throat. It may also help treat nausea, vomiting, and pain. The fresh or dried ginger root can be made into a tea or added to food to help relieve symptoms of colds or other respiratory issues.
For best results, use ground ginger to make tea to soothe a sore throat. You can take 2-3 grams four times per day. If you are making tea to ease chest congestion, it's best to use fresh ginger root because it has anti-inflammatory properties that dissolve mucus. Let each dose steep for 10 minutes before drinking it.
Avoid ginger if you take blood thinners or medications for high blood pressure or diabetes, as it may cause your condition to worsen. It may also interact with migraine medication, NSAIDs, and anti-inflammatory drugs.
Most people should be able to take ginger without side effects, but you should avoid it while pregnant or breastfeeding because not enough research has been done. The general rule of thumb is to consult your doctor before taking any herbs while pregnant or breastfeeding.

Other Native American herbs can help with respiratory issues like Yarrow, Peppermint, and Comfrey. Comfrey is a type of plantain used to treat sores, wounds, and other skin disorders. Yarrow can be used to soothe sinuses, reduce inflammation and prevent pain from the common cold. Peppermint contains menthol, which can help clear nasal passages and relieve coughs.

Which herbal remedies will work best for you, and which ones will even help you? It all depends on what health issues you have or what type of pain you are experiencing. If you have a health issue resulting from a bacterial infection, it might be best not to use any herbal remedies unless your physician has recommended them. But, if you suffer from a disease that has a viral basis or a disease that affects your neurological or nervous system. In that case, these herbs may be beneficial in alleviating the symptoms they address.

The Endocrine System

What Is the Function of the Endocrine System?

An endocrine system is a group of glands that secrete hormones into the bloodstream. These hormones play a critical role in many physiological processes, such as causing growth, developing an individual's sex characteristics, and regulating body composition.

The hormones are transported in the bloodstream by lipoproteins, which bind to receptors on cells; the overall process is called endocytosis. They then release their signals into the bloodstream and travel through nerve fibers. These signals cause various events at their contact sites or target cells.

These events include biochemical reactions that alter specific proteins, affect digestion and absorption of nutrients, alter blood sugar levels, stimulate specific types of tissue growth or cell division, regulate body temperature, and control the production of certain fluids in body tissues.

The endocrine system works in concert with the nervous system to maintain homeostasis (the stability of internal conditions like temperature and chemistry). The endocrine system is divided into two broad categories: the exocrine and endocrine glands.

Anatomy of the Endocrine System:

Exocrine glands: A group of organs that produce and secrete materials into membranous or serous cavities outside the body, such as sweat glands, salivary glands, sebaceous glands, and mammary glands.

Endocrine glands: A group of organs that produce and secrete substances directly into circulation through ducts.

Endocrine glands are located throughout the body, even in remote areas like your face. Different endocrine glands produce hormones, while others produce enzymes. Endocrine glands include the thyroid gland, pituitary gland, muscle cells, and adrenal cortex (the outer layer of adrenal glands).

The function of the endocrine system is to produce and secrete hormones from a gland, establishing a link between the nervous system and internal organs. Hormones are critical to maintaining homeostasis within an individual's body.

How Does Stress Affect Endocrine System?

The endocrine system plays an essential role in the body by regulating hormones, those chemical messengers that are produced by endocrine glands and control various bodily functions.

The endocrine glands, or hormone-producing glands, release hormones directly into the bloodstream, signaling cells to regulate specific processes in the human body. Endocrine glands produce hormones in response to autonomic nervous system (ANS) signals, such as the body's circadian rhythms.

Hormonal regulation is primarily regulated by the hypothalamic-pituitary-adrenal (HPA)axis. The HPA axis is responsible for producing cortisol to counter-regulate stressors. The HPA axis also receives signals from other organizations, primarily the central nervous system (CNS). The CNS releases hormones passed to the HPA axis via blood vessels, and these hormones further stimulate cortisol production within the body.

The hyperactivity of the HPA axis can be seen through elevated levels of cortisol in a person's bloodstream after a stressful situation occurs. That can be observed when there is a lack of sleep; the body is under chronic stress or in difficult situations. The long-term use of prescription drugs or overuse of recreational drugs can also trigger the HPA axis to become hyperactive. These conditions can cause long-term damage to adrenal glands and their ability to produce cortisol.

Chronic stressors are also known to affect the HPA axis by initially increasing cortisol levels within the body. This initial increase in cortisol lasts only four days, after which there is a decrease in levels until they are once again at baseline levels.

There are two main components of the HPA axis: the hypothalamus and the adrenal glands. The hypothalamus is located close to the pituitary gland at the base of the brain and triggers chemical reactions that produce cortisol in the adrenal glands. With chronic stress or trauma, such as an accident or attack, these chemical reactions can become depleted and stop working properly, leading to depletion of the HPA axis.

Exhaustion of this system can manifest in many illnesses. Chronic stress or trauma may cause post-traumatic stress disorder (PTSD) or major depression. PTSD is a mental illness that may cause long-term brain dysfunction and trigger fluctuations in cortisol levels. It can lead to adrenal exhaustion, which causes chronic depression or cause long-term insomnia or other sleep disorders. The HPA axis exhaustion can also trigger major depression.

The Native American herbalists have helped an individual deal with stress by increasing the production of endorphins, allowing a person to deal with symptoms such as anxiety and stress. Also, the individual improved the metabolism of fat cells. Herbalists have increased the functioning of the endocrine system, which is affected by the stress hormone cortisol produced by the adrenal glands. The latter regulates blood sugar levels and utilizes energy sources in the body cells. It creates an immune response against infections, reduces inflammation, and triggers the storage of calories in fat cells and their excessive use for energy.

Native American herbalist helps improve fat cell metabolism, increase or support energy production in body cells, and boost immunity against infections.

The stress hormones are released when prolonged exposure to severe injuries caused by accidents, calamities like earthquakes, floods, etc. These stress the mind and body, alter blood sugar levels, and trigger fat cells to store calories, overusing them for energy.

Many Native Americans historically used the herb yucca to treat stress-related conditions. Yucca root is known as "yappo" in Navajo medicine.

Native American Herbs Known for Their Positive Effect On Hormonal Balance

The word "hormonal" has become so commonplace in modern culture that it's hard to believe people have been unaware of this hormone system for millennia.

The medical world has understood just how powerful hormonal balance can be, both by regulating bodily functions and influencing our moods. Of course, the benefits of herbalism are no secret either—centuries ago, Native American tribes relied on herbs like black cohosh for fertility purposes.

Today, we are more aware of the importance of a healthy diet and lifestyle that affect hormonal balance. And herbs can help with that too.

Following herbs and plants are known for their positive impact on hormonal regulation:

Black Cohosh

This herb is known for its ability to prepare the body physically for pregnancy, and it is also said to help regulate menstruation and reduce symptoms associated with PMS. It is available in the form of teas, capsules, tinctures, and creams.

Sage

This herb is known to help regulate estrogen levels, which can be especially helpful for women who are experiencing menopause. It also relieves symptoms associated with PMS. You can use sage in teas, topical applications, or capsules, depending on your preference.

Chasteberry (Vitex)

Women dealing with PMS, menstrual irregularity, or infertility are told to try this herb! It is thought to help regulate estrogen levels while promoting other parts of the reproductive system to function more efficiently. This herb is available in capsules and teas.

Cayenne Pepper

This herb is well-known for its ability to help regulate estrogen levels, promote menstrual regularity and relieve painful periods.

You can use it in teas, capsules, or topical applications, depending on your preference.

Fenugreek Seeds

This herb is known to support healthy fertility during both pregnancy and menopause by regulating the hormone estrogen. It's also thought to help promote menstruation and fight menstrual irregularity and other reproductive system issues. It is available in capsules and teas.

Raspberry Seed Oil/Berries/Fruits/Leafs/Twigs/Herb Tea

These are herbal superpowers! It has been used for centuries to support healthy hormone levels in both men and women. This herb is well-known for supporting menstrual regularity, helping combat PMS symptoms, regulating estrogen levels, and encouraging breast health. Raspberry leaf tea also helps treat menstrual irregularities, hormonal imbalances, progesterone deficiencies, and other issues in women. You can find it in capsules and teas.

Dandelion Root

This herb is known for its ability to help regulate the hormones estrogen and progesterone in women.
It can also help regulate menstrual irregularity, PMS symptoms, and pregnancy, especially for women who have trouble conceiving. Dandelion root is available in capsules and teas.

B- Complex Vitamins

They are not often included in our modern diet, but they're essential for people dealing with hormonal imbalance. This vitamin complex is needed to support proper hormone levels.
You can find them in foods like breakfast cereals and multivitamins or minerals supplements.

Broccoli

This vegetable is high in the hormone indole-3-carbinol, which can help regulate estrogen levels in women. It's also thought to support healthy liver function, which can help with hormone processing and elimination. It is available in capsules, tablets, and teas or as a food.

Green Tea

This herb has become very popular for its ability to encourage weight loss, but it's also helpful for hormonal health!

Green tea has natural chemicals called catechins that help regulate hormone levels and support healthy estrogen balance in both men and women. Depending on your preference, you can prepare tea to drink or take dietary supplements.

Evening Primrose Oil

It can support healthy estrogen levels and regulate the menstrual cycle, and it can also promote breast health, relieve PMS symptoms and help support overall hormonal regulation. It is available in capsules or dietary supplements.

Flaxseed Oil/Flax Seeds/Whole Flax Seeds/ Sprouts/Leafs/Hulls/Hulled Hemp Seeds/Raw Hemp Seed Powder

This herb is also popular for promoting healthy hormone balance in both men and women. It's thought to be effective in supporting healthy estrogen levels, regulating menstrual cycles, and supporting overall reproductive health. It is available in capsules, teas, or dietary supplements.

Fennel Seeds/Fennel Seed Tea/Whole Fennel Seeds/ Fennel Seed Capsules

This herb is thought to support healthy estrogen levels in both men and women. It also helps regulate PMS symptoms, menstrual cycles, and other reproductive system conditions. You can find this spice in teas, capsules, or dietary supplements.

Oregano Oil/Oregano Leaf Extract/Oregano Tea/Whole Oregano

This herb supports healthy estrogen levels in both men and women. It's also thought to help regulate the menstrual cycle while supporting breast health. You can use this herb in teas, capsules, tinctures, and topical applications.

Cordyceps Powder/Herb Tea

Cordyceps is a traditional Chinese medicinal mushroom. It is beneficial for people struggling with fatigue because it has anti-fatigue properties that are thought to help boost energy and stamina. This herb is specific for its ability to promote healthy hormone levels in both men and women, regulate menstrual cycles, and relieve PMS symptoms. It is available in capsules, teas, and dietary supplements in the US.

Parsley

This herb is commonly used to relieve stomach upset and encourage proper liver function, but it's also helpful for hormonal health! It supports healthy estrogen levels in men and women. You can use it as a food or in teas or dietary supplements.

What Native American Herbs Help with PCOS Syndrome and Endometriosis?

PCOS and endometriosis are two common female reproductive system disorders that cause many symptoms such as irregular periods, heavy or light menstrual bleeding, mood swings, weight gain, or difficulty losing weight. Many women with PCOS and endometriosis also experience infertility.

Fortunately, research has found that specific herbal remedies can help relieve some of these symptoms and improve the quality of life for afflicted women.

Dandelion

This herb helps with an imbalance in estrogen levels, leading to menstrual irregularities and endometriosis.

Raspberry leaf

Women with PCOS who drink this tea regularly may find reduced testosterone levels (and thus better insulin sensitivity). It also helps regulate periods.

Black Cohosh root

This herbal remedy can help with hormonal imbalance, leading to endometriosis. It also helps regulate periods.

Burdock root

This herb strengthens the immune system and is a natural anti-inflammatory. As endometriosis is an inflammatory condition, this herb may be beneficial in treating it.

Red clover flowers

The flowers of this wildflower are high in estrogenic compounds that can help balance an imbalance of estrogen caused by PCOS or other conditions.

Oatstraw

This herb is beneficial for women with PCOS trying to conceive, including reducing excess hormone levels associated with the syndrome.

Barberry bark

This herb can help reduce inflammation, which can help with endometriosis.

Herbal remedies that contain no estrogens and phytoestrogens, such as black cohosh root, dandelion root, and red clover flowers, are more likely to be safe for use by women with PCOS.

In addition to these herbal remedies, some foods may also help relieve symptoms of PCOS. For example, eating more fibrous fruit and vegetables and more protein from fish or poultry can help balance hormones and keep a woman feeling healthier during hormonal changes.

Studies have also found that specific diets may be beneficial in treating endometriosis. For example, eating plenty of fiber and avoiding sugary foods or alcohol can help prevent inflammation.

Many women find that meditation, yoga, or other stress management techniques help control hormonal imbalances, including those caused by PCOS and endometriosis. Finally, acupuncture may also benefit many women with PCOS syndrome or endometriosis because it helps balance hormones.

The Gastrointestinal System

Why Is Gut Microbiome So Important For Whole-Body Immunity?

Native American Herbalism is a culture and system of healing that has been around for over 4,000 years. This traditional form of healing uses plants as the primary source of medicines, and plants have been used to treat physical and mental health disorders since ancient times. The Native American herbalists use plants as natural allies in the fight to maintain good health. In addition to this, herbalists believe that ingredients from plants can help balance the composition of the body's microbial ecosystem, which mainly resides in the gut microbiome.

That further supports a holistic approach toward healing for practitioners who want to simultaneously target internal and external processes because it is a crucial component for good health overall.

Recent studies have shown that an individual's gut microbiome makes up more than 80% of the body's immune system. Many bacteria and other microbes live inside the gastrointestinal tract, which is vital for good health. These microbes help control the immune system by modulating its responses to pathogens and autoimmune diseases. The microbial components also produce metabolites that help control inflammation which is one of the main components of chronic diseases. Furthermore, research shows that specific cells within the immune system act as microbial surveillance stations or "sentries" that monitor these microorganisms for potential threats. The sentries then respond to these messages by activating pathways to produce cytokines proteins. These proteins ensure the immune system's response to infection or disease and control the normal growth of cells in the body.

How To Keep Gut Microbiome In Good Condition?

The first step is eating fresh food daily and practicing home-cooked meals, daily probiotics, and protein supplementation. The next step is to ensure that you are safe from pathogenic stressors such as pesticides, antibiotics, and vaccines. The third step is ensuring that you are doing everything possible to support your immune system, which includes promoting the production of beneficial gamma-aminobutyric acid (GABA) through dietary supplements such as valerian root extract or Rhodiola Rosea root extract (which has traditionally been used for conditions like anxiety, insomnia, and depression).

The fourth step an individual must take is to avoid any antibiotic usage, which can cause significant damage to the gut microbiome. It can lead to candida infections, severe leaky gut syndrome, poor digestive function, and even autoimmune diseases. Another step is to avoid food allergies that further harm the gut microbiome. It is also important to avoid gluten items that are genetically modified because they have similar proteins to the proteins found in the human body's tissue.

Gluten aggravates inflammation which can be damaging to our immune system. Antibiotics have been linked with a leaky gut syndrome, which allows toxins and other harmful pathogens for easy access into your bloodstream leading to more inflammation throughout your entire body.

What Herbs Have Positive Effects On Gut Health And Boosting Immunity?

Many Native American herbs have been commonly used for centuries to support gut health, such as stinging nettle, burdock root, red clover, Oregon grape root, and burdock.

Native American herbalists typically mix these plants in tinctures or encapsulated form, which can be taken daily to improve the composition of the gut microbiome and maintain immune function.

Stinging nettle is particularly beneficial because it suppresses the growth of unfavorable bacterial flora and yeast imbalance in the intestinal tract. It also helps promote the production of lactobacillus probiotics which help restore balance to the system. Nettle also helps regulate blood.

Herbalism Today

Herbalism has been a part of human culture for thousands of years, and it still has an important role in modern medicine. Herbalists have always been the first people to try to repair or cure a sick person's ailment or disease. In today's society, taking herbs is considered alternative medicine, but it is not always accepted as mainstream medical care because there are no strict guidelines from the American pharmaceutical industry.

In this book, you'll learn how herbalism originated and attained its current status as an alternative healing method.
This book will also include exciting folklore and historical information, where you'll learn about the sources, benefits, and risks of herbs.
This book aims to give you a knowledge base on herbalism so that you can make informed decisions based on your own needs. You will also be able to separate the facts from the myths so that you aren't misled by misinformation. This book will offer you enough information to discuss herbalism with your doctor.
Herbalism has been practiced for thousands of years, and its roots go back to ancient Egypt and Palestine. It was very prominent during the Middle Ages, causing many to take up herb gardening. Herbs were used as medicines, pest repellents, aromatherapy aids, and culinary ingredients. The popularity of herbalism has continued into modern times, with people using herbs for their healing properties or as alternative medicine options. In today's society, herbalism is as popular as more people turn to natural cures for their ills.

Herbalism is the use of plants and herbs for medicinal purposes. It can range from using a cup of tea with a few herbs to using a single herb that treats a specific ailment. Herbalists learn about each herb they wish to use through experience and study. For example, they learn about medicinal effects and how to use one of the most common herbs, aloe vera. The leaves of this herb are often found in sunburn creams and are used to treat burns and other skin ailments like eczema and psoriasis.
Herb gardens can be a good way for aspiring herbalists to educate themselves on the medicinal values of herbs and learn how to grow them. Herb gardens can also be a source of income if the herbalist decides to sell their produce or excess stock to others. Some herbalists do not wish to grow their herbs but prefer purchasing them from experienced growers instead.
Practitioners of herbalism are commonly called herbalists but are not necessarily the same thing. A practitioner of herbalism is someone who simply uses herbs, while an herbalist is a person who studies the effects of plants on health. An herb gardener would not necessarily call themselves an herbalist but may be so because they learn medicinal plants and know which ones are good for remedies.

Many people who practice herbalism are also called apothecaries, but they are not necessarily the same. Apothecaries are skilled in creating natural remedies and formulating tinctures, balms, teas, tonics, salves, and ointments. But they are not always skilled at treating illness or injury with their prescriptions.

Herbology (the study of herbs and herb-like substances) was one of the subjects taught to aspiring physicians in Western universities during the Middle Ages until the faculty of medicine at Paris prohibited such studies in 1219 (ostensibly for having no scientific value), and the other faculties followed suit. In this system, herbal remedies were prescribed by an academic physician who used herbs and concoctions of his creation.

Herbalism is an ancient art that may have faded from popular culture except for its continued use as alternative medicine by many. It was once the main form of treatment for many ailments but has slowly been replaced by modern medicine. Herbalism is still valid today as it has proven effective in treating certain conditions or symptoms. If someone wants to become an herbalist, they can learn through books and practical experience.

Conclusion

The Native American Herbalism Encyclopedia is filled with information on the medicinal properties of plants and their spiritual uses. It covers many topics that include how to plant, harvest, dry, and store herbs; the medicinal properties of plants; how to prepare herbal remedies for specific uses such as healing wounds or relieving chest congestion; the effects of nature on the teachings of the philosophy of Eastern medicine - the mystical view that all things happen in cycles. There are also recipes for herbs based primarily on wild foods gathered by natives.

Native American herbalism is an ancient practice of using plants and natural elements to achieve health, happiness, and spiritual purification. It can be found in pueblo (North America's southwestern native Americans) shamanism and the Hawaiian "kahuna" practice of traditional medicine.

This encyclopedia was created as a gateway to information for those who want to learn about the history, beliefs, culture, and traditions of Native American sacred plants and for those who want to learn more about their use as a healing system or as a lifestyle tool.

The goal is to provide an easy-to-use, smooth-sided reference source to make learning about Indian sacred plants easy and enjoyable.

Many things should be considered when trying to heal a body or cure a person; one of those items should be the Medicine Wheel, an ancient symbol representing the four directions and a scale for balancing out all of the elements needed for survival. In today's society, research on indigenous peoples around the world has found that this sacred symbol brings balance, harmony, and unity to those who follow its teachings. In short, it is an ancient system of healing and restoring life through nature itself.

Native Americans have been using herbal remedies for various diseases and ailments since ancient times. Many people may think that these healing techniques are outdated, but it may surprise you that old herbal remedies are making a comeback in today's medical field. While new methods are constantly being tested and developed, some texts have been discovered from studying ancient Native Americans that reveal the old ways were the best alternative to cure an illness or heal a human body. Some of these ancient texts date back over twenty-five hundred years, and a great deal of information written on these ancient scrolls still has yet to be translated into English. One of the most well-known ancient texts comes from the Iroquois tribe, who describe their herbal remedies with stories about how plants, herbs, and trees came into existence. According to the writings of this tribe, plants began to appear on Earth after various gods seeded them with life. All of the plants were created and placed on Earth from this original seed by these gods. There is information about where these plants originated and how they can be used to heal an illness or disease that may affect a person's body.

Other ancient texts explain that certain herbs were placed on Earth before man appeared. During this time, it is believed that these plants provided medicine for animals that had begun to evolve at the time. Some of the most exciting writings are the ones that describe how humans were placed on Earth by gods who grew tired of looking after them.

It may seem incredible that there was no life on Earth at one time, but it is still something that many American Indians believe is true.

APOTHECARY GARDEN

Introduction

The different forms of herbs used in herbalism (herbology / herbal medicine) use the word "medicinal plant." It is the application and analysis of the uses of plants as medicine. Nowadays, the term herb applies to some portion of the plant, such as fruit, stem, seed, grass, herb, bark, leaf, root, a stigma, and a plant (non-woody). Previously, only (non-woody) plants, such as those derived from shrubs and trees, were defined by the word "grass." These species are also used for food, flavonoids, medication, perfume, and some spiritual practices.

Plants were used for medicinal purposes even before prehistoric times. There is evidence that Indian Vadis, Unani hakims, and indigenous communities such as Rome, Iran, Africa, America, Egypt, and European and Mediterranean communities have used herbs as medicine for over 4000 years. For example, early Unani manuscripts identified the use of herbs in Egyptian papyri and Chinese writings. Herbal remedies are routinely used also in Western medicinal systems, Ayurveda and Chinese Medicine.

In several respects, the methods of conventional medicine seem to be the most followed. Increasing population, limited availability of pharmaceuticals, the prohibitive cost of drugs, adverse effects of several synthetic drugs, and the emergence of tolerance to commonly available drugs for infectious diseases have contributed to the increasing attention to the use of herbal materials as the basis of medicinal products for a wide range of human diseases.

Ancient civilizations have recognized India as a rich repository of medicinal herbs. Many medicinal herbs, harvested mainly as raw materials for the manufacture of medicines and perfumery products, are the key repository of the forest in India. In India, AYUSH programs have codified about 8,000 medicinal herbs. The main frameworks of indigenous medicines are Ayurveda, Siddha, Unani, and folk (tribal) medicines. Ayurveda and Unani medicine are the most evolved and commonly followed systems in India.

Recently, 80% of people worldwide rely on herbal medicines for some of their primary health care needs, as reported by WHO. According to WHO, some 21,000 plant species have the potential to be used as medicinal herbs. According to available statistics, about three-quarters of the world's population relies predominantly on herbs and plant extracts for their medical needs. About 30% of all types of plants have been used for medicinal purposes at some point in time. However, the economic value of medicinal plants is much higher for countries such as India than for the rest of the planet. These countries supply two-thirds of the plants used in the Western medical system, and the rural population's health care system depends on indigenous medical systems.

Medicinal plant therapies are considered very healthy, as they have zero or minor side effects. Such treatments are in harmony with nature, which is also the most significant gain. The golden truth is that all ages, demographic groups, and genders are independent of the use of herbal therapies.

Ancient authors claimed that herbs were the only way to treat many ailments and illnesses related to physical fitness. We conducted extensive research on the subject, coming to specific conclusions about the potency of medical benefits in various herbs. Many herbal medicines are free of adverse effects or reactions, hence their formulation. As a result, herbal medicine is becoming increasingly common throughout the world. These medicinal-grade herbs offer a reasonable way to cure many internal disorders that are often challenging to treat.

Numerous natural diseases are cured with medicinal plants such as Tulsa, Neem, Aloe, Turmeric, and Ginger. These are known in certain parts of the world as home remedies. It is understood that many customers use Basil (Tulsa) in their daily lives to create medicines. Many herbs are used in some parts of the world to respect their rulers, presenting them as a sign of luck. After discovering the role of herbs in medicine, many consumers in their home gardens have started planting Tulsa and other medicinal plants.

It is recognized that medicinal plants are a rich supply of ingredients that can be pharmacopeia/non-pharmacopeia or synthetic medicines used in drug production. In addition, these plants play a vital role in the growth of human societies worldwide. Some plants are considered a source of essential nutrients and are therefore recommended for their medicinal properties, such as ginger, nuts, green tea, pepper, aloe, and turmeric. Many plants and their extracts are an essential source of active ingredients found in aspirin, toothpaste, and other products.

In addition to medicinal purposes, the plants are also used as a natural dye, rodent prevention, fruit, perfume, tea, etc. In many countries, various medicinal plants/herbs are used to prevent ants, bugs, and rats from invading homes and workplaces. Medicinal herbs are already an essential part of therapeutic development since a few years ago.

Traditional medicine practitioners have very successful formulas for treating prevalent diseases such as hypertension, diarrhea, constipation, poor sperm production, dysentery, poor male genital erection, coated tongue, piles, menstrual irregularities, bronchial asthma, leucorrhea, and fevers. Therefore, much research is being done today on herbal medicines.

Modern Medicine vs. Traditional Medicine

In some parts of the world, health treatment has been revolutionized over the last 100 years by the invention and industrial manufacture of chemically synthesized drugs. However, in developed countries, a significant part of the population relies on conventional physicians and natural remedies for their primary treatment. Up to 90% of the people in Africa and 70% in India rely on conventional treatment to meet their medical needs. Traditional medicine accounts for almost 40% of all healthcare provided in China, and more than 90% of general hospitals have conventional medicine systems. According to one study, the most commonly practiced complementary treatment (18.9%) was holistic therapy or medicinal resources other than minerals and vitamins, while the use of all prayers was omitted. A study conducted in Hong Kong in 2003 revealed that, compared to Western medicine, 40 percent of respondents showed a marked reliance on herbal medicines. 12.8 percent were taking at least one herbal supplement in a study of 21,923 people in the United States. In another survey, 42% of respondents were taking dietary or nutritional supplements, with multivitamins and minerals being the most common, supplemented by saw palmetto, flax, garlic, and ginkgo at the time of the interview.

The most important explanations for the use of alternative medicines are that they are more affordable, fit better into the consumer's philosophy, alleviate concerns about the harmful effects of artificial (synthetic) drugs, address the need for more individualized treatment and provide the public with better access to clinical knowledge. The main application of herbal medicines for recurrent disorders, and not for life-threatening ones, is wellness promotion and therapy. However, as conventional medication proves unsuccessful in treating diseases such as advanced cancer and, in the face of modern emerging disorders, the use of alternative remedies is growing. In comparison, conventional medications are commonly accepted, i.e., they are not poisonous but normal and healthy. That is not generally valid, primarily when herbs are used with prescription narcotics, over-the-counter medications, and other herbs, as is very popular.

Whether or not people have financial or physical access to allopathic medicine, Traditional Medicine represents an essential health care service, regardless of why an individual uses it. It is a thriving global commercial enterprise. In 1990, spending in the United States related to "alternative" treatments amounted to $13.7 billion. By 1997, this figure had doubled, with herbal medicines increasing more than all other complementary medicines. Annual spending on conventional medicine in Australia, Canada, and the United Kingdom is expected to be $80 million, $1 billion, and $2.3 billion, respectively. These figures represent the introduction into many healthcare structures of herbal and other alternative medicine and its integration into the medical training of physicians in many areas of the developing world.

We should not underestimate the aggregate economic attractiveness of the ethnobotanical industry. In 1995, for example, the overall turnover of over-the-counter herbal remedies in pharmacies contributed to approximately 30% of the total turnover of over-the-counter herbal medicines in Germany, and annual sales figures for herbal medicines in the United States are valued at $5.1 billion. In India, herbal remedies are a traditional activity, and the herbal medicine industry uses around 960 plant species, of which 178 are large, exceeding 100 metric tons each year. The overall volume of herbal medicine developed in 1995 reached 17.6 billion yuan (about $2.5 billion) in China. This pattern has persisted, and in 2003-2004, annual sales in Western Europe reached $5 billion. Sales of herbal medicines amounted to $14 billion in China in 2005, and sales of herbal supplements in Brazil amounted to $160 million in 2007. Annual demand for these products worldwide is estimated to have exceeded $60 billion.

Herbs are currently used to cure chronic and severe diseases and different disorders and problems, such as heart disease, prostate disorders, depression, and inflammation, to name just a handful, to enhance the immune system. Traditional herbal medicines played a prominent role in the control and treatment technique of SARS (severe acute respiratory syndrome) in China in 2003. The traditional herbal medicine, African flower, has been used in Africa for decades to control HIV-related wasting symptoms. Herbal medicines are still very popular in Europe, with France and Germany leading European countries in over-the-counter sales, and essential oils, herbal extracts, and infusions can be found in pharmacies selling prescription medicines in most developed countries.

Herbs and seeds, including whole herbs, herbal teas, infusions, syrups, essential oils, salves, ointments, capsules, rubs, and tablets comprising a raw ground or powdered plant or its dried extract, can be manufactured and taken in numerous forms and types. Plant and herbal extracts differ in terms of the solvent used for extraction, temperature, and extraction period and include vinegar (acetic acid extracts), alcoholic extracts (tinctures), hot water extracts (tisanes), usually roots or barks (decoctions), long-term boiled extract and cold infusions of plants (macerates). There is little standardization, and the ingredients of a medicinal extract or substance can differ considerably between batches and manufacturers.

Plants have many rich compounds in them. Most are secondary metabolites containing aromatic compounds, mostly phenols, such as tannins, or their oxygen-substituted equivalents, the protective effects of several of these substances. Ethnobotanical products are relevant when plant components are used primarily as therapeutic agents for pharmacological research and drug production and as starting materials for drug synthesis or as templates with pharmacologically active compounds.

About 200 years ago, morphine, the first purely pharmacologically active compound, was developed from opium, derived from the pods of the opium poppy Papaver somniferum. This finding revealed that drugs from plants, regardless of their origin or the age of the substance, can be distilled and administered in specific doses. The detection of penicillin improved this method. With this ongoing pattern, plant and natural products (such as fungi and marine microorganisms) and their inspired analogs have been substantially incorporated into today's industrial drug formulations.

About 60 percent of cancer therapies, mainly marketed or under the study, focus on natural ingredients. More than 70 percent of the 177 drugs licensed worldwide for cancer therapy focus on natural/mimetic products, several of which are enhanced by combinatorial chemistry.
Here are a few examples. Paclitaxel, extracted from the bark of the Pacific yew tree (Taxus brevifolia), contains plant-based cancer therapeutic agents. Camptothecin, an anti-cancer alkaloid obtained from the Chinese "Happy tree" (Camptotheca acuminata), is used to prepare anti-cancer drugs irinotecan and topotecan. Combretastatin is obtained from the South African Bush Willow tree.

It is estimated that approximately 25% of the drugs administered worldwide are extracted from plants and that 121 such active substances are used. Thirteen drugs derived from natural resources were approved in the United States between 2005 and 2007. One hundred drugs based on natural products are in clinical trials, and 11% of 252 drugs on the WHO essential medicines list are predominantly of plant origin.

Sourcing Herbs

You can get fresh herbs, which you can grow or buy, or get dried herbs readily available in the store. You also have the option to purchase seeds so you can grow these herbs yourself to make essential oils and flower essences, depending on how you want to use them.

How to Source Fresh Herbs

However, due to climate and location, this is not always possible. Ideally, you should have a garden to grow herbs in; there are some herbs that you can also grow indoors, but your options will be limited.

You can buy fresh herbs at the farmers' market or online, but they tend to be expensive and spoil quickly. Most garden herbs are not difficult to grow, but growing some medicinal herbs can be tricky.

You can grow your basic herbs by following the steps outlined:

1. Decide Which Herb to Grow

You can grow specific herbs in a sunny spot in your garden or even plant them indoors in a pot where sunlight comes in through the window. The simplest herbs to grow are basil, mint, chives, tarragon, and rosemary.

Chives

Chives are a great garnish and can easily be grown in your garden. Growing chives can also help repel insects from your garden.

Mint

Mint is the best herb for a novice to grow, as it is hardy and difficult to spoil. You can grow mint in moist, fertile soil in a partially shaded or sunny area. Mint makes a great garnish and can be added to beverages for flavor.

2. Do You Want Fast or Slow Growing Herbs?

Herbs grow in different cycles. Ask yourself if you want an annual, perennial, or biennial herb. Annual and biennial herbs include cilantro, dill, and parsley. They grow fast, and you may need to plant them at regular intervals throughout the spring and summer to have a supply. Perennial herbs include thyme, mint, sage, oregano, rosemary, and chives.

3.   Grow a Cutting or Buy Seeds

You can buy seeds and start to grow your herbs from scratch or buy potted plants already growing. You can also grow many herbs from small cuttings of a mature herb. You get seeds and cuttings from any nursery. If you want to use a cutting to grow your first herb, consider mint because it is the easiest.

4.   Do Your Research

You need to make sure you spend a good amount of time researching the individual requirements of the herbs you decide to grow. You need to find out how much and how often to water them, how much light they need, and the optimum temperature for their growth. Some herbs also have specific needs in terms of soil texture, soil moisture, and pH level.

5.   Water it Right

Don't overwater or underwater a plant, as that can be the main reason why your herbs may fail. You can always let the top of the soil dry out between watering sessions, but don't let the soil dry out completely. Make it a routine, and you will get used to the needs of your plants.

6.   Take Care While Harvesting

When harvesting your herbs, be sure to cut them down to a leaf or a pitch. It looks better than leaving the stems and is also healthier for the plant, and will allow it to heal faster. Cut off the tip of the stem to allow new leaf growth along with the plant's nodes because the plant's hormones distribute this way.

7.   Increase Production

You can make your plant more productive by dividing it, and you can also grow a cutting to increase production.
That is an excellent way to grow more herbs without spending money on a new plant. You can follow these steps to grow essential herbs in your garden and home. You can also do some research on the Internet to find out how to grow specific herbs. Once you have the tools, the actual cultivation is not that complicated.
However, if you don't think you have a green thumb, you can always buy your herbs online or at the farmer's market.

How to Get Herbal Tinctures

In this book, you will find detailed recipes on how you can make herbal tinctures at home. You can also buy herbal tinctures at local pharmacies and herbal stores. Do a little research to see which ones sell these tinctures at a discount.

However, if you have the herbs for it, there is no reason for you to spend extra money on herbal tinctures when you can make them yourself, according to your needs.

How to Get Flower Essences

Flower essences are used in aromatherapy to achieve energetic reactions similar to homeopathy. Flower essences act more on emotions than on the body. They are made from an infusion of plants placed directly in the sunlight. After some time, certain parts of the herbs are separated, and the remaining liquid essence is kept mixed with brandy. They are that easy to make at home.

However, many stores sell flower essences if you don't have time to make them yourself. You can find them at your local herbalist/botanist and on the Internet.

How to Obtain Essential Oils

Essential oils are the easiest to buy, as they are available in many different places. The trick is to find good-quality essential oils. You can purchase essential oils from local stores, as they make them in smaller batches and put more time and effort into their oils. If you buy from a big brand, make sure it is legitimate to get the best quality for your money. Or you can make your own.

Be careful as many fake essential oils are synthetically manufactured and available cheaply.

How to Source Dried Herbs

Dried herbs are available in most supermarkets and whole food stores. You can also find good deals on dried herbs on the Internet. Or dry your herbs in the oven or place them in the sun.

If you don't grow a particular herb in your garden, you can order it by the pound from various websites. You can research and find the websites closest to you to get the best deals. At first, you can order small batches to check the quality. Make sure they are freshly harvested and well dried, and you can get superior-quality dried herbs. If you can't find good-quality dried herbs online, you can check local farms in your area. Some of these farms also sell their dried herbs online. If it is a hard-to-find herb, you can also check national listings to see the shipping process and place your order accordingly.

How to Obtain Herb Seeds

Many online nurseries sell organic herb seeds. You can do a little research to see which local nurseries in your area have an online presence. If you don't mind going out and doing some physical shopping, there is nothing better than going to local farms and nurseries and hand-selecting seeds.

You can start by ordering small batches of seeds and see which ones have the best germination success. Some websites also sell books and guides on how to grow specific herbs from seeds and use them as plant-based medicine, so be sure to check them out.

Many seed companies also sell in stores or farmer's market stalls. Similarly, you can buy seeds from garden stores, co-ops, and online.

You can also try exchanging seeds with like-minded local gardeners. A good practice is to save seeds from your garden whenever you can so you have more options.

How to Obtain Herbal Plants/ Seedlings

You can buy organic herbaceous plants or seedlings from local growers. You can check your local gardens for pollinator plants to start growing your herbs, and you'll find that you can get hundreds of different varieties of herbs.

Some gardens and nurseries offer plants by mail, so you won't even have to leave home to get them. You can call ahead and see what sales options these places have or check their online catalog.

Many local farms grow organic produce and sell herbs and vegetables from early spring to early summer. Some sell their merchandise online and at their farm and farmers' market.

You can check your local co-op chain to see what kind of organic herbs and vegetables they sell.

You can recycle these herbs by cutting parts of the plants you buy to grow more in your garden.

Foraging

Have you ever gone foraging for wild blackberries? Are you ecstatic when you find an edible mushroom on the forest floor? If so, you're a picker! Picking plants and mushrooms from nature is a great way to eat healthily and enhance your connection with nature. But whatever you choose for your plate or pot, remember to treat it with care and respect. You'll see weeds and wild critters in a new light after learning the basics of foraging and wildcrafting.

Foraging is traveling and investigating the physical environment searching for edible plants (or fungi). According to behavioral ecology theory, foraging influences the fitness of animals, as it is fundamental to their ability to live and reproduce. Humans indeed seem to be able to survive and reproduce without relying on hunting for food in natural areas. Nevertheless, we believe that this ancient practice has a beneficial effect on physical, mental, and emotional health.

What is the difference between foraging and wildcrafting? Not much. They are just different names for the same thing. Most often, foraging refers to the act of gathering food. On the other hand, wildcrafting is more often associated with herbal and mushroom remedies. However, this difference is not set in stone. You will almost certainly hear of people foraging for plants or making wild food.

Check with your local council (or whoever is in charge of the area you are interested in) to see if foraging is allowed where you want to go. Consider presenting your message as an effort to eradicate invasive species. Many delicious foods are invasive, so your foraging can contribute to environmental stewardship. Laws against foraging, according to some, unfairly affect blacks, Native Americans, and people of color, as well as rural residents.

Ethical Wild Foraging

It is a beautiful experience to go out into the forest or field and come back with a huge pile of food and herbs.

With each new plant, you learn to recognize and use, you feel more able to take care of yourself and your family. You also become less dependent and susceptible to big business. However, with greater independence comes the duty to protect your safety.

In addition, dangerous pesticides can be sprayed on numerous so-called wastelands on the edge of the inhabited world and along stream banks and roadsides.

Runoff from vehicles waters the ditches when it rains. Herbicides will also be sprayed on the sides of rural roads in several villages.

That saves money over running mowing vehicles. However, it destroys many little-traveled places where it might otherwise forage. Streams and rivers can carry hazardous material for hundreds of miles.

If you consume something, make sure it does not come from a poisoned region. The more experience you gain, the more deviations from the rules you will see and know when to ignore them.

But, since no one wants to be a cautionary tale, we encourage the beginner to follow
them all.
The first guideline is to take things slowly when dealing with new plants. Allergies or
intolerances to wild plants are as common as allergies or intolerances to commercial
foods. Use a small amount the first few months you try a plant. You should also
experiment with only one new plant at a time. This way, if you experience a response,
you will be able to determine which plant is the culprit.

Talk to a Local Expert

Local specialists often know small details that books and websites may miss and
expert knowledge of how plants appear and act in your region.
If you can't locate a local expert, books and the Internet are good ways to learn about
wild agriculture. However, they can't warn you when you're going to make a mistake.
To reduce your risks, be careful and ask for advice from several sources.

Know Your Environment

Thorns, pits, ledges, dangerous animals, moving cars, quicksand and volcanoes are all
physical hazards. Just stay alert and avoid putting your hands and feet in places where
you can't see them. Chemical hazards are more difficult to identify. Avoid wilderness
tourism in areas that have been treated with herbicides or pesticides. If you are not
sure, ask. It's not something you want to consume.

Respect Private Property

After dark, don't forage around someone's house or through someone's private land.
For starters, why were you foraging in the dark?

Use All Your Senses

What does the plant look like? What kind of tendencies do you notice? What are the
colors? What is the general shape of the object? What does it feel like to you?
(Rough? Fuzzy? Soft?) Does it have a strange sound? Plants can make different
noises.
Sometimes you'll come across a seemingly right plant, but something is missing. You
may have discovered a subspecies or a variant. On the other hand, it may be a deadly
double. For this reason, you'd better leave it alone until you can get a more accurate
identification.
Mints (Lamiaceae) are known for their stems that are square or opposite to the leaves.
As they move up the stem, these leaf pairs rotate 90 degrees back and forth. Avoid
plants that look like mint but don't smell like mint.
Animals can consume various foods that could sicken or kill humans. They usually
have a solid sense of what is healthy for them, but they have no idea what is suitable
for people. Don't try to be like the animals.

Avoid Plants with White Sap

Dandelions, for example, are entirely harmless, and others may be safe if they have been properly prepared. However, if a plant contains white sap, it should be left alone.

Avoid Plants with White Berries

Plants that have white berries are not ones to fool with. Don't even go near them. If you find a crop with umbels, you should be very sure what it is before harvesting and using it. Elderberry, yarrow, or carrots produce attractive umbels. Poison hemlock also has packaging techniques because of its lethal properties. However, many of these crops look similar to each other. I'm not saying you shouldn't do them in the future, but you should practice with safe plants first. When you are ready for umbels, always check their qualities. No matter how smart or experienced, anyone can poison themselves if they become arrogant or careless.

Beware of Mushrooms

The word "poisonous" is taken as a personal target by mushrooms. Mushrooms, on the other hand, are tasty and entertaining. If you select the right type, you can grow them safely. Some mushrooms, such as morels or puffballs, are quite safe for novices to collect. Just be cautious, study their appearance and look-alikes, go out with an expert guide, and you'll get the hang of it. This guideline also applies to garlic. However, the plant you discover should look and smell similar to onions or garlic. There are some dangerous look-alikes, and none smell the same.

All Mustards Are Edible

Mustards (family Brassicaceae) are edible and can be found all over the world. It's a wonder. So how does mustard appear? Flowering is the most reliable method of identification. Plants in the mustard family have four petals and six stamens (4 tall and two short). Since the blooms are usually tiny, it may be necessary to use a magnifying lens. Several members of this family are very intense with a pungent smell and should not be consumed in large quantities.

Know Your Local Environment

Although you are unlikely to look for prickly pears in the humid Pacific Northwest, it is helpful to understand and appreciate what is abundant and what is considered "endangered" in your region. Get a guide to your area from your local public library, bookstore, or the Internet, and learn about the flora of your area. Pay close attention to plant characteristics, growth circumstances, and flowering/fruiting period. Seek out expert plant foragers and herbalists who lead foraging walks and sign up for their next event.

Local farmers, hunters, and anglers have proven to be excellent sources for finding some wild and abundant plant materials.

Have a Foraging Plan

Never go into the woods (or anywhere else) if you don't have a strategy. Remember what you're looking for and where to look for it, and then stick to your objective. If you encounter something interesting, note where you are, take a photo or a small specimen, and consult identification materials or field guides if you have time and resources.
This technique will probably save you time and the possibility of misinterpretation and influence your decision whether or not to collect it, e.g., if it is endangered or at risk.

Identify

We cannot stress this enough, learn to recognize your herbs or mushrooms correctly! Never rely on a single identifying feature, such as a flower or leaf, to identify a plant. Use three or more forms of identification. Color, leaf, flower, stem, fruit, bark/branch, odor, location, plant life cycle, soil conditions, and spore track are factors to consider (in the case of mushrooms).
Cottonwoods, for example, develop shoots of sticky, aromatic leaves on brittle, gnarled branches in late winter or early spring, usually near rivers or in wet, often marshy soils. Aspen is recognized by location, life cycle stage (leaf bud), scent, and branches; four identification criteria.

Leave Nature the Same or Better Than You Found It

As an outdoor enthusiast, nothing is more annoying than seeing your favorite places ruined, pillaged, and ravaged by less-than-grateful individuals. Remove all trash, and consider carrying an extra bag to pick up any mess or trash you may find.
Do NOT radically change the environment for your purposes— don't cut down trees/limbs, drag fallen trees over rivers to make bridges, don't go off the roadway, don't disrupt nests, burrows, etc. Do not.
Notify appropriate authorities, such as Fish & Wildlife, the Forest Service, Parks and Recreation, and state police, of dangerous circumstances.

Prepare and Report

Someone else always has to know where you're going and how long you plan to be gone!
Be prepared with the tools you'll need and clothing to wear. You could carry a lightweight "parachute" type cross-body bag with a large front pocket to hold your cutters, several survival guides, plus small zippered type pouches, while the body of the bag has more than enough room for your finds.

A basket might be a suitable option for softer harvests, such as nettle leaves, mushrooms, flowers, and petals. Use pruners or a good sharp, compact knife to make clean cuts.

Wear sturdy, weather-appropriate footwear and long sleeves if possible. A decent, sturdy pair of protective gloves is always a wise choice.

Buying Herbs

Ideally, find a local herbalist for advice if you start with herbs and herbal remedies. You can find an herbalist by going to your local health food store. There are many health food stores in cities and towns across America. You can also find them in many large grocery stores. However, places to buy herbs are not limited to health food stores. There are specialty stores that sell herbs, as well as online stores. The Internet has made it easier than ever to find what you are looking for, the best herbal remedies at your fingertips.

The following website is one of my favorites for buying Native American herbs.

https://mountainroseherbs.com

What Are the Benefits of Buying Herbs?

They don't usually cost as much as some prescription drugs. Prescription drugs often have some side effects, and usually, they are more expensive. Herbal remedies are less likely to have side effects because they contain fewer chemicals than prescription drugs, which can cause adverse reactions in the body.

But it is important to know how herbs work, so you know their possible side effects before you buy them.

If you are a beginner with herbs, you want to be sure you are using the right herb. You are confident about their quality by buying them from a local nursery or herbal store. You can get valuable advice from local experts or herbalists.

Growing Herbs

Finding herbs for your home garden can be done at many different places. The grocery store is the best place for some; others might prefer to purchase their herbs at a nursery or garden center. You'll want to choose an herb that's the right size and color for your needs and one that's not too expensive because you'll need plenty of it. The trick is finding what type of herb you want and where you can find it!

Garden Center

A garden center allows you to purchase various herbs such as rosemary, oregano, and thyme. You'll want to make sure that the herb is easy to grow and take care of. Most garden centers require their herbs to be grown from seeds indoors before putting them out for sale. If the herb is grown using cuttings, it should be able to bloom and produce fruits without any problem. If the herb is in a container, it should be labeled and easy to identify.

Nursery

Another source for herbs would be a nursery. A nursery might specialize in herbs such as aloe, lemon balm, or forsythia. You'll want to make sure that the herb grows well and bloom without any problems. If it's not labeled, make sure it's safe to take home with you.

Seed and plant stores

Several seed companies carry a wide range of herb seeds. You can grow these plants for culinary purposes.

Online

If you're looking to buy seeds or potted plants online, you can check out this website https://strictlymedicinalseeds.com/ which will provide you with the product you need and valuable information.

Growing Your Herbs

A lot of herbs can be grown indoors in pots on your windowsill, but some need a bit more work to grow well. However, no matter what type of herb you want to grow, some things make life easier when growing herbs indoors.
When choosing which herb to grow, please consider what it's good for and the smell. For instance, you can grow basil and cilantro to make your food taste better, repel bad odors and flies, and keep yourself healthy. You might even want to keep a plant of each kind.

It's easy to grow them in some containers, but choose herbs that require more water to get the most out of your pots. You can also use bigger pots, but make sure they're at least 4 inches deep (or more) and at least 9 inches across (or more).

Propagation From Seeds

You can grow numerous plants from seeds. Plant the seeds in pots or indoor pads toward the finish of winter. They need a radiant window and cool temperatures (60 degrees F) to develop best. Treat young plants for the nursery as you would treat youthful sage or pepper plants. A few plants take more time to create than others. Start those with more modest seeds first, ideally in February. You would then be able to relocate them into individual pots and plant them in the nursery after the danger of frost has passed. The better the seeds are, the shallower the planting. Some herbs do not transplant well. Use soil from your garden or purchase potting soil mix, which is lighter and contains organic material.

For direct sowing outdoors, plant in spring after all danger of frost has passed and the soil begins to warm up. Make the soil a fine, level seedbed. As a general rule, sow the seeds at a depth of twice their diameter.

Sunlight

Most herbs are easy to grow, but selecting the right location to grow them is necessary. Most herbs need a sunny position, and only a few, including angelica, woodruff, and sweet woodruff, are best grown in partial shade. The oils, which are the basis of the herbs' flavor, are produced in more significant quantities when the plants are exposed to 6 to 8 hours of full sunlight each day and if you can put them out on the ground for part of the day, even better. If you don't have a sunny windowsill, try placing pots on a table or shelf in front of a south-facing window. Many herbs will tolerate light shade if you do not have a good sunny location, but their growth & quality will not be as good.

Watering

Some herbs need more water than others, so it's best to be informed about this before you start growing them. For instance, chives don't need as much water as parsley or mint (this depends on the variety you choose). If they get too much water, they'll begin to wilt or mold.

It's also important to grow the same kind of herb every year, but you can use different pots and containers and keep some herbs in pots and others in bigger pots. To grow your herbs indoors, you'll need either an herb pot for each plant (you can buy 4-10) or one enough big pot for all of your plants. It is necessary to put drainage holes in the bottom of the pot, and the holes should be around 1/4" wide and 1/4" deep to allow proper drainage.

Before putting your plants in their pots, soak them in water (if needed) and let them dry before planting them. That will eliminate the risk of them molding or wilting.

When it comes to watering, if your herbs are in pots, make sure they get water daily (or every other day) and if you keep them in their final pots, make sure they get poured with plenty of water (enough to fill the entire pot). Also, make sure that the soil gets watered enough.

Harvesting Herbs

Harvesting herbs is a time-honored practice at best. But it's also a task that cultivators, farmers, and naturalists have been involved in for centuries. Some herbs are often collected from the wild, while others are grown on farms and hedgerows. Herbal medicine is all about respecting the plants you use, whether wild or grown by hand. That means harvesting them when they're in their most potent form. For example, harvesting mint during its blooming period will yield a far more potent product than if you harvest it before or after this period.
Other herbs have to be harvested in a certain way or at a specific time. For example, many types of ginger are considered to be "hot" rather than "cold," as one might assume. Therefore, the root is harvested when it's dormant to avoid getting burned from it.
Depending on the herb, the harvest may include one or more plant parts such as leaves, flowers, seeds, roots, or sometimes even the whole plant. Handle flowers as you would handle leaves. Often the flowers are collected with the leaves and mixed. To cut any part of the plant, always use a sharp cutting tool to avoid damage to the live plant. Before cutting, always check for any signs of pest infestation or other damage such as mold or insect damage.

Leaves

It is essential to gather leaves when they contain the ideal measure of fundamental oils, and these oils give herbs their unique taste or aroma. Preferably you should cut your herbs soon after the dew has dried from the leaves toward the beginning of the day, during mid-morning, as after that, the sun starts to evaporate the oils from the herbs.
Cut the stems for gathering when the bloom buds start to open. Mints, be that as it may, have more oil in their leaves when the spikes are in full sprout. When harvesting many herbs, use a basket or crate with an open binding that allows air to circulate. Try not to stuff herbs into plastic sacks, which can warm up and make the herbs break down rapidly. Never cut more stems than you can dry at one time.

Flowers

Like leaves, harvest flowers in mid-morning after the dew has dried from them and the plant is relatively dry.

Cut six or more inches of the stem so you create a bunch of them and can them easily hang up for drying. After drying, you can cut them shorter if needed.

Flowers will continue to open even after has been cut and can lose their petals as they dry. That's why I choose to cut ones with not fully-opened buds.

Roots

Angelica and lovage produce usable roots. Dig these roots in late autumn or early spring. Wash them thoroughly after digging. Then slice or split the large roots. Put the pieces in thin layers on drying racks and turn the slices several times a week. After they are partially dry, finish them off in an oven over low heat before putting them in an airtight container for storage. The roots can take six to eight weeks to dry out completely. When they are dry, the root piece should break when you bend it.

Seeds

You can grow and process dill, caraway, fennel, and anise seeds at home. Then the seeds should fall out of the heads quite easily. Remove the husk and let the seeds continue to dry for another week. Stir them often. Store the seeds in airtight jars after they have dried completely.

Drying Herbs

Drying herbs is a perfect low-tech project for the summer. It takes up little time and results in beautiful, aromatic herbs that can be used to flavor dishes or just as decorations for your kitchen. Here are some key tips to get you started!

How to begin

To start, rinse them well and pat them dry with paper towels. Separate the leaves from the stems and place them on a drying rack or tea towel-lined baking sheet. Far away from light sources, dust, pests, etc.
Use scissors to snip the ends off the stems, if necessary. Remove any small leaves or bits of debris from the leaves. For longer stems, leave them on! They make beautiful decorations when dried.

A dim, very much ventilated room where the temperature is between 70 and 90 degrees F is an ideal space for drying.
In general, herbs with more robust leaves contain more oil and are easier to dry, such as thyme, sage, rosemary, or bay leaves.
On the contrary, herbs with wider and more tender leaves are more sensitive to moisture, making them more challenging to dry. It is essential to dry them straight away after harvesting to avoid them turning moldy.
Native American herbs can be dried in many places and for many different amounts of time. For example, sage dries in about 3 weeks, cinnamon in 2 weeks, and thyme in 1 week. Other herbs can be dried in 4-5 days with proper care.

If you are drying herbs outside, make sure they are exposed to the sun most of the day. Or tie them onto drying racks. If you are drying herbs indoors, you should keep windows open for proper air circulation and place your herbs in a shady place with plenty of air flow.
If you plan on using your herbs soon after they are dried, it is best to dry them for about 4-5 days, then store them in airtight containers with plastic wrap over the top to slow moisture loss. That will help the seasonings retain the flavor and color better than if they dried out longer than five days.
Drying herbs for a long time can cause them to lose their flavor and aromatic properties. Take care not to dry longer than necessary.

Air or low heat drying is a traditional way of preserving herbs—the canvas bags or cheesecloth help protect the herbs from dust and other contamination during drying.
Hang bunches of herbs in a warm, dry, and well-ventilated area out of the sun.
A simple frame that has a mesh attached to the bottom works well. Spread a single layer of herbs on the mesh and place these frames in a warm, well-ventilated area out of the sun. It may be necessary to turn the leaves regularly to ensure even drying.

Drying with heat

Drying with heat may involve using conventional ovens, microwave ovens, or dehydrators, and this may be the only way to dry herbs effectively in very humid places.

For both oven and microwave drying, removing any excess moisture from the herbs is essential because it can lead to them cooking and not drying. However, it is important to realize these drying methods consume large amounts of electricity or gas.

Domestic dehydrators do an excellent job of drying herbs. Refer to the owner's manual for specifications and settings.

Oven drying works well if temperatures can be closely monitored. Often, oven temperatures cannot be set low enough, resulting in a loss of flavor and color. However, if the oven temperatures can be maintained in a range of 100°F to 145°F, this would be the ideal temperature for oven drying. Setting the temperature too hot may burn the herbs. Leaving the oven door a little bit open ensures important good air circulation.

Using microwaves for drying herbs could be a simple but also risky method. Always try first with a small amount of herbs to avoid ruining the whole harvest. Place the herbs on the paper towel, leave enough space among the pieces and cover them with another paper towel. Place them in the microwave for 1min at a high temperature. After 1 min, let them cool, turn them and place them again in the microwave for 20-30 seconds. Repeat the process until the herbs are thoroughly dry. Don't let them sit in the microwave too long, and if you start smelling them burning, immediately stop the process.
After drying with heat, place the herbs on a rack and allow them to cool before storing.

Drying seeds

To dry the seeds of herbs, cut off the stems with the seed heads as soon as the heads start to turn brown. Once dry, shake out the seeds from the seed heads. Rub the seeds carefully to separate the seeds from the capsules. Laying seeds on a clean flat surface and gently blowing on them will help remove debris and trash. Collect the seeds and store them in sealed containers. Seeds can take longer to dry than leaves.

Storing dried herbs

Dried herbs stored improperly may lose some flavor and color and become bitter. Before storing dried herbs, always make sure they are completely dehydrated. Try to rub them between your fingers, and if they crumble easily and feel crispy, you can store them.
If they feel tender and don't crumble well, let them dry a little longer or place them into a dehydrator to dry them.

Keep these 4 key factors in mind when storing dried herbs:

Container

It is best to store herbs in an airtight container away from light sources, dust, pests, etc. Exposure to air for too long makes your dried herbs stale quickly. Mansons jars work well with a screw cap lid to seal tight. Some herbs don't have to do well in metal tins, so using a glass container is better.
After placing your dried herbs into a container, always put a label with the herb's name and the harvest date or date you purchased your herb. It is important to have a reference point because even properly stored herbs lose their potency after some time, so it is good to know when to replace them or use them before that to avoid wasting them.

Sunlight and heat exposure

Store dried herbs in a dark, cool, and dry place to keep them longer in shape. Sunlight and heat decay dried herbs and cause a change of color.
You may keep them in cabinets or drawers of your kitchen pantry or by using dark-colored jars if keeping them out of the cabinet. Avoid keeping them close to the cooking area where is a lot of heat and moisture produced.

Temperature and humidity

Don't store your dried herbs in the attic or basement, as temperature changes and higher humidity can cause molds on your dried herbs. Always find a room with a stable temperature and low humidity to make your dried herbs last longer.

Shelf life of dried herbs

The average shelf life of dried herbs depends on the part of the plant it's from and its form.

- Ground or powdered dried herbs from leaves, seeds, and bark will last a maximum of 1 year.

- Ground or powdered dried herbs from roots last up to 2 years.

- Dried roots can last up to 3 years before they start to decay.

- Dried seeds and barks last for 2 to 3 years.

- Dried leaves and flowers last for up to 2 years if stored properly.

Native American Herbs and Remedies– Part 1

Agave

Common Names: Agave, Century Plant, Maguey, or American Aloe

Scientific Name: Agave Americana

Family: Asparagaceae (Asparagus)

Origin: Native to semiarid and arid regions of America, particularly the Caribbean and Mexico

About Agave:

The agave plant has numerous plant species used for the production of tequila. It is a plant that takes a long time to grow, between 5 and 7 years. Its low glycemic index helps keep blood sugar levels under control. It is a beneficial plant for strengthening the immune system.

Medicinal Parts: The sap, leaves, seed

Habitat & Foraging: The agave plant is a monocarpic plant that dies after fruiting. It only blooms once after 10 years in a warm climate or 35 years in a cool climate. In its native range, this plant blooms from June to August.

Influence on the Body: It helps improve metabolism and heart health and can help with depression.

Traditional Uses: Wound healing agent. Hand skin treatment. Soap production.

Possible Side Effects: Digestive system irritation – if taken in large quantities. Allergic reactions for those who are allergic.

Alder

Common Names: Red Alder

Scientific Name: Alnus rubra

Family: Betulaceae (Birch family)

Origin: Native to Northwest America (California)

About Alder:

Alder is a tree whose leaves and bark are used to make medicines by Native American Indians. This medicine helps the body fight sore throats, rheumatism, swellings, mouth inflammations, and fever. The individual dosage depends on the age and severity of the health condition. For this reason, people taking other medications should be careful when using Alder and always consult with their health practitioner.

Medicinal Parts: The bark and leaves.

Habitat & Foraging: Alder grows in open woodland on most soil types with a flowering period between March to April.

Influence on the Body: It helps to combat fever or headaches. It reduces symptoms of diarrhea.

Traditional Uses: For bleeding.

Possible Side Effects: Inner bark is emetic when fresh and must be thoroughly dried.

Alfalfa

Common Names: Buffalo Herb, Lucerne

Scientific Name: Medicago sativa

Family: Fabaceae (Legume family)

Origin: Native to Asia and introduced to North America

About Alfalfa:

Alfalfa is native to Asia but only came to North America beginning in the 1860s. This deep-growing plant is also seen around Virginia as far west as Maine and westward to the Pacific coasts of the United States. This herb has seeds, shoots, and leaves adapted for medicinal use, especially for kidney, bladder, and prostate conditions. It contains many essential nutrients, making it popular for constant use.

Medicinal Parts: The seeds and leaves.

Habitat & Foraging: The alfalfa plant is usually found in vacant lots, abandoned fields, and railroads.

Influence on the Body: It helps improve metabolism, lowers cholesterol levels, and contains healthy antioxidants.

Traditional Uses: Relieving menopause symptoms because of its high content of phytoestrogens.

Possible Side Effects: It can be harmful to those who have the following complications: pregnant women; people who take blood thinners; those who have autoimmune disorders or other immune issues. Can cause drug interactions.

Amaranth

Common Names: Wild Amaranth Pigweed, Purple Amaranth

Scientific Name: Amaranthus

Family: Amaranthaceae

Origin: Native to Central America (Mexico)

About Amaranth:

Amaranth is a group of grains with more than 60 species cultivated since long ago (about 8000 years). This ancient grain provides a healthy dose of protein, fiber, and other essential micronutrients, and it is naturally gluten-free. The leaves are also rich in soluble and insoluble fiber, which helps reduce weight.
The seed is easily prepared by soaking it in water for about three days and allowing it to germinate. That facilitates the breakdown and digestion of all the anti-nutrients, which might hinder the absorption of the necessary nutrients. Then, it can be used for different tasty dishes. It has a nutty, earthy taste.

Medicinal Parts: The leaves and seeds.

Habitat & Foraging: Amaranth is easy to plant. Found in North America and South Asia. It needs to be planted for a long season, close to 120 days.

Influence on the Body: Lowers cholesterol levels, contains antioxidants, and reduces inflammation. Amaranth is a rich source of manganese, which is essential for healthy brain function. Other essential micronutrients include high levels of magnesium, phosphorus, and iron.

Traditional Uses: Weight loss.

Possible Side Effects: None known.

Amaranthus retroflexus

Common Names: Redroot Amaranth, Pigweed, Wild Beet, Common Amaranth, Common Tumbleweed

Scientific Name: Amaranthus retroflexus

Family: Amaranthaceae

Origin: Native to Central America (tropical parts)

Habitat & Foraging: Diffused almost all over the United States and Canada in meadows and prairies. You won't find it growing in the shade, but preferably in moist soils.
Its flowering period is between July and September. Seeds are collected from August to October.

Characteristics: This flowering plant is roughly 4 feet tall and has gray-green, oval-shaped, rough leaves. The flowers are hairy at the end of the branches, aments red or purple depending on the species. Inside the flowers, you can find numerous tiny, black seeds during fall. The taproots are red.

Medicinal Parts: Leaves and flowers.

Preferred solvent: Water.

Main effect: Astringent.

Uses: The decoction or raw consumption of leaves was used for its astringent characteristic and to reduce excessive menstruation (hypermenorrhea). The decoction of leaves was also used as gargling for throat inflammation.
Seeds were used as food for sustainment. You grind them and prepare bread or cakes. Leaves (raw and cooked) and roots (boiled) are edible.

American Licorice

Common Names: Wild Licorice

Scientific Name: Glycyrrhiza lepidota

Family: Fabaceae

Origin: Native to Canada and Northwest America (Texas, California, Virginia)

About American Licorice:

American licorice root is one of the oldest herbal remedies in the world today. This root has been popularly used to treat various medical conditions in the form of teas, tinctures, supplements, powders, and medications. Although this root has been around for a long time, it is supported by scientific research but should be taken with caution.
It has been used to treat coughs, viral infections, hot flashes, heartburn, and acid reflux. It also helps control sore throats and similarly clears difficult skin conditions. Although this root does not have a standard dosage, it is advised not to take more than 100 milligrams daily, and a safe and effective dose should be first discussed with your health practitioner.

Medicinal Parts: The leaves and roots.

Habitat & Foraging: American licorice is primarily found in prairie and other grassland communities. It is grazed in summer and early falls.

Influence on the Body: It protects against cavities and helps treat peptic ulcers.

Traditional Uses: Reduction of menopause symptoms, weight loss, excess blood sugar aid, skin condition aid. An infusion was used as a birthing aid to speed placenta delivery.

Possible Side Effects: Not fit for pregnant and breastfeeding women. Bad interaction with certain drugs.

American Mistletoe

Common Names: Eastern Mistletoe, Guy American, Guy de Chine, Mistletoe, Oak Mistletoe

Scientific Name: Phoradendron leucarpum

Family: Santalaceae

Origin: Native to North America (New Mexico, Florida, Illinois)

About American Mistletoe:

American mistletoe has been used since the early 1920s and is a helpful plant with numerous uses. All parts of this plant are medicinal from the stem, leaf, fruit, and flower. The chemicals in the American mistletoe plant affect the muscles and are used to treat low blood pressure and constipation. Although American mistletoe is considered a great and healthy herb, it is always advisable to avoid complications by taking the berries and leaves in small amounts.

Medicinal Parts: The flower, root, stem, and leaves.

Habitat & Foraging: American mistletoe grows as a host on trees like lime, blackthorns, willows, and apple. This herb prefers open space with a lot of light.

Influence on the Body: Constipation, low blood pressure

Traditional Uses: Easy emptying of the system.

Possible Side Effects: Taking a lot of berries or leaves can lead to complications such as diarrhea, heart problems, vomiting, and nausea. Toxic in large quantities. Pregnant and breastfeeding women must avoid this plant.

American Raspberry

Common Names: American Red Raspberry, Blackberry, Dewberry, Grayleaf Red Raspberry

Scientific Name: Rubus idaeus

Family: Rosaceae (Rose family)

Origin: Native to Europe and introduced to North America

About American Raspberry:

The American raspberry, also known as Rubus strigosus, is a species native to North America. It is found in different colors and contains many nutrients that help lower blood pressure. This herb contains omega-3 fatty acid, which helps prevent heart complications and even strokes.
This herb helps keep the body healthy, protecting the skin and bones with consistent but healthy consumption. American raspberries have a distinctive flavor – depending on the color – and to get all the nutrients from them, you can use them as a topping for cereals, muffins, and fruit salads. There are countless recipes for getting the most out of raspberries.

Medicinal Parts: The fruit and leaves.

Habitat & Foraging: American raspberries grow in the most temperate regions of the world. It is found in many North American regions, and it grows for most of the year.

Influence on the Body: It contains numerous healthy nutrients, like folate, Vitamin C, and fiber. It has antioxidant properties which protect against cancer and other complicated diseases.

Traditional Uses: It is used as a face mask for keeping the face safe.

Possible Side Effects: None known.

American Spikenard

Common Names: Small Spikenard, Indian Root, Life-of-Man, Petty Morel, Spice Berry, Signet

Scientific Name: Aralia racemosa

Family: Araliaceae

Origin: Native to Quebec and North America (Georgia, Missouri, Kansas)

About American Spikenard:

American spikenard is a North American plant whose root has thick, branched yellow rhizomes and a colored latex. Herbalists have used American spikenard root to treat any infection and lung disorder.
It is also taken directly on the skin to help treat numerous skin diseases. People tend to sweat out some of the things that lead to these complications when they consume American spikenard. It is a functional root plant that has been used for decades and is known for its effectiveness.

Medicinal Parts: The oil and roots.

Habitat & Foraging: It originates in the wooded mountains of North America, and it grows randomly along rocky and rich riverbanks. The American spikenard flowers from July to August.

Influence on the Body: Asthma, coughing, arthritis

Traditional Uses: Reducing cold symptoms, improving overall balance.

Possible Side Effects: None known.

Arnica

Common Names: Wolf's Bane, Mountain Arnica, Mountain Tobacco, and Leopard's Bane

Scientific Name: Arnica montana

Family: Asteraceae

Origin: Native to North America (Alaska, Montana, Nevada, Oregon, Utah)

About Arnica:

Arnica is a herb commonly used to treat bruises, and the leaves are also used to treat certain conditions related to muscles. It is usually administered orally and applied in gel form, and it has often been taken topically to avoid overdosing on the drug. Homeopathic solutions are the best way to take arnica, and they should be allowed to dissolve until it is completely diluted before ingestion. It is dangerous for your health to take the plant directly as it is.
Arnica is beneficial for treating pain. And compared to other medicines, people do not become addicted to it.

Medicinal Parts: The flower and leaves.

Habitat & Foraging: Arnica likes partial shade and grows in open woods of higher elevations. This hairy flower blooms during the flowering season in central Europe, which is between May to August.

Influence on the Body: It helps reduce inflammation, and it helps bring down joint pains and swellings.

Traditional Uses: Aches and pain relief, a cure for bruises.

Possible Side Effects: It can cause skin irritation if left on the affected surface for too long. It may cause allergic reactions in hypersensitive people. Not advisable for pregnant women. The plant itself is poisonous when eaten.

Arrowwood

Common Names: Southern Arrowwood, Arrowwood Viburnum

Scientific Name: Viburnum dentatum

Family: Adoxaceae (Elderberry family)

Origin: Native to Canada and North America (Texas, Florida)

About Arrowwood:

Arrowwood, also known as Arrowwood Viburnum, is native to southern Minnesota and Georgia. Native Americans named it for the arrowwoods they made from its roots.
The fruit of this plant is eaten boiled or raw for its sweet taste and stomach-soothing properties. The fruit of arrowwood is small, but it works effectively in small doses, so do not take too much.
On the other hand, a stem poultice of Smooth arrowwood (sub-specie Viburnum dentatum lucidum) was applied to the swollen legs of women who had just given birth for quick relief. To prevent conception, women used a decoction of smooth arrowwood twigs.

Medicinal Parts: The fruit and stem.

Habitat & Foraging: This herb grows on moist soils. It can be propagated using the seed, and while it can take some time to germinate – 18 months and propagation can take place between July and August.

Influence on the Body: It is helpful for calming pains in the body.

Traditional Uses: The vigorous shoots were traditionally used for making arrow shafts.

Possible Side Effects: None known.

Aspen

Common Names: Populus Tremella, Alamo Templon, American Aspen, European Aspen, Quaking Aspen, Trembling Aspen, Interpupil, Pulpier Faux-Tremble, Populi Cortex, Populi Folium, Populus Tremolites

Scientific Name: Populus tremuloides

Family: Salicaceae (Willow family)

Origin: Native to Canada and Central America (Mexico)

About Aspen:

Quaking aspen thrives in cool summers and cold regions, especially in the high mountains, plains, and high altitudes. Many people in North America refer to quaking aspen as trembling aspen because of the way it shakes in the wind.
This tree is dominant in regions with other conifer species and has grown and adapted continuously for a long time. Quaking aspen does not thrive in areas with a lot of shade, as the seeds have difficulty growing and developing. One of the most popular outdoor uses of quaking aspen bark is the manufacture of paper, matchsticks, and other constructions when allowed to thrive and dry.
The bark and leaves of quaking aspen also have medicinal purposes, such as treating joint, nerve, and bladder problems. It contains chemical compounds similar to those found in aspirin, known as silicon, and this is known to help reduce inflammation.

Medicinal Parts: The bark and leaves.

Habitat & Foraging: Aspen reproduces both by seeds and roots, and it germinates within a few days of planting.

Influence on the Body: It helps treat rheumatoid arthritis and helps to manage nerve pain.

Traditional Uses: It helps treat swellings that come from infections.

Possible Side Effects: Skin reactions when you handle the leaves or bark.

Balsam Fir

Common Names: Sapin Baumler, Canada Balsam

Scientific Name: Abies balsamea

Family: Pinaceae (Pine family)

Origin: Native to Canada and North America (Minnesota, West Virginia)

About Balsam Fir:

Balsam fir is North American spruce found in eastern and western Canada and the northeastern United States. This evergreen tree is usually medium-sized with dark green leaves (needle-like), which are medium in size and have a narrow conical crown. Native Americans have long used balsam fir for therapeutic and medicinal purposes. Humans then and even now take small amounts of the needles directly from the tree. There are two varieties: Balsam fir var. Balsamic and Balsam fir var. Phaneroses and both are used for numerous medical purposes. When applied directly to the skin, it kills germs instantly and helps treat hemorrhoids.
Natives used balsam fir to treat different types of burns and sores and relieve pain. Today it is a component of many ointments and creams for its superior skin-soothing properties.

Medicinal Parts: The buds, resin, and sap.

Habitat & Foraging: Balsam fir grows in cold climates with a growth rate of 12 inches per year. It goes well with a maximum of four hours of sunlight daily.

Influence on the Body: It helps to combat inflammation.

Traditional Uses: Burns, cuts, sores, chest pains, sore throats, and colds.

Possible Side Effects: Avoid while pregnant and breastfeeding. The resin may cause skin irritation.

Balsam Poplar

Common Names: Bam, Bamtree, Tacamahac Poplar, Tacamahaca, Eastern Balsam-Poplar, Hackmatack

Scientific Name: Populus balsamifera

Family: Salicaceae (Willow family)

Origin: Native to Canada and North America (Alaska)

About Balsam Poplar:

It is a North American tree and hardwood species that grows in floodplain sites where it attaches. It is a fast-growing tree that is usually short-lived except in particular situations. This tree has a sweet, strong fragrance that comes from sticky buds. Its scent is profound to the point that it has been compared to balsam fir, and its softwood is used for construction. Animals also use the twig of this herb as food. Balsam poplar is good for the body for numerous reasons, such as coughs, wounds, sunburn, and frostbite. Sticky spring buds are a highly prized ingredient in medicinal salves and other herbal preparations in indigenous North American traditions.

Medicinal Parts: The leaf buds.

Habitat & Foraging: The balsam poplar tree is usually found in waterways and floodplains.

Influence on the Body: Hemorrhoids – direct application. Frostbite cure – direct application. Chest congestion and cough.

Traditional Uses: Relieving skin injuries – direct application.

Possible Side Effects: It can be harmful to pregnant and breastfeeding women.

Balsamroot

Common Names: Arrowleaf Balsamroot

Scientific Name: Balsamorhiza sagittata

Family: Asteraceae (Sunflower family)

Origin: Native to Canada and North America

About Balsamroot:

The Arrowleaf Balsamroot is a plant of the sunflower family. It has caudices and fleshy taproots with basal leaves and erect stems. The entire plant is nutritious and edible, although some parts are bitter, with those below the plant being more palatable than those above the ground. This plant can be easily found on the dry mountain slopes of western North America. Its root has antibacterial properties, which have medicinal properties eliminating respiratory problems such as colds and flu. The leaves and roots are equally helpful for soothing sores, burns, blisters, and other wounds. Root infusions and decoctions have been used for headaches, fever, tuberculosis, and whooping cough. The natives also used smoke from the roots to relieve body aches and pains. For instance, the Cheyenne tribe steamed the entire plant and, by inhaling the vapors, cured stomach aches and headaches.

Medicinal Parts: The entire plant.

Habitat & Foraging: The balsamroot blooms in May and lasts through to July. This herb also prefers to bloom in the sun and can manage a partial shade. Harvesting flowers and leaves is ideal for early spring, and roots are best harvested in late autumn.

Influence on the Body: It helps to cure respiratory disorders.
An alcohol tincture from fresh root is excellent for colds and flu symptoms and treats sore throats. For sore throats, you can combine a few drops of tincture with a spoonful of honey and swallow.

Traditional Uses: It keeps away the cold and flu.

Possible Side Effects: None known.

Barberry

Common Names: Common Barberry, European Barberry

Scientific Name: Berberis vulgaris

Family: Berberidaceae – Barberry family

Origin: Native to Europe and introduced to North America

About Barberry:

Barberry is found mainly in North America and has been used for many years to treat skin complications, digestive problems, and infections. Barberry is full of antioxidants and helps treat pimples, dental infections, and diabetes.
It is very nutritious and rich in vitamins, fiber, and minerals, and its consumption even goes as far as treating and managing cellular damage. It is easy to add to the diet, as it has sweet flavors that make it easy to consume raw or even as a component of salads and other savory dishes.

Medicinal Parts: The fruit – for appetite stimulation. The root – as a tincture and astringent. The leaves – for coughs.

Habitat & Foraging: Barberries grow on basically any soil. They require enough drainage for proper growth.

Influence on the Body: It protects against dental infections, and it helps to improve the skin, managing any complications.

Traditional Uses: Treating coughs and diabetes.

Possible Side Effects: It can be harmful if taken in large quantities.

Black Cohosh Plants

Common Names: Black Cohosh, Black Snakeroot, Fairy Candle, Black Bugbane

Scientific Name: Actaea racemose or Cimicifuga Racemosa

Family: Ranunculaceae

Origin: Native to North America (Ontario, Missouri, Georgia, Arkansas)

About Black Cohosh:

Black cohosh is a flowering plant of the Ranunculaceae family native to North America. It grows in forests, and its rhizomes and roots are used for medicinal purposes in the home.
Black cohosh will be your best friend if you experience painful or uncomfortable menopausal or PMS symptoms. The mixture of its ingredients—tannins, resins, fatty acids, 27-deoxyactein, isoflavones, triterpene glycosides, and formononetin—mimic the hormone estrogen and has been clinically shown to alleviate congestion, cramps, bloating, mood swings, depression, and much more. Native Americans treated gynecological conditions, kidney problems, malaria, snake bites, coughs, and colds with black cohosh. Herbalists have since primarily focused on women's pain related to the uterus, ovaries, infertility, and labor pains. It also helps with other conditions such as lowering blood pressure, arthritis pains, and period regulation. At the same time, it's also used in alternative remedies for neurological and lung ailments.
One of the primary uses of black cohosh is the treatment of menopausal symptoms, used since the early 1950s.
Black cohosh root and subway stems are extracted and consumed in powder or liquid forms.

Medicinal Parts: The rhizome and roots.

Habitat & Foraging: The black cohosh thrives in moist and rich soil, which contains high organic matter, and must undergo a completely warm and cold cycle to heat until the seeds germinate. Ensure success by putting mature seeds in autumn; therefore, it experiences the process and up your odds of growing throughout its first spring. It is found in well-shaded areas which are well-drained.

Traditional Uses: Curing menopause symptoms, curing painful periods and other period problems, treatment for rheumatic diseases, improving weak bones
Natives widely used black Cohosh root decoction to cure cough and as a blood purifier. Another wide use was the treatment of hypo-menorrhea (poor menstruation flow).

A simple preparation of the black cohosh you can do in no time is the alcohol tincture. This preparation is highly effective in curing rheumatism. The instructions to prepare it are pretty simple: soak black cohosh fresh root in alcohol with a weight ratio of 1:8 for 1 week. The recommended dose is 2 to 4 ml of the alcoholic tincture in a cup of water 1-3 times a day.

Possible Side Effects: It causes mild side effects like headaches and potential weight gain.

Caution:

Researchers urge not to take black cohosh if you are breastfeeding, pregnant, diagnosed with breast cancer, or possess hormone-sensitive problems that could be triggered by the herb, which stimulates estrogen in the body. Should you take the herb internally, take a rest after one year. Also, stop if you are experiencing unwanted effects like upset stomach, headaches, cramps, weight gain, spotting, or bleeding between menstrual periods.

Avoid black cohosh while pregnant as it can irritate nerve centers and may cause abortion.

Large doses of black cohosh are poisonous. It must be used with caution.

Before starting using black cohosh, consult with a certified herbalist or your health practitioner.

Black Gum

Common Names: Sour Gum, Black Tupelo, Tupelo, Black Gum

Scientific Name: Nyssa sylvatica

Family: Nyssaceae (family of flowering trees)

Origin: Native to North America (Ontario, Texas, Florida)

About Black Gum:

It is found in many wetlands and upland habitats, and its flowers are an essential source of fruit and honey.
This tree grows as an ornamental plant in extensive gardens and parks, where it serves as a shade tree. It is an essential source of wild honey, and beekeepers use it like bee gum.

Medicinal Parts: The fruits – raw or cooked. Bark and roots are collectible parts for medical use. It dissolves preferably in boiling water and has diuretic, diaphoretic, expectorant, sedative, and emmenagogue effects.

Habitat & Foraging: Black gum is found along swamps and streams. It prefers well-drained soils.

Influence on the Body: It is used to prevent vomiting.

Traditional Uses: The decoction obtained from black gum bark will help treat minor respiratory conditions, and bark infusion was also effective as a wash during a difficult childbirth.
Native Americans used twigs to clean teeth.
Finally, the "jelly juice" (ooze) of the root was used as an eyewash.
Wood for making shoes and boxes

Possible Side Effects: None known.

Black Haw

Common Names: Black Haw, Blackhaw Viburnum, Sweet haw, Stag Bush

Scientific Name: Viburnum prunifolium

Family: Moschatel family (Adoxaceae)

Origin: Native to eastern North America (Kansas, Texas, Alabama)

About Black Haw:

Black haw is a shrub native to North America, and the root bark is used for numerous medicinal purposes. It has many health benefits, such as remedying asthma, dysmenorrhea, and even labor pains. Black haw contains many chemicals that soothe the uterus, reducing many of these prominent symptoms.
The parts to collect for medical purposes are the bark and root bark. Its preferred solvent is water and alcohol, and it has diuretic, astringent, nervous, and antispasmodic effects.
Native American healers used black haw root bark decoction to prevent miscarriages in women who had shown a tendency to it by their history or having symptoms of uterus contractions.
The benefits of the root bark decoction did not limit the prevention of miscarriages: it is known for its use as a powerful febrifuge and in case of diarrhea when other treatments failed.
Lastly, it positively affects heart palpitation issues, menstrual disorders, and cramps.

Medicinal Parts: The bark.

Habitat & Foraging: The black haw grows in floodplain forests. Black haw has a bloom time in spring.

Influence on the Body: Miscarriage prevention. Asthma. Diarrhea. Labor pain Urine production. Menstrual cramps

Traditional Uses: Premenopausal symptoms relief, menopause symptoms relief.

Possible Side Effects: None known.

Black Locust

Common Names: Black Locust, False Acacia, Green Locust, Pea Flower Locust, White Locust, Yellow Locust

Scientific Name: Robina pseudoacacia

Family: Fabaceae (Legume family)

Origin: Native to North America (California)

About Black Locust:

Black locust tree is native to North America but was brought to western America by gold miners who needed trees for timber for the mines. In this way, they obtained a good wood that was then taken to France to manufacture ships. They also used the flowers for cooking and the fruit as a coffee substitute.
The black locust is a medium-sized melliferous tree found in North America. Native Americans have used the dried leaves of black locust to treat burns and wounds. It can also treat internal conditions such as stomach burns and for people suffering from stomach ailments.
It simply aids and covers some of the complications related to digestion. It also has soothing effects on the body, and this is great for adults and children who have insomnia and general difficulty falling asleep.

Medicinal Parts: The leaves, flowers, and fruit.

Habitat & Foraging: Black locust is native to the Appalachian Mountain, and it grows pretty fast.

Influence on the Body: It helps to improve digestion.

Traditional Uses: Pain reliever, easing digestion.

Possible Side Effects: Reaction with certain medications. Toxic if not heated.

Black Walnut

Common Names: American Black Walnut, Green Walnut, Persian Walnut, Carpathian Walnut, Madeira Walnut.

Scientific Name: Juglans nigra

Family: Juglandaceae (Walnut family)

Origin: Native to North America (Florida, South Dakota, Ontario)

About Black walnut:

Compared to the usual nuts we are familiar with, black walnut is not grown in orchards. Instead, it grows in most Native American locations. It is rich in protein and contains many other vitamins, minerals, and fiber. It contains many antioxidants that make the body healthy, preventing some of the worst diseases like diabetes and cancer.
Adding it to your meals gives you a tasty and healthy diet.

Medicinal Parts: The nut.

Habitat & Foraging: Black walnut grows in rivers and valleys and at the base of the lower slopes of bluffs.

Influence on the Body: Reduces diabetes, cancer, and even heart complications risks.

Traditional Uses: Beauty and radiance support, digestive support.

Possible Side Effects: Topical use is not safe. Avoid black walnut if you have any nut allergies. It may cause drug interactions. Avoid while pregnant and breastfeeding.

Blazing Star

Common Names: Blazing Star, Button Snakeroot, Gay-Feather, Snakeroot

Scientific Name: Liatris

Family: Asteraceae

Origin: Native to North America, Canada, and Mexico

About Blazing Star:

The blazing star is a perennial flowering plant that belongs to the sunflower family. This herb flowers quickly and usually blooms in mid-summer. The flowering process of this plant begins with a new flower and other offshoots emerging after the first one, and this process lasts until early fall. The blazing star is an excellent target for numerous pollinating insects in North America.
Used by the Cheyenne tribe, this herb also serves humans to alleviate health problems, such as earaches and headaches. Burning star root also helps with more complicated diseases like smallpox and measles. The leaves are also helpful for treating upset stomachs, while others are used as antiseptic washes.

Medicinal Parts: The root.

Habitat & Foraging: The trees grow well in well-irrigated soil.

Influence on the Body: It helps treat kidney disorders. It helps treat gonorrhea.

Traditional Uses: It is used to improve blood flow.

Possible Side Effects: Nausea.

Bloodroot

Common Names: Bloodwort, Coon Root, Indian Plant, Sanguinaria, Sanguinaria Canadensis, Snakebite, Sweet Slumber, Red Puccoon, Red Root, Black Paste, Sang-Dragon, Sang de Dragon, Tetterwort, Indian Red Paint, Paulson, Red Indian Paint, Sanguinaria, Sanguinaria du Canada

Scientific Name: Sanguinaria canadensis

Family: Papaveraceae (Poppy family)

Origin: Native to Canada and eastern North America (Florida)

About Bloodroot:

Bloodroot is a beneficial plant, and people use the subway stem to make medicines. Medicines made from bloodroot are used to empty the bowel and make people vomit up everything bad they have ingested. It is very versatile, helping to treat other problems such as sore throat, muscle and joint pains, and fever.
It is also used topically around wounds and cuts to enhance the healing properties and remove all dead tissue from the affected area. In the early 19th century, bloodroot extracts were applied to the breast to help treat mammary tumors and other breast-related complications.
That was not all; bloodroot was applied to the teeth to prevent plaque buildup. That left the tooth and gums healthy and protected from any tooth-related diseases.

Medicinal Parts: The underground rhizome.

Habitat & Foraging: Bloodroot thrives in rich soil under deciduous shrubs and trees.

Influence on the Body: It helps to cause vomiting and emptying of the bowels, and it helps with the treatment of sore throats.

Traditional Uses: Treatment of fever.

Possible Side Effects: Nausea and vomiting. Long-term use is unsafe.
Cause interactions with certain drugs. Avoid it for pregnant and breastfeeding women and children.

Blue Cohosh

Common Names: Squaw Root, Blueberry Root, Caulophyllum, Papoose Root, Blue Ginseng, Yellow Ginseng

Scientific Name: Caulophyllum thalictroides

Family: Berberidaceae (Barberry family)

Origin: Native to North America (Missouri)

About Blue Cohosh:

Blue cohosh is a plant with a name derived from an Indian Algonquin word meaning "rough," which points to the representation of the root, which is rough. Its root is used to make medicine, but consuming it alone is not safe. Still, it can be used as a much better and safer medicine than direct ingestion.
One of the essential things about blue cohosh is that it stimulates the uterus and makes it easier for women to give birth. It also helps calm menstruating women, preventing some of the pain that comes with menstruation, such as muscle spasms. It also helps treat certain internal complications related to internal organs and joints infection.

Medicinal Parts: The rootstock with roots, collected in autumn.

Habitat & Foraging: The blue cohosh thrives in a mixed hardwood forest.

Influence on the Body: Sore throat treatments, treating uterus infections.

Traditional Uses: It is used for stimulating labor.

Possible Side Effects: When taken by mouth, it can lead to chest pains and stomach cramps. It is unsafe for pregnant women and nursing mothers. Not suitable for children.

Blue Flag

Common Names: Blue Flag, Harlequin Blue Flag, Nothern Blue Flag

Scientific Name: Iris versicolor

Family: Iris

Origin: Native to Eastern America and Eastern Canada

About Blue Flag:

The beauty of this lily-like flower is easily recognized. It has more than eight hundred species in about fifty genera, mostly in tropical America. It is characterized by two rows of leaves and flowers of different shades. In addition to its beauty, the rhizome and root tissue have a corrective influence on human tissue.
The blue flag is a plant with a subway stem that has been used as a medicine by Native Americans. One of its main benefits is preventing and remedying bloating situations for women and men. When there is swelling, vomiting, or even certain skin conditions, the blue flag has always been used with good results.

Medicinal Parts: The rhizome – underground stem.

Habitat & Foraging: Blue flag thrives in moist black soils. It also grows along roadsides or railroads.

Influence on the Body: It helps to relieve bloating and vomiting.

Traditional Uses: It treats skin swellings.

Possible Side Effects: It can cause headaches. Not safe for pregnant and breastfeeding women.

Blue Spruce

Common Names: Colorado Spruce, Colorado Blue Spruce, Green Spruce, White Spruce

Scientific Name: Picea pungens

Family: Pinaceae (Pine family)

Origin: Native to North America (Montana, Wyoming, Utah)

About Blue Spruce:

Although the blue spruce grows relatively slowly, it has lived for more than 800 years and was first discovered on Pikes Peak in Colorado. It belongs to the pine family and grows up to 80 feet long. Its unique color is due to the white color that forms on the new needles.
This evergreen tree has its genus name derived from the Latin word pix, meaning sticky resin. The benefits of using blue spruce are numerous and range from treating lung problems, colds, throat problems, and measles.

Medicinal Parts: The cones, central portion, and inner bark.

Habitat & Foraging: Blue spruce usually grows on stream banks and the bottoms of canyons.

Influence on the Body: It reduces tension and stress in the muscles and brings emotional balance. It helps to tackle lung challenges.

Traditional Uses: Teas and salves for cold. Poultice on rheumatic joints, chest, and stomach to relieve congestion and pain.

Possible Side Effects: None known.

Blueberry

Common Names: Blue Huckleberry, High Blueberry, Swamp Blueberry, Tall Huckleberry, Swamp Huckleberry

Scientific Name: genus Vaccinium, section Cyanococcus

Family: Ericaceae (Heath family)

Origin: Native to North America

About Blueberry:

It is a perennial flowering shrub that produces blueberries. When used fresh, blueberries are eaten as fruits and can be a great additive to cereals and other exciting foods. You can make homemade nourishment for personal enjoyment, such as juices and wine from blueberries.
They contain many healthy nutrients such as protein, fat, and water, all in the right amounts. They have the right amount of micronutrients such as manganese, vitamin C, and K, which is great for leading a healthy life.

Medicinal Parts: The whole fruit.

Habitat & Foraging: Blueberries can be found in rocky or sandy soil with a pH level of 4.5 to 5.5.

Influence on the Body: Reduces cholesterol in the body. It helps to prevent heart complications.

Traditional Uses: Preventing cataracts and glaucoma and treating ulcers, urinary infections, chronic fatigue syndrome, colic, and fevers. Improving varicose veins and circulation.

Possible Side Effects: It causes mild side effects like weight gain or headaches.

Boneset

Common Names: Common Boneset, Augueweed, Thoroughwort, Sweating Plant, Feverwort

Scientific Name: Eupatorium perfoliatum

Family: Asteraceae

Origin: Native to Canada and North America (Texas, Florida)

About Boneset:

It is a plant cultivated in the warmer regions of the Antilles and even America. It has more than 150 species, and some of them can grow in cold regions such as Eastern America.
The flower has anti-inflammatory properties, which help reduce fever symptoms, such as constipation and vomiting, as it also increases urine production. It helps treat many other conditions, such as nasal inflammation, flu, and influenza.
Boneset has the same benefits as taking aspirin and even more. It keeps your muscles fit and strong, mainly because it contains protein.

Medicinal Parts: The leaf and flower.

Habitat & Foraging: Boneset thrives in floodplain forests and edges of rivers. It prefers well-drained soils.

Influence on the Body: Hot infusions are used to reduce fever. It helps to treat swine flu and influenza.

Traditional Uses: Traditionally used for treating joint pains. Leaf poultices were used to treat broken bones.

Possible Side Effects: It can lead to diarrhea and vomiting when taken by mouth due to the pyrrolizidine alkaloids. People with liver damage must avoid it. Long-term use of boneset is unsafe. It may cause interactions with certain drugs. Avoid while pregnant and breastfeeding and for children.

Borage

Common Names: Bee-bread, Bugloss, Burrage, Starflower

Scientific Name: Borago officinalis

Family: Boraginaceae Juss (Borage family)

Origin: Native to the Mediterranean and introduced to America

About Borage:

Borage is a plant with seed, flower, and leaf oils used for numerous medicinal purposes. It is known as the starflower of North America for its vibrant purple flowers. It is the annual herb in the flowering plant family, Boraginaceae Juss. This plant can be easily grown in your gardens and can also be grown commercially to extract borage seed oil. It also contains alkaloids that are both carcinogenic and healthful.
Oil derived from borage seeds treats skin disorders such as rashes, eczema, and other topical skin conditions. It can also be used for other inflammation-related internal conditions, such as pain and swelling. It is also added to infant formulas to add fatty acids, which are necessary for the development of premature infants.
The leaves and flowers help fight coughs and even hormonal problems, as they help purify the blood. Both leaves and flowers are edible, and they can be consumed in salads and other tasty foods to get the best out of the herb.

Medicinal Parts: The flower, leaves, and seeds.

Habitat & Foraging: Borage grows in pastures and woodlands but can likewise be cultivated in gardens.

Influence on the Body: Prevents inflammation and treats coughs and fevers.

Traditional Uses: It helps to dress and soften the skin.

Possible Side Effects: It can be dangerous when taken in high quantities. May cause interactions with certain drugs. Avoid it for pregnant and breastfeeding women and children. It is not recommended for people with epilepsy.

Broom Snakeweed

Common Names: Broomweed, Snakeweed, Matchweed, Snakebroom

Scientific Name: Gutierrezia sarothrae

Family: Asteraceae (Sunflower family)

Origin: Native to Canada, northern Mexico, and North America (Montana, Colorado)

About Broom Snakeweed:

Broom snakeweed is a subshrub native to the western side of North America. Broom snakeweed is known for its healing properties, as North American peoples used it to treat snakebites on animals such as sheep and dogs.
The plant can be smooth or with short hairs, and when it is touched, it is sticky due to resin. When grown, this plant can produce about 8000 seeds, which is one of the main reasons for its high availability. It grows in late winter with an average of about three years.
This plant has numerous medical and health properties, making it a great component for health and wellness. It possesses antidiuretic, anthelmintic, antimicrobial, and anti-asthmatic properties, which help combat and cure different health problems. Its internal properties ensure the health of the intestine and the general prevention of fungal and amoebic infections in the body.
As we said before, it is anti-asthmatic, which means that when used, it relaxes the whole body. The plant's juice is used to treat pains in the abdomen; when crushed, the leaves are used to prevent wounds and body openings from bleeding; the other parts of the plant help fight colds, coughs, and other minor health complications.
The decoction obtained from the whole plant was used to treat colds and coughs by drinking it and gargling it in case of sore throats or toothache.
A curious use done by the Navajo was to rub the ashes of the burned plant all over their body to treat headaches.
The poultice of the plant was used as a topical analgesic for swollen joints, insect bites, wounds in general, and snakebites.

Medicinal Parts: Roots, leaves, and flowers.

Habitat & Foraging: This small, perennial bushy subshrub is widely diffused in many environments, from prairies to semi-arid sites, and thrives in dry and open plains. The alternate leaves that populate the stems are small and almost linear. At the top of the stems, clusters of small, yellow flowers bloom from July to September.

Influence on the Body: Helps to treat abdominal pains and cold and cough.

Traditional Uses: Used for stopping bleeding.

Possible Side Effects: Poisonous when taken in high quantities due to its high content of alkaloids. Must avoid during pregnancy and lactation.

Buckthorn

Common Names: European Buckthorn, Common Buckthorn, Purging Buckthorn

Scientific Name: Rhamnus cathartica

Family: Rhamnaceae

Origin: Native to Europe and introduced to America

About Buckthorn:

Buckthorn contains vitamins, minerals, and amino acids beneficial for a healthy life. The buckthorn leaves, flowers, seeds, and berries make healthy oils and teas for many medical complications. Its antioxidant properties help cleanse the body and eliminate free radicals in the blood.
That helps treat intestinal problems, regulate overall blood pressure, prevent heart problems, and improve immune functions. It is also applied topically as a sunscreen or cosmetic to maintain healthy skin.

Medicinal Parts: The leaves, flowers, berries, and seeds.

Habitat & Foraging: The buckthorn grows in forested upland habitats but can likewise thrive in grasslands. Buckthorn grows from May to June and then matures from July through September.

Influence on the Body: Combats upset stomach, prevents heart diseases, and improves blood cholesterol.

Traditional Uses: Treats obesity and improves dry eyesight.

Possible Side Effects: Long-term use is unsafe.
Cause interactions with certain drugs. Don't take it if you have any underlying health conditions. Unsafe for pregnant and breastfeeding women and children.

Agrimony

Scientific name: Agrimonia eupatoria

Family: Rosaceae

Habitat: Widespread throughout the United States, at the margin of woods and in meadows.

Characteristics:
Agrimony is a perennial infesting flower. From the small rhizome, a single, erect stem emerges from the ground and can reach up to 30 inches. Leaves are lance-shaped with a serrated margin and have two smaller leaflets with slightly different shapes. At the top of the plant are clusters of small yellow flowers with five petals and protruding stamens. The fruit is a small achene with hooks for hooking onto animals passing nearby.

Medicinal Parts: Flowers.

Preferred solvent: Water.

Main effect: Astringent, diaphoretic, febrifuge.

Uses:
Iroquois and Cherokee used root decoction to treat diarrhea and reduce fever, while the tea prepared from leaves and flowers treated urinary tract infections.

Possible Side Effects: It can be dangerous when taken in large doses. Causes interactions with diabetes medications. Avoid it for pregnant and breastfeeding women and children.

Aloe Vera

Scientific name: Aloe barbadensis Miller

Family: Asphodelaceae (Liliaceae family)

Habitat: The Southern United States, especially Southeastern ones.

Characteristics:
At the base of the plant, there is a basal rosette of long, pointed succulent leaves with toothed edges. Its color is olive green, sometimes mottled in yellow. It creates a group of red or yellow tubular flowers from a central spike.

Medicinal Parts: Leaves latex (juice) has a yellow color. Leaves gel has a transparent color.

Preferred solvent: Water.

Main effect: Tonic, emmenagogue, vermifuge, cathartic, depurative.

Uses:
The poultice of fresh leaves was used to treat wounds, insect bites, and burns in general.
An almost unknown use of this fresh leaf poultice is as follows: the poultice was placed in a tow to dry. Then the dried poultice was ground into a fine powder used as a topical treatment for open wounds to stop bleeding and blisters to absorb moisture and prevent infection. If diluted in water, the powder was used to regulate the menstrual cycle or expel intestinal worms.
Preparations from aloe also help relieve constipation or heartburn.

Caution:
Do not administer in case of pregnancy, liver or gallbladder disorders, or hemorrhoids. It is not recommended for breastfeeding mothers. If you are taking any medication, consult your doctor first before using aloe.

Aromatic Clove

Common name: Clove

Scientific name: Syzygium aromaticum (Myrtaceae family)

About Clove:

Clove is an incredibly nutrient-dense spice whose active ingredient, eugenol, has been extensively studied.
Packed with manganese, magnesium, iron, vitamin K and fiber, this miracle flower bud is admired for its anti-inflammatory, antiviral, antibacterial, and antimicrobial properties.
Clove essential oil is traditionally used for its analgesic effects for toothaches and other dental pains.
Since the 8th century, cloves have been an essential part of Asian and European trade. Wars have been fought over the spice.
Clove is considered safe when taken in typical food amounts, but no studies have been conducted on taking the herb for long-term medicinal use. The active ingredient in cloves, eugenol, slows blood flow. For this reason, avoid eating cloves after surgery or when taking blood thinners.
Cloves are the flower buds of recurrent clove trees. They grow easily in moist tropical locations or rich, reddish soils, and their perfect requirements are shade and rain.

Bach Flowers – Flower Essences

About Bach Flowers:

In the 1930s, British physician Dr. Edward Bach discovered 38 Bach Flower Remedies; however, Ancient Native Americans have used healing therapy flower essences since long ago.
Body health and mood are not divided. Bach flowers work on both fronts, and each one of them adapts to different personalities, produces effects, and acts on emotions in different ways. Some people are predisposed to certain emotions more than others. Some people tend to be hyperactive, while others are carried away by inertia. Dr. Bach indicated the most appropriate flower remedy for each state of mind. Bach had understood that, for example, a person with a fear of losing control could not be treated and cured as someone who wanted to overcome the trauma of any nature. Taking care of ourselves through Bach flowers, therefore, also pushes us to know better who we are deep down, through that delicate phase which is the choice of the remedy that suits us.

Bach flowers will not cure the disease but aim to unblock the reactive force of an individual and mobilize the inner forces to trigger a positive change. The indicated essence works on rebalancing negative emotional attitudes that promote the onset of various disorders.

Caution:
There are no particular contraindications, except for what is called a crisis of consciousness, which is a worsening of symptoms just before healing.

Balsam Poplar

Common names: Balsam Poplar, Bam, Black Cottonwood

Scientific name: Populus balsamifera (Salicaceae – Willow family)

Habitat: Balsam poplar grows wild in wet environments all over the northern part of the North American continent, from Labrador, west to Alaska and northwestern Canada.

Characteristics:
This massive tree can grow up to 100 feet tall. From the wide central trunk (covered by a gray-green and smooth bark), depart heart-shaped leaves with serrated margins populate many branches. Flowers are in the shape of white catkins. A resinous, fragrant substance covers new buds, making them sticky.

Medicinal parts: Leaves, barks, and buds.

Preferred solvents: Water.

Effects: Diuretic, febrifuge, analgesic.

Uses:
It is not a case that salicin, widely contained in the bark of the poplar, is considered a predecessor of aspirin. Native Americans benefited from this tree's analgesic and febrifuge properties by preparing a bark decoction to treat colds, flu, and rheumatism. In addition, the inner bark decoction was used for its strong diuretic properties as a cleansing and detoxifying drink.

Another beneficial use of this plant is the one that involves the sticky resin that covers its buds: the salve obtained from it is perfect to seal wounds and ensure proper healing without infections.

The instructions are pretty simple: mix the resin and a vegetable oil of your choice (e.g., olive oil, canola oil) in a weight ratio of 1:8 into a non-metallic container; cook the mix in the oven for 10 hours at 170°F. Let the mixture cool, transfer it to a pan, and gently reheat it; add beeswax to thicken it to the desired consistency.

Caution: It may cause an allergic reaction. Try a small amount first on a small part of the skin and observe 24-48h for any reaction.
Do not use poplar if you are allergic to aspirin or similar drugs, propolis, or balsam made from resins (e.g., Peruvian balsam). There is insufficient research and evidence if poplar is safe for children and pregnant or breastfeeding women.

Bee Pollen

The name pollen is derived from the Latin pollen or di farina. It appears as a powder of variable color (yellow-red). Pollen consists of microscopic structures to which plants entrust the transport of their germ cells. Bees collect it and use it to produce royal jelly and feed the larvae.
It contains 21 of the 23 known amino acids;
Minerals such as potassium, calcium, and magnesium;
Proteins (35% of pollen content);
Vitamins, especially A, B, C, and E;
Carotenoids, flavonoids, and phytosterols;
All essential trace elements.

Uses:
It is a nutritional dynamo, a pure and immediately available energy source.
It is a support for anticancer therapies. It reduces the adverse effects of radiation and chemotherapy and increases the number of immune cells to fight tumors better.

Beeswax

Scientific name: Cera Alba

About beeswax:

Therefore, beeswax has been a material of enormous importance to man for many years, being the only natural product of its kind available. Today, beeswax's application has been reduced, replacing it with similar, sometimes less expensive, materials. Beeswax is a by-product of honey extraction: it is believed that bees have to fly 530,000 kilometers to collect one kilogram of honey.

Types of beeswax:
Depending on the procedures to which it is subjected after collection, we can distinguish two types of beeswax whose uses are, however, superimposable:

> **Yellow wax -** is the one obtained by simple collection and extraction from the honeycomb.
> **Sunrise wax** - is the one obtained by purifying and bleaching the yellow wax by the action of air.

Properties:
Beeswax has several properties that allow wide use in different sectors due to its particular composition.

> **Emollient properties** – are water-repellent and protective properties (as it forms a kind of film on the surface to which it is applied).

> **Emulsifying and viscous properties** - In ancient times, beeswax was also believed to have healing properties and was therefore applied hot (and then melted) on wounds to facilitate healing. However, it is most likely that beeswax facilitated wound healing, not because it had true healing properties but because it was able to create a barrier that protected the wound from the external environment and prevented the development of possible infections.

Beech

Common names: American Beech, North American Beech

Scientific name: Fagus grandifolia (Fagaceae family)

Habitat: The Eastern United States and southeast Canada. It grows in sunny environments.

Characteristics:
This beautiful, tall tree can reach 120 feet. The central trunk is covered by a smooth, gray bark and bears long, thick branches populated with many leaves. These are deeply veined, oval-shaped, and toothed edges. Leaves fall in autumn, as per all the deciduous trees. Fruits are small four-lobed nuts covered with soft thorn-like red hair.

Medicinal Parts: Bark, leaves.

Preferred solvent: Water.

Main effect: Antibacterial, astringent.

Uses:
The decoction of beech bark and leaves helps treat dysentery and diarrhea due to its astringent characteristics. This decoction was used to treat liver conditions (also used by modern physicians to treat diabetes) and bladder infections. The recommended dose and use for this treatment is one teaspoon of dried leaves or bark for each cup of boiling water, to be drunk three tablespoonfuls at a time before the main meals.

Blackberry

Common Names: American Blackberry, Dewberry, Brambleberry, Gout Berry.

Scientific name: Rubus villosus (Rose family)

Characteristics:
There are several species of Rubus (blackberries); two types are known, trailing or dewberries and erect blackberries. However, there are many intermediate types both in the wild and in cultivation. This unique variety is endemic to the northern United States and Canada and central and Western Europe, among other regions.
The blackberry has a root that lasts several years and a crown that grows juicy, black, flavorful berries one year and fruit the next. As for the typical raspberry, the berries adhere to the core when they are regular rather than withdrawing from the receptacle. When out of season, this creeping vine dies in the field. Spring finds clean, prickly tips forming rootlets in sandy or dry soils. The flowers are white.

Medicinal Parts: Fruit, stems, leaves.

Solvents: Tobacco, water.

Influence bodily: Astringent, tonic.

Uses:
Blackberries are listed as an astringent healing agent and are much more medically beneficial than most of our generation understands. The Native Americans used the berries as food and medicine. Today, from their history and clinical studies, we know that the plant is beneficial for chronic diarrhea in children, dysentery, cholera, and summer ailments. Sometimes, it is the only thing that produces results.
Four or five times a day, a decoction of the root or leaves, or both (the root is more astringent than the leaves), may be used openly. This agent is helpful in prolonged menses and is very productive in fevers and hot distempers of the body, ears, skin, and other parts, which is pleasant to the mouth.
The berries can be made into aspic, brandy, jam, jelly, and vinegar and have tasty properties.

Dose:
One teaspoonful of root or leaves, steeped for 15 minutes to 1 cup of boiling water; 3–4 cups a day, depending on age. 1/2–1 dram of the tincture, 3–4 times a day.

Note:
The swollen and outwardly rubbed leaves can serve as an astringent for hemorrhoids. Gargle the tea of the roots and leaves regularly for sore mouth and inflamed throat; they may be used green or dried.

Blackroot

Common Names: Culver's root, Culver's physic, Tall Speedwell, Leptandra

Scientific name: Veronicastrum virginicum (Plantain family)

Characteristics:
The black root is endemic to North America and southeast Canada.
The soil in which the plant is grown significantly influences its virtues, and it can be observed in cool soils, wet forests, swamps, etc. The calcareous soil enhances the medicinal benefit, guaranteeing the consumer its attributed impact.
The right time for harvesting is in the autumn of the second year. The most agreed procedure is the dried root (fresh is too irritable), but it should be used cautiously. With simple, straight, smooth, herbaceous roots, the plant reaches 2-5 feet. Upright in fours or sevens, the leaves are low and finely toothed. The flowers are white, almost sessile, and are very numerous.
It has an acrid and very bitter taste.

Medicinal Parts: Dried root.

Preferred solvent: Tobacco, water.

Main effect: Emetic-cathartic, alterative, tonic, antiseptic.

About Blackroot:

Blackroot is a Native American remedy of a long tradition. It was invented as a therapeutic agent by Dr. Culver as medicine for whites and is beautifully known as Culver's physic.
The key importance of black root is that, when there is inadequate bile flow, it acts on the bowels in chronic constipation and is quite often used in chronic liver disease. It works moderately and without depressing the brain as with other purgative medicines.
It removes the frightful matter from the intestines without reducing their tone or leaving the dangerous stinging that remains even after using calomel. It is used very successfully in treating pleurisy and in certain dyspepsia cases. As a cathartic for dysentery, it is one of the best medicines available when given in moderate doses. Traditionally, herbal remedies used for centuries were decoctions from a small Chinese rhubarb root (Rheum palmatum) and blackroot.

Caution:
Do not use fresh roos as it is toxic. It is recommended to use blackroot under medical supervision.

Bloodroot

Common Names: Red puccoon, Canada puccoon, Redroot, Back paste, Bloodwort

Scientific name: Sanguinaria Canadensis (Poppy family)

Habitat: Diffused all over the eastern part of North America, from the Eastern coast of Canada in the North to the Great Lakes region, down to the Mississippi River in the South.

Characteristics:
This small, low-growing plant can reach, at its best, 7 inches tall. The stem emerges from a red, twisted rhizome that releases a red sap if squeezed (hence the name) and usually has 4-5 leaves. These are grayish-green and have many lobes (5-7). The flower is white with 10-12 petals and yellow central stamens.

Medicinal Parts: Root.

Preferred solvent: Water, alcohol.

Main effect: Antibacterial, expectorant, sedative, emetic.

About Bloodroot:

Bloodroot was renowned by natives to be a potent emetic, and it can cause vomit if eaten in excessive quantities. It was used in case of food poisoning.
Another use for this root is the topical application of its juice to treat warts.
The double extraction of the root is used in moderate quantities to treat respiratory diseases from mild to severe, such as cough, laryngitis, bronchitis, and asthma.
The root alcoholic extraction contains sanguinarine, which is nowadays used for the topical treatment of skin cancer.
Another non-medical use of this root extraction is a repellent for mosquitos and insects. Natives applied it on their bodies to prevent insect bites, and that's why Native Americans were called red skins by the first Europeans.

Caution:
Do not use bloodroot without the supervision of your health professional. And it lowers blood pressure and may cause drug interactions. Not safe during pregnancy and breastfeeding.

Burdock

Common Names: Greater Burdock, Edible Burdock, Lappa, Gobo

Scientific name: Arctium lappa (Asteraceae family – Daisy family)

Medicinal Parts: Root, leaves, and seeds.

Main effect: Blood purifier, reduces fever, treating skin problems, diuretic and digestive.

About Burdock:

It is native to Japan, Nothern Asia, and Europe and was introduced to North America. In Asia, it is widely consumed as a vegetable.
Burdock is the herb you want to use when you need to get rid of toxins from your blood. But it does not mean that you use it as a cleanse. Instead, burdock is used to help get rid of infections, boils, rashes, acne, and fevers. Burdock's root works the best with elimination through the skin as an exceptional treatment for chronic skin diseases from eczema to psoriasis.
It is an antibiotic plant and is also antiseptic and anti-inflammatory. It has been used as a cancer treatment for over a hundred years, and it is one of the main herbs used in Essiac tea.
Burdock, although very useful, is not usually used alone. It is a remedial plant used in combination with other plants. The use of burdock alone can result in contact dermatitis or cause a flare-up of recurring skin conditions.
You can use burdock root as food or create tinctures and decoctions.

Caution:
Can interact with certain medications, consult with your doctor before use. Do not take it if you are scheduled for surgery. There is not enough research if it is safe to use during pregnancy or lactation. People with an allergy to the Asteraceae family should avoid burdock.

Calendula

Common Names: Calendula, Pot Marigold, Common Marigold

Scientific name: Calendula officinalis (Asteraceae family – Daisy family)

Medicinal Parts: Flowers.

Main effect: Anti-inflammatory, antimicrobial, anti-thrombogenic, antidiabetic, anticancer.

Preferred solvent: Oil, water, alcohol.

Habitat: Canada and USA. USDA Zone 2-9. Calendula tolerates any type of well-drained soil. Flowers last longer in partial sun or in shaded areas.

Grow and Harvest:
Plant seeds indoors in early spring or outdoors after the last frost. Water occasionally once plants are established. The plant prefers cooler temperatures to bloom best in filtered sun or shade. Calendula will bloom from spring through fall or even longer, provided it is deadheaded regularly. It may not bloom during the warmer months in warmer climates but will bloom in spring and again in fall.
After harvest, place the flowers in a single layer in a cool, dry place and let them dry for up to a week until completely dry. Store the dried petals in an airtight container.

About Calendula:

Natives used calendula topically to heal wounds and other skin ailments such as inflammation, rashes, infections, pain, or swelling. Its flower petals are rich in flavonoids – anti-inflammatory, anti-thrombogenic, antidiabetic, anticancer, and neuroprotective compounds of calendula.
Tea from calendula flowers is a traditional herbal remedy for treating the mouth and throat thanks to the chemical compounds that help decrease swelling and help new tissue grow in wounds. It can be a gargle for sore throats or a mouth rinse for blisters, gum inflammation, or other mouth sores.
Native Americans drank calendula tea to help heal gastric ulcers or used compresses for itchy and inflamed skin. Calendula footbath makes a good remedy for athlete's foot condition.
Calendula extract is often used in oils, ointments, and tinctures, and it is rich with antioxidants that combat oxidative stress in your body and may have anti-cancer benefits.

Caution:
Do not take it if you are scheduled for surgery. It is unsafe to use during pregnancy or lactation by mouth, and it is recommended to avoid topical use as well during pregnancy. People with an allergy to the Asteraceae family should avoid calendula.

Cayenne

Common Names: Cayenne pepper, Hot chili pepper

Scientific name: Capsicum annuum (Solanaceae family)

Habitat: Native to North America, northern South America, Caribbean, USDA zone 9-11.

Medicinal parts: Fruit.

Main effect: Digestive, antirheumatic, antiemetic – prevents vomiting, antispasmodic – calms nerve pain and irritation, relaxes muscle spasms and cramps.

Grow and Harvest:
Seeds can be planted in the garden 10-14 days before the last frost, plants 2 to 3 feet apart. When planting or transplanting from a greenhouse, compost or other organic matter should be mixed into the well-drained soil with a neutral pH. Soils with low nitrogen levels will favor plant growth with more fruit and fewer leaves. The plant requires at least 6-8 hours of direct sunlight per day and needs approximately 1-2 inches of water per week or more when the weather is warmer.
Harvest when peppers are red, about 70-80 days after planting. Pods should be 4-6 inches long at harvest.

How to store: Peppers do not last long once picked and should be dried to keep them longer. You can use a food dehydrator or place a single layer in the oven on the lowest setting for 2 to 3 hours, turning them frequently to make sure they dry evenly. Once dry, store them in an airtight container. Prune the plant often to make it grow more compact and produce more fruit.

Uses:
Cayenne is used primarily for culinary purposes. It stimulates digestion and muscle movement in the intestines, which can help restore digestive secretions and aid nutrient absorption. It can stimulate circulation and blood flow, especially in the extremities, when applied topically. It helps stimulate mucus release from the respiratory tract and causes sweating by stimulating blood flow to the skin.
When added to an herbal preparation, cayenne helps improve the absorption and circulation of other herbs in the body. It is often used to treat high blood pressure and high cholesterol, and it can prevent platelets from clumping together and allow blood to flow more easily. It can also be used as a compress or oil to soothe sore muscles and joints.

Caution:
May cause interaction with certain medications, consult with your doctor first. Do not take it if you are scheduled for surgery. It can cause stomach or skin irritation, and large doses are not recommended.

Chickweed

Common Names: Common chickweed, Chickenwort, Birdweed, Starweed, Winterweed, Mouse-ear, Satin flower

Scientific name: Stellaria media (Carnation family)

Habitat: Native to North America and Europe. Chickweed can be seen globally in moist, cultivated soil and is often regarded as a weed. USDA zone 4-11.

Medicinal parts: The whole plant is harvested from May to July.

Main effect: Astringent, soothe itching, diuretic, reduces inflammation and promotes wounds healing, expectorant – remedy for respiratory diseases

Grow and Harvest:
Grows in many different soils but does best if compost or manure is added before planting to ensure a good start for seeds or seedlings. The best time to plant is late spring or early summer. Requires shady areas, even at the base of trees, and prefers moist soil.
If harvested in the wild, be careful because chickweed is considered a weed in many areas and is sprayed with pesticides. Cut the stems when the leaves are green. Discard yellow or brown leaves before drying.

How to preserve: Tie the stems together and hang them upside down in a dark, cool place. Once dried, store in an airtight container.

Uses:
It is often used in ointments and poultices for burns, rashes, and other skin irritations. It is a mild diuretic and may be suggested for fluid retention. In addition, chickweed is a rich source of nutrients, such as potassium, calcium, and iron. It can also be juiced and mixed with lemon juice, for example. A gentle infusion of chickweed is incredibly soothing. This herb does not dry or store well, so to preserve it for future use, consider tincturing a quantity of the next chickweed crop that appears in your yard. Instead of seeing it as a sprout, it is a small, tender, stubborn, reclaimed plant.

Caution:
Avoid it while pregnant or breastfeeding and for children, as there is not enough research about its safety. Large amounts of herb are toxic, and it is recommended not to use the herb orally. People with an allergy to plants from the daisy family can develop skin irritation when used topically. Before topical use, always do the patch test first.

Dandelion

Common Names: Dandelion, Common Dandelion, Carnkerwort, Lion's Tooth, Blowball

Scientific name: Taraxacum officinale (Asteraceae family)

Habitat: Introduced to North America from Europe and Asia. It prefers moist soils and grows in lawns, on roadsides, on shores of waterways, etc. USDA zone 3-9.

Medicinal Parts: Leaves, flowers, roots.

Main Effect: Dandelion preparations have cholagogue, antirheumatic, laxative, stimulant, tonic, and powerful diuretic properties.

About Dandelion:

Dandelion contains vitamins A, B, C, D, iron, potassium, and zinc. For hundreds of years, the leaves have been eaten as a vegetable, the flowers are used to make wine, and the root is used as a coffee substitute.
The roots are harvested between June and August, when they are at their most bitter, split lengthwise, and dried. The leaves are most tender for consumption when picked in spring, but you can harvest them at any time of the year. Pick the flowers soon after they bloom and long before they become the white balls of seeds we all know.

Uses:
The main medicinal uses of dandelion are for liver problems, such as jaundice, hepatitis, and cirrhosis, and it is a potent liver cleanser and healer. It is also helpful for cases of kidney disease, gallbladder problems, bloating, skin problems, heartburn, and upset stomach. Significantly, it can stimulate kidney function without the loss of potassium. Most treatments for kidney function cause potassium loss, but since dandelion is high in potassium, this is not a problem.

Caution:
Some minor side effects of dandelion use may include allergic skin reactions, upset stomach, heartburn, or diarrhea. Avoid if you have eczema or blood disorders. Avoid it while pregnant or breastfeeding and for children as there is not enough research.

Devil's Claw

Common Names: Devil's Claw, Wood Spider, Grapple Plant

Scientific name: Harpagophytum procumbens (Sesame family)

Medicinal Parts: Roots.

Characteristics:
The drug is the taproot of Harpagophytum procumbens, an herbaceous plant that grows wild in the Kalahari Desert (South Africa). Other species of Devil's Claw are found in the southwest United States and northern Mexico. The genus name has its origin in the Greek "harp ago" (rampion) and alludes to the fruits provided with hooks that adhere to animals' legs, thus spreading the seeds. The plant's root is formed by a taproot, called a primary root, which penetrates vertically into the soil, and by secondary roots spread in a radius of about 1.5 meters around the plant.

Uses:
Devil's claw is anti-inflammatory, analgesic, and antirheumatic. Therefore, it is indicated in cases of chronic rheumatism, rheumatoid arthritis, osteoarthritis of various locations (coxarthrosis, osteoarthritis of go, cervical osteoarthritis), joint pain in general, tendonitis, neuritis of the traumatic base.
You can find devil's claw as an herbal supplement for alternative treatment for muscle and joint pain, back pain, and rheumatic pain.

Caution:
Because of its bitter-tonic action, it is advisable to take the devil's claw on a full stomach. If you have inflammation of the stomach mucosa, like all bitters, it should be avoided in case of an ulcer. Its use is also discouraged in case of taking anticoagulant drugs and during pregnancy or lactation. It is unsafe for people with any heart problems. Can interact with certain medications; please consult with your doctor first.

Dogwood

Scientific name: Cronus Spp. (Cornaceae family)

Dogwood or boxwood is a flowering tree native to a large area of North America along the eastern seaboard and west to present-day Minnesota, Kansas, and Texas.

Uses:
Dogwood has astringent, antiperiodic, diaphoretic, tonic, and mildly stimulant properties.
When used internally, the inner bark, berries, and twigs treat malaria, fever, pneumonia, and colds, and it was used a lot during the American Civil War for these purposes. Infusions help treat diarrhea and may help improve the patient's digestion and appetite. A decoction of the bark is soothing to sore muscles and is used to promote sweating and break fevers.
External preparations, such as poultices of the bark, berries, and twigs, treat ulcers and sores, and the Menominee used the bark to create an enema for intestinal problems.
The people of the New England area also used the twigs of the dogwood as a kind of toothbrush or toothpick, and European settlers observed that they had very white and healthy teeth.
The Cherokee people chewed the dogwood bark for headaches, used a bark decoction for children to treat worms, measles, and diarrhea, and used poultices for various wounds and skin disorders.
The Chippewa used dogwood infusions to make eye compresses.
Some cultures, such as the Arikara, used some dogwood species in smoking mixtures and mixed it with sacred tobacco.
Aside from its medicinal uses, the inner bark of dogwood can also be used in mixtures to make red, black, and yellow dyes. The bark is hard and therefore suitable for carving. Tradition says that it is time to plant corn when the dogwood blossoms.

Echinacea—Echinacea Spp.

Uses:
Echinacea is the most commonly used herb in American folk herbalism. There are
nine species in North America, and all have similar properties. It is widely available as
a dietary supplement in health food stores, and the flowers grow wildly in many parts
of North America in rocky, disturbed soils in open fields. Echinacea is grown in
many home gardens for its medicinal properties, its beauty, and attraction to
butterflies and bees to the garden.

Its purple petals and orange/brown cone-shaped center allow the flowers to be
identified. Use the dried roots for preparations such as decoctions, tinctures, or
capsules. Use the leaves and flowers to make infusions, tinctures, or capsules.
Actions of the different parts of the plant include antimicrobial, alterative,
antibacterial, antifungal, antiviral, and anti-inflammatory.

The Cheyenne, Dakota, Fox, Kiowa, Montana, Omaha, Pawnee, Ponca, Teton, Sioux,
and Winnebago are known to use E. angustifolia as an infusion to treat mouth, gum,
and throat pain. They also value the plant as an antidote for many poisons and toxic
substances and use the crushed root as a poultice to extract venom in case of
snakebite, insect bites, and septic diseases. A compress is made to wash burns and
relieve pain, and an infusion is used for stomach cramps and intestinal pain.

The Cheyenne and Dakota used a decoction of E. pallida roots to treat rheumatism,
arthritis, smallpox, mumps, measles, and as a wash for burns and fever. The roots are
chewed to relieve cold symptoms, and a poultice is applied to alleviate inflammation.

The Choctaw and Delaware used E. purpurea primarily to treat coughs and
dyspepsia, either by chewing the root or drinking an infusion.

The primary use of Echinacea is to support healthy immune function; it is effective
against bacterial and viral attacks and can help the body get rid of microbial
infections. A root decoction strengthens the immune system and helps relieve cold
and flu symptoms. Echinacea is the main ingredient in many over-the-counter
products marketed to boost the immune system and fight illness.
Using a poultice helps heal sores and wounds and relieve swelling. The roots and
seeds are often chewed to alleviate toothache and sore throat or lozenges to ease
congestion.

Caution:
Possible side effects of Echinacea may include diarrhea, indigestion, nausea, rash, or a
bitter-tasting tingle in the mouth. Do not use Echinacea remedies with steroids or
liver-toxic prescription drugs.

Elder Herb

Common Names: Black Elder, Common Elder, American Elder, Elderberry, Sambucus, Elderflower

Scientific name: Sambucus nigra (Adoxaceae family)

Medicinal Parts: Bark, leaves, flowers, fruit.

Main Effect: Febrifuge, diaphoretic, antiviral, expectorant – clears mucus from the airways.

Uses:
In the U.S., elderberry syrup and tincture are popular remedies against cold and flu germs, although they are more likely to be found in grocery stores than in pharmacies. Both the berries and the flowers are diaphoretic - they cause sweating and reduce fever. Elderberry also has strong immunological and antibacterial properties and can be much better when combined with Echinacea. Elderberries produce some of the best syrups I have ever tasted. Every summer, I pick the significant and aromatic horizontal clusters of elderflowers and make elderflower fritters, my special summer treat.
Several different varieties of elderberry grow in the U.S. People who eat elderberries say they are safe to eat, although most men and women agree that it is best not to eat the fruit raw and that it is better to cook, soften or dye it. Elderberry syrup is also delicious for lemonade or a mocktail.

Caution:
Red berries growing on a blue-green tree at a high elevation are not edible. Do not eat red elderberries.

Eyebright

Scientific name: Euphrasia officinalis (Orobanchaceae family)

Characteristics:
Eyebright is characterized by small white flowers that bloom in late summer or early fall. When the flowers bloom, the flowers, leaves, and stems can be collected and dried for herbal preparations. Eyebright's many uses for acute or chronic eye conditions give the herb its name.

Uses:
Eyebright's actions include anticatarrhal, astringent, anti-inflammatory, antioxidant, and anti-mucosal. Above all, it is antibacterial, with properties similar to goldenseal but slightly less potent, making it suitable for use on mucous membranes such as the eyes. In addition, infusions help with nasal catarrh, sinusitis, and other congestive conditions, including irritations of the nose, throat, and esophagus. Add dried eyebright leaves to smoking mixtures as a helpful pain reliever for bronchitis and coughs.
The combination of anti-inflammatory and astringent makes it suitable for many conditions related to mucous membranes.
An infusion of eyebright at room temperature used as a compress effectively relieves chronic eye conditions such as redness, stinging, watery eyes, and hypersensitivity to light. Eyebright washes help weak eyes or those suffering from eyestrain. It helps aging eyes and is believed to restore vision.

Caution:
Rare side effects of eyebright may include confusion, nausea, sweating and pressure in the eye, itchy eyes, and allergic reactions in those allergic to ragweed. It can be unsafe for people with any eye procedures or wearing contact lenses, and it might lower blood sugar levels. Do not apply directly to the eye. There is no research about using eyebright for pregnant and breastfeeding women.

Feverfew

Scientific name: Tanacetum parthenium (Asteraceae family – Daisy family)

Uses:
This garden flower has an excellent reputation for treating migraines and headaches.
Recent clinical studies have shown that it also relieves inflammation and stress.
Because it is relatively bitter, I often combine feverfew with lavender and California
poppy to create a tincture. For migraine prevention, take a half teaspoon of the
tincture two or three times a day for five days, then two days rest, and repeat the
cycle.
Feverfew is best for treating migraines when taken for 2 to 3 months, although it will
also eliminate acute migraine symptoms when taken at the first signs of a migraine.
While the fresh herb is ideal for a tincture, I have found that properly dried, and high-
quality feverfew also works well.

Caution:
It is unsafe for pregnant women, and there is not enough research about safety while
breastfeeding. If you are allergic to ragweed, avoid feverfew. It might slow blood
clotting, so it is not safe for people with blood disorders.

Garlic

Scientific name: Allium sativum (Amaryllidaceae family)

Uses:
Garlic is used primarily as a culinary herb, but it also has antiseptic, antioxidant, expectorant, antimicrobial, antibiotic, antifungal, antiviral, diaphoretic, cholagogue, hypotensive, and antispasmodic properties. Garlic provides health benefits in many aspects, especially those centered on the heart and antibacterial. Garlic cloves are consumed raw or cooked, and the bulbs keep well if stored in a cool, dry place. Among its several beneficial properties, garlic contains volatile oils that some experts believe can assist in clearing congestion from the lungs and bronchial tubes. Garlic also includes sulfur compounds, which contribute to the unique smell of garlic and may be poisonous to intestinal parasites. Garlic is one of the best antimicrobial agents available, and long before researchers discovered these chemicals, Native Americans used garlic to treat bacteria, viruses, parasites, and worms.

The antibacterial action of garlic is widely known. It helps eliminate lung infections, such as chronic bronchitis, respiratory catarrh, recurrent colds, and flu, and may help treat whooping cough.

Garlic is a preventive for most infectious diseases of the digestive and respiratory systems. In the digestive system, garlic promotes the growth of natural bacterial flora while eliminating pathogenic organisms. In particular, it helps fight H. pylori bacteria, the cause of stomach ulcers.

Garlic increases heart health and the overall health of the body. It prevents, slows, fights disease, and protects against free radical damage.

It accomplishes this in three ways: by lowering blood pressure, decreasing harmful LDL cholesterol levels in the blood, and reducing the blood's propensity to produce dangerous, potentially life-threatening clots. According to some studies, as little as one clove of fresh garlic per day may be sufficient to exert these preventive effects. It can increase the body's resistance to colds, flu, viruses, and infections and reduce the duration of colds, coughs, flu, croup, bronchitis, earaches, and respiratory illnesses.

As an aid for diabetes, garlic can help lower blood sugar.

The antifungal properties of garlic help treat athlete's foot and nail fungus when used as a feet bath.

Caution:
Garlic is generally safe for long-term use, but it is reserved only for culinary purposes during pregnancy. Nursing infants may reject milk if the mother consumes garlic. Rare side effects may include headache, fatigue, loss of appetite, muscle aches, skin rashes, indigestion, bloating, bad breath, and body odor.

Ginger

Scientific name: Zingiber officinale (Zingiberaceae family – Ginger family)

Medicinal Parts: The underground rhizome. Dig up ginger root when the leaves have dried. Wash the root and dry it thoroughly in the sun.

Uses:
Ginger is used extensively for culinary purposes, and it also has powerful carminative, stimulant, rubefacient, diaphoretic, analgesic, anti-inflammatory, antibacterial, antiemetic, antispasmodic, and digestive properties. Use the fresh and powdered root to make decoctions or tinctures.

Ginger is great for indigestion. Drinking ginger tea can help relieve bloating and indigestion, help to promote gastric secretion, and is used for dyspepsia, stomach cramps, flatulence, diarrhea, belching, nausea, vomiting, and colic. It also helps relieve nausea and vomiting associated with motion sickness and morning sickness.

Ginger is an effective remedy for earache and ear infections, and it can stimulate digestion, relieve bloating, and heal bronchial infections.

Ginger also helps to fight bronchial infections and nausea. It can fight or even prevent colds and flu, fever, chills, cough, sore throats, sinus congestion, and sinusitis. A ginger lozenge or a gargle is highly effective for a sore throat.

Ginger can help to stimulate circulation and relieve cramps either internally as a tea or externally as a salve

Caution:
Ginger's mild side effects may include heartburn, stomachache, diarrhea, and burping. It can cause skin irritation when applied topically on sensitive skin. When pregnant, breastfeeding, or for children, consult with your health practitioner first.

Ginkgo Biloba

Ginkgo biloba is a large, slow-growing perennial shrub that can live in an ancient wild era. The sole survivor of the oldest known genus of trees, Ginkgoaceae, dates back more than 200 million years; and possibly stands as an actual living fossil tale due to its extraordinary ability to aid with recall and memory.

Uses:
Ginkgo works as a "brain food" and is an excellent memory aid. In addition, it increases energy and improves circulation. I propose ginkgo as a regular tonic herb for anyone experiencing memory loss or "brain exhaustion."

Recently, it has been shown to stop the development of Alzheimer's disease if administered in therapeutic doses (i.e., standardized extracts) within a period.

Ginkgo should be used regularly for many weeks until you discover its benefits. Generally speaking, ginkgo is thriving as a tea, tincture, or capsule to strengthen the brain and blood flow.

Caution:
Due to its effects on the blood and circulatory system, ginkgo must be discontinued at least two weeks before and after an operation. It causes interaction with certain drugs and might cause seizures. Avoid ginkgo during pregnancy and breastfeeding.

Goldenrod

Scientific name: Solidago (Asteraceae family)

Habitat: Widespread all over the North American continent, from coast to coast in meadows and on the sides of cultivated fields.

Characteristics:
This perennial plant is made of a group of stems that can grow up to 7 feet tall from a central rhizome. These round and thin stems are smooth at the base and slightly hairy on the top. Leaves are alternate, lance-shaped, and serrated margins. The small, yellow flowers are positioned at the top of the stem in racemes.

Parts to collect for medical purposes: Leaves and flowers.

Preferred solvent: Water.

Main effect: Carminative, astringent, diaphoretic, diuretic.

Uses:
Native Americans used the goldenrod flower and leaf decoction to treat many conditions. It was used as a preventive treatment for colds and fever.
This drink was also proven effective in allergies to pollen and dust to soothe the inflamed mucosae and have a cleansing effect on the whole body (and kidneys in particular) due to its strong diuretic properties.
Lastly, this decoction was used as a topical wash for ulcers and wounds.
Once dried and powdered, flowers and leaves were applied topically on wounds and burns to stop bleeding and absorb excess moisture.

Caution:
Avoid it while pregnant and breastfeeding women for insufficient research. It can cause allergic reactions in those allergic to ragweed and latex, and it can cause skin allergy reactions for some when applied topically. It might be unsafe for people with high blood pressure.

Goldenseal

Scientific name: Hydrastis canadensis (Ranunculaceae family – Buttercup family)

Habitat: Widespread in forests and well-drained grounds of the Eastern United States and South-Eastern Canada. It usually grows near Indian Ginseng (Ashwagandha).

Characteristics:
This small flower reaches 10 inches at best, and it can be found in dense colonies in the forests. It grows from the yellow underground rhizome as a hairy stem with serrated margins with lobed leaves (usually seven). At the top of the plant, the flower blooms during spring. It is a hermaphrodite flower with no petals, but only white stamens encircle a green calyx. It will fall soon after the blooming, giving space to the round scarlet fruits with shiny black seeds.

Parts to collect for medical purposes: Rhizome.

Preferred solvent: Water, alcohol.

Uses:
Native Americans used the decoction of dried rhizomes and roots to treat dysentery due to its specific astringent characteristics. This decoction was also used for its emollient and anti-inflammatory properties as a wash for skin inflammation or conjunctivitis. The raw consumption of the root was indicated to benefit from these characteristics in the treatment of cough and sore throat.
The root extraction was widely used for curing scrofula and as a panacea for every liver and gallbladder condition.
The powdered dried rhizome was applied on wounds and burns to prevent infections due to its antiseptic properties. Also, it was considered a potent anti-fungal.

Caution:
The consumption of this herb is not allowed during pregnancy or lactation. In addition, excessive consumption may result in food poisoning. Goldenseal's rare side effects may include nausea, vomiting, or reduced liver function. It is not safe for long-time use. Consult safe dosage with your health practitioner.

Gooseberry

Scientific name: Ribes uva-crispa (Currant family)

Habitat: In the forests of the Middle and Eastern parts of the North American continent. Both in the United States and Canada.

Characteristics:
This many-branched perennial shrub can grow up to 4 feet tall and spread widely in forests on low ground. Branches can either have or have no thorns on the same plant and are densely populated by three to five-lobed, palmate leaves. The green-whitish flowers are small, tubular, and grouped in clusters. After the pollination, they develop into round, red, and spiky fruits with many red-brown seeds inside.

Parts to collect for medical purposes: Fruits and roots.

Preferred solvent: Water, alcohol.

Uses:
Besides the raw consumption of fruits, Native Americans used the plant for medical purposes. In fact, the tea obtained from the dried fruits was gargled to soothe sore throats.
Also, the decoction of roots was used as a wash for eye inflammation or drunk directly due to its vermifuge characteristics to treat intestinal worms. Finally, the poultice of fruits and leaves was used to cure skin inflammation due to its emollient feature. It was believed that it cured snakebites because snakes were frightened by the plant.

Caution:
Fresh leaves are not recommended to use because they contain hydrogen cyanide toxins. An excess of this toxin can cause respiratory failure.

Gravel Root

Common names: Joe Pye weed, Queen of the Meadow, Sweet Joe Pye weed

Scientific name: Eupatorium purpureum (Asteraceae family)

Habitat: Widely diffused in wet environments of the Eastern part of North America, both in the United States and in Canada.

Characteristics:
This perennial shrub can grow up to 10 feet tall. The stems grow straight from the central, underground rhizome, bearing many oblong leaves grouped in whorls. These leaves have serrated margins and are hairy to the touch. At the top of the stems, pink, bell-shaped flowers are grouped in umbrella-shaped clusters.

Parts to collect for medical purposes: The whole plant.

Preferred solvent: Boiling water.

Effects: Diuretic, tonic, vermifuge, febrifuge.

Uses:
Native Americans used gravel root leaves to treat a plethora of conditions.
For example, the tea obtained from the dried leaves and flowers was used as a topical wash on infected wounds to reduce inflammation and infections. Also, tea was drunk to treat all the urinary tract infections and kidney stones, using its diuretic properties. The diaphoretic qualities of this tea also helped reduce fever and promote cleansing. Leaves were also used raw by pounding them and applying the poultice directly on wounds and burns to promote healing and prevent infections from the injury. Lastly, natives also used the gravel root rhizome decoction to cure asthma and menstrual problems for its anticonvulsant qualities.

Caution:
Avoid this herb during pregnancy or lactation. It can cause allergic reactions in those who are allergic to ragweed. Consult with your doctor first, as gravel root use may affect liver or lung function.

Hawthorn

Common names: Hawthorn, Common Hawthorn, May tree, Whitethorn

Scientific name: Crataegus monogyna (Rose family)

Habitat: Temperate regions of Noth America, USDA zone 5-7.

About Hawthorn:

Hawthorn is a tree belonging to the rose family. The berries are collected and dried to use for creating herbal preparations. Hawthorn has been used to treat digestive complaints such as indigestion, diarrhea, and stomach pain. It can also be used as a sedative to reduce anxiety. As a compress, it can be used to help with skin conditions such as boils, itching, and frostbite.
Hawthorn is very possibly the best hub tonic herb there's. It's been admired and surrounded by legend for centuries and can be employed as a curative plant in each nation it develops in.
Hawthorn dilates the veins and arteries, allowing blood to flow more freely by discharging cardiovascular constrictions and blockages. Additionally, it can help maintain healthy cholesterol levels. As it's regarded as food instead of medicine, it's usually considered safe to use together with heart medicine. But if you are taking any type of pharmaceutical, you should check with your healthcare practitioner before using herbal supplements. Hawthorn is yummy as a tea, syrup, and shake, and it could also be tinctured.

Grow and Harvest:
Hawthorn can tolerate several soil conditions, including clay and alkaline soils in full or partial sun. For watering, keep the ground moist, though the tree is reasonably drought tolerant.
The tree can be grown from seed but will take several years to grow large enough for berries to grow. Seedlings should be planted in early spring while they are dormant. Berries are collected starting in early October. The tree should be pruned back in winter to remove dead branches and to cut back any branches that grow vertically. Gloves should be worn when harvesting because of the large thorns on hawthorn branches. Flowers can be harvested in the spring, but some flowers should be left on the tree if the berries are harvested in fall.

How to preserve: Flowers or berries can be preserved by drying them for several days in a single layer in a cool and dry place.

Caution:
It might cause interaction with certain drugs - consult with your doctor before use. Stop using at least two weeks before a scheduled surgery as it might increase the risk of bleeding. There is not enough research on its safety during pregnancy and lactation.

Lavender

Scientific name: Lavandula angustifolia (Mint family)

Habitat: USDA zone 5–9.

Grow and Harvest:
Lavender likes well-draining soil. An alkaline or chalky soil will enhance the scent of lavender, where an excess of organic matter will make the flowers less fragrant. The plant requires full sun and water frequently until it is established. Once the plant grows well, water it about once per week if there is no rain. Lavender enjoys being in a tight space, so it will do well in a container.
Harvest from late spring to early summer when the flower stalks are fragrant. The plant can be pruned to about one-third of its size in the fall or early spring.
Tie stems of lavender together and hang them upside down in a cool, dark place for one week or more until they completely dry out.

Uses:
Lavender is no one-hit-wonder. It is also one of the few essential oils which herbalists recommend applying directly to the skin for healing cuts, wounds, scrapes, and bruises with zero side effects. A pound of lavender blossoms would set you back about a month's salary if you were a farmworker in ancient times. The Greeks discovered early that crushed and properly treated lavender could release a relaxing smoke when burned. Later it was also used for mummifying and perfuming. French chemist René-Maurice Gatehouses, who coined the term aromatherapy, endured terrible burns after a laboratory explosion. In a last-ditch effort at recovery, he rubbed his traces with lavender essential oils, which sped healing and left his skin almost scar-free.
Inhaling lavender aroma can improve sleeping issues or sleep quality in general.
You can make the sachets by placing dried lavender into small pillows or bags made from cotton or linen and keeping those in a drawer with pajamas and bed linens to infuse the relaxing smell of lavender into the fabrics. The relaxing qualities of lavender can also be pleasant in a bath, combined with oats and chamomile, or in a salve for a soothing bedtime massage.
Lavender is an effective herb to lower anxiety levels or calm down headaches or migraines.

Caution:
Lavender might cause skin irritation when applied topically, do a patch test before use. Lavender essential oil is possibly unsafe for children to apply on the skin as it might disrupt normal hormones. There is insufficient research on its safety for children when taken by mouth, and pregnant women and breastfeeding women should avoid it. If using any medication or anesthesia, avoid lavender due to its effect on the nervous system. Consult with your doctor first.

Magnolia

Scientific name: Magnolia officinalis (Magnolia family)

Habitat: From North Carolina to Florida, Western Texas, USDA zone 7-9.

Uses:

It is used for weight loss, stomach disorders, constipation, inflammation, anxiety, stress, depression, flu, headache, stroke, and asthma.

Magnolia flower bud is used for a stuffy nose, runny nose, common cold, sinus discomfort, hay fever, headache, and dark facial spots.

For toothaches, some individuals add magnolia flower buds directly to the gums.

Magnolia bark is an ingredient of traditional Chinese and Japanese (Kampo) medicine of Hange-koboku-to, consisting of 5 plant extracts, and Saiboku-to, which consists of 10 plant extracts. These extracts are used to relieve anxiety and nervous stress and enhance sleep. Some scholars claim that what makes these drugs work is honokiol, a compound in magnolia bark.

Magnolia seems to influence animal behavior by decreasing fear. It could also increase the development of steroids in the body to fight asthma. Both studies were conducted in laboratories.

Sleepiness and drowsiness may be caused by alcohol, but sleepiness and drowsiness may also be caused by magnolia bark. It could induce too much sleepiness to take large quantities of magnolia bark along with alcohol.

Dose:

The appropriate dose of magnolia depends on various considerations, such as the patient's age, physical condition, and some other circumstances. There is no adequate clinical evidence available at the moment to establish a reasonable dose range for magnolia. You can find magnolia bark extract supplements in pill form. Be sure to follow the guidelines required on the product label and contact your pharmacist or doctor, or other healthcare providers before use.

Caution:

Magnolia is not safe during pregnancy and possibly during lactation. It might interact with drugs and alcohol. Always consult with your health practitioner first before use. It might slow blood clotting and increase the risk of bleeding.

Mountain Arnica

Common names: Mountain Arnica, Mountain Tobacco, Mountain Daisy, Leopard's Bane, Wolf's Bane

Scientific name: Arnica montana (Asteraceae family)

Habitat: Canada, northwestern North America, USDA zone 4-9.

Plant some arnica in your garden, and you're going to have this perennial for two springs. You will realize this medicinal attractiveness due to its glowing yellow, daisy-like appearance and round hairy stalks.

Uses:
Though its active ingredients are primarily regarded as analgesic and anti-inflammatory, some herbalists use it as an antibiotic, especially for topical skin ailments. It was revered since the 1600s for its pain-relieving ability, and German philosopher Goethe is rumored to have smoked its leaves and drank its tea to ease chest discomfort. Many studies have recently concluded that the herb effectively relieves muscle pain because of vigorous exercise. In reality, a 2003 study published in Homeopathy revealed it worked better than the placebo for treating muscular soreness in runners who had just finished a 26.2-mile marathon. Arnica is usually considered toxic in amounts more significant than what you'd see in cosmetics or food. In fact, the amount you discover in herbal or homeopathic remedies is generally so diluted they are deemed secure.

Caution:
Do not use it on broken skin, before or after the operation (it increases flow), or when you have digestive conditions. It's considered unsafe to inhale or use as aromatherapy.

Nettle

Common names: Stinging Nettle, Common Nettle, Nettle, Urtica

Scientific name: Urtica dioica (Urticaceae family – Nettle family)

Habitat: North America, USDA zone 3-10.

About Nettle:

Often regarded as a pesky plant by anglers, nettle is nonetheless appreciated by herbalists worldwide. It's a flavorful wild green when steamed and rich in minerals and vitamins, particularly calcium and iron.

It's an age-old treatment for allergies, hay fever, and respiratory ailments. Due to its nutrient density and bio chelated calcium, nettle is great for kids and is remarkably suggested for growing pains as soon as their joints and bones ache. A superb reproductive tonic for women and men, nettle is used to relieve the symptoms of PMS and menopause and enhance fertility in both men and women once the infertility is a result of inadequate nutrition. Nettle is also known as a scalp and hair tonic; it is believed to maintain a complete head of healthy hair. It may be utilized to substitute spinach in almost any recipe; however, it should always be well cooked; if undercooked, it will sting you! It's also tasty as a tea that may be served many times each day to stop allergies.

The above-ground parts and roots of stinging nettle are utilized as medicine.

Sharp spines cover the stems of this plant, which cause the skin to be irritated and become itchy. When harvesting nettle, always be sure to have skin covered to prevent irritation. Despite this, nettle is a very nutritious vegetable. Boil the stems and leaves to neutralize their irritant quality.

Uses:

Nettle is astringent, diuretic, tonic, antihistamine, anti-inflammatory, analgesic, and anti-asthmatic. It acts as an effective pain reliever, lowers blood pressure, and reduces bleeding. In an infusion or tincture, nettle is an excellent remedy for respiratory diseases, allergies, and all conditions that produce excess mucus, including hay fever, bronchitis, pneumonia, colds, and flu.

Infusions are also effective for BPH (prostate gland enlargement) and other prostate issues. Nettle helps increase breast milk supply, reduce heavy menstrual bleeding, and increase libido. Compresses or salves work well on skin wounds, stings and bites, and rashes and can help to reduce hair loss and clear dandruff. Nettles are beneficial for all forms of eczema, especially nervous eczema, and childhood eczema.

Nettles strengthen the entire body, and many Native American nations rely on nettle as general medicine and as a tonic for the whole body. A decoction of roots helps with intermittent fever or rheumatism. The diuretic properties work well for treating burning and difficult urination, aiding weight loss, and help with arthritis, gout, diarrhea, and dysentery.

Stinging nettle is used for osteoarthritis and diabetes.

It is often used for urinary tract infections (UTIs), kidney stones, swollen prostate glands, muscle discomfort, and other disorders. However, to confirm these applications, there is no solid scientific research.

In persons with type II diabetes, taking stinging nettle leaf prep for 8–10 weeks tends to decrease blood sugar.

In people with osteoarthritis, taking nettle leaves by mouth or applying it to the skin can relieve discomfort. The need for pain relievers could also be minimized by taking nettle leaves by mouth.

Ingredients that could minimize inflammation and improve urinary output are found in stinging nettle.

Interactions:
Lithium, diabetes medicines (antidiabetic drugs), high blood pressure medications (antihypertensive drugs), sedative drugs (CNS depressants), and warfarin (coumadin).

Caution:
Pregnancy/breastfeeding, diabetes, and low blood pressure: people with renal issues must use it with caution.

Some of the possible side effects of nettle include skin rash, edema, gastric irritation, and electrolyte imbalance.

Oregon Grape

Common names: Oregon Grape, Holy-leaved Barberry, Holly Barberry, Mahonia, Holly Mahonia, Oregon Barberry

Scientific name: Mahonia aquifolium (Barberry family)

Habitat: western North America, USDA zone 5-9.

About Oregon Grape:

The origins of the gorgeous holly-like plant are gaining popularity since they contain berberine, a compound like the active ingredient in goldenseal.

It is a therapeutic herb. The plant was also used for appetite enhancement in indigenous societies long before the Europeans, and other settlers started moving in. Today, it is widely used as a replacement for goldenseal, which has similar antimicrobial properties and is now known to be an endangered species owing to over-harvesting.

Uses:
Collect the underground parts of the Oregon grape, the root (golden yellow), and rhizome in the fall. Clean them and cut them into slices before drying.

Oregon grape is an alternative, antibacterial, anti-inflammatory, antimicrobial, antifungal, cholagogue, laxative, antiemetic, anti-catarrhal, and tonic.

External preparations of Oregon grape work well to treat chronic and scaly skin conditions like eczemas. In a skin disease called psoriasis, the Oregon grape is often known to reduce immature skin cells' overproduction and decrease inflammation. Use Oregon grape as a douche for treating vaginitis.

Internally, Oregon grape root helps alleviate chronic constipation, nausea, vomiting, and stomach, and gallbladder conditions. It can also be effective for indigestion, gastritis, abdominal bloating, irritable bowel syndrome, arthritis, jaundice, and fever. It works as a blood purifier, tonic, immune enhancer, cleanses the liver, gallbladder, and spleen, and clears out microbial diseases.

The Oregon grape root has been used to cure numerous illnesses, including colds, flu, hepatitis, herpes, syphilis, upset stomach, tumors, skin conditions, yeast infections, and much more, as herbal medication. The usage of the Oregon grape has been touted by herbalists, saying it successfully stimulates liver activity, cures illnesses, and improves digestive health.

In patients with insulin resistance, it has reduced blood sugar. It has cholesterol-lowering properties as well.

Oregon Grape is considered to have antifungal and antibacterial effects as an alkaloid derivative of several herbs, including barberry, goldenseal, and other plants.

It is known that alkaloids help in battling different kinds of infections. It has been used to relieve conditions such as diarrhea, persistent candidiasis, and more.

Interactions:

Some drugs can interact with the Oregon grape but might conflict with the body's ability to break down certain forms of liver medications.

Examples of drugs with which Oregon grape should not be taken include: Cyclosporine (Neural, Sand immune), Doxycycline, Tetracycline, and all drugs that change in the liver.

Dose:

It has been commonly used as a tea by boiling a few teaspoons (5–15 grams) of chopped roots in 2 cups (500 milliliters) of water for 15 minutes, then cooling and straining the mixture.

Though further research evidence is required to ensure Oregon grape ingestion protection, herbalists suggest that no more than 3 cups (750 milliliters) of tea should be drunk every day.

It is used as a tincture, an alcohol-based herbal blend, supplied at 1/2–3/4 teaspoon (3 milliliters) doses and taken per day 3 times.

A particular mixture of 10 percent extract cream of Oregon grape bark is commercially manufactured as a topical psoriasis cream, to be applied to the infected region (around 2 months) of the skin 2–3 times per day. Often available are creams with a 10 percent Oregon grape root tincture.

Caution:

Do not use Oregon grape long-term. Oregon grape should not be used while pregnant or breastfeeding. Side effects can include low blood pressure and heart rate, vomiting, lethargy, nosebleed, irritation of the eyes, skin, kidneys, and liver toxicity. Never use it for children, not even breastfeeding mothers, as it can affect the newborn baby through breast milk.

Pine

Scientific name: Pinus Spp. (Pine family)

Uses:
Use pine bark, resin, and needles for their therapeutic effects. The Chippewa people use a decoction of pine bark to cleanse and heal all types of cuts and wounds. Collect the needles, young buds, and twigs in the early spring as they begin to form.
Pine has a stimulating action and is especially good for rheumatism and arthritis pain either as an infusion or as a bath, which can also help ease fatigue, nervousness, and sleeplessness.
Pine is especially good at dealing with upper respiratory catarrh, and steam is excellent for bronchitis, sinusitis, or other respiratory tract inflammation.
The resin forms a sticky and firm substance, which is very helpful in removing small splinters.

Caution:
There is insufficient research and evidence that pine bark is unsafe, and most people tolerate it well. Although some groups of people like pregnant women, breastfeeding women, and older people, people on medication can be sensitive to pine bark and avoid using it.

Pumpkin

Scientific name: Cucurbita pepo (Cucurbits family)

Habitat: north-east Mexico, southern USA, USDA zone 3-9.

Uses:
Pumpkin seeds have medicinal as well as culinary purposes. They are high in fiber, zinc, beta-carotene, and minerals. Remove the pumpkin seeds from the pulp after harvesting the pumpkin in late summer or early fall. Dry and powder the seeds for medicinal use. Add the seeds to a liquid or food, or place the powder into capsules.
Pumpkin seeds have anthelmintic, antioxidant, anti-inflammatory, and diuretic properties. They can help to raise the immune system response of the body. The use of pumpkin seeds helps lower cholesterol and reduce depression in patients.
The strong anti-inflammatory property makes it an ideal remedy for arthritis, gout, and rheumatism, and it can also help prevent osteoporosis and provide pain relief.

The diuretic properties are beneficial for cases of irritable bladder, inflamed or blocked urethra, inflamed kidneys, cystitis, water retention, and swollen ankles and knees. Internal use of pumpkin seeds increases the production of male hormones and can help in benign prostatic hyperplasia (BPH) cases.

Use pumpkin seed preparations for expelling tapeworms and roundworms.

Externally, use pumpkin seeds for wounds and burns, and they can help heal chapped skin.

There are no known side effects of the use of pumpkin medicinally.

Purple Passionflower

Common names: Passionflower, Wild Apricot, Maypop, Maracuja, Wild Passionflower, Apricot Vine

Scientific name: Passiflora incarnata (Passifloraceae family)

Habitat: From southeastern to the central USA, USDA zone 7-11.

Uses:

Its compounds have calming, sleep-inducing effects. The plant has been FDA-approved as an over-the-counter remedy for sleeplessness and sedation. However, it was withdrawn from sale in 1978 because of insufficient proof of its safety and efficacy. If you'd like those effects today, boil some passionflower tea, stash a few of these fresh herbs beneath your pillow, and allow the Zazas to start.

Passionflower can likewise be Mother Nature's cure for emotional and mental difficulties associated with stress, mood, and anxiety. A study and research published in the Journal of Clinical Pharmacy revealed that plant extract could handle pressure without affecting job performance, which exists with the standard pharmaceuticals. Another study demonstrated the herb successfully reduced stress related to undergoing an operation.

Caution:

Passionflower is usually considered secure, with a couple of exceptions. Avoid if pregnant since the herb was known to cause uterine contractions.

Additionally, avoid at least 2–3 weeks before the surgery as it might increase anesthesia's effects to dangerous levels. Don't combine with any other sedatives.

Red Clover

Common names: Beebread, Wild Clover, Cow Clover

Scientific name: Trifolium pratense (Legume family)

Habitat: Southern Canada, northern USA, USDA zone 4.

A part of the pea family, red clover has long, slender roots that penetrate several layers of earth and draw vitamins, minerals, and other components usually not located close to the surface.

Uses:
It's famous for its ability to repair nitrogen from the soil, thus functioning as a natural fertilizer. As a medicinal herb, red clover is among the finest respiratory tonics, helpful for young kids and adults, and it's also among the most excellent detoxification herbs. It's one of those ingredients in conventional anticancer formulations like the Hoxsey formula and Essiac tea. Red clover produces flavorful tea. Combine it with other herbs like mullein for chronic respiratory difficulty or use nettle for tea to construct the bloodstream and enhance it. The tea or tincture may be used to stop and remove unwanted growths such as tumors, cysts, and fibroids. Red clover is effective in relieving menopause symptoms such as hot flashes.

Caution:
Hemophiliacs, or individuals with "lean" blood (people who snore heavily or have problems with blood clotting), shouldn't use red clover. It's referred to as a blood thinner and may encourage prolonged bleeding.

Red Raspberry

Common names: Red raspberry, Raspberry, Framboise

Scientific name: Rubus idaeus (Rose family)

Habitat: California, Washington, Oregon, USDA zone 3-9.

Uses:
It was a beneficial treatment for the North American continent's indigenous peoples, which believed it was a nourishing tonic and therapeutic cure for nursing and pregnant women. It's been utilized as a uterine tonic and anabolic supplement since. Raspberry leaves are full of minerals and vitamins, especially iron and calcium.

It helps reduce excessive menstruation and is among those exceptional tonics for childbirth and pregnancy. Also, it makes a fantastic mouthwash for sore or infected teeth. It can also be ready in tincture and capsule types or made into a yummy syrup. Raspberry fruit is delicious food full of Vitamin C, fiber, minerals, antioxidants, and other beneficial plant compounds that protect against cell damage. You can just add them to your diet.

Caution:
Raspberry leaf is not safe in early pregnancy, but it can be used in late pregnancy or labor under the supervision of your health practitioner. If you have any estrogen or other hormone-sensitive condition, please avoid raspberry leaf.

Rosehips

Common names: Rosehip, Rose Haw, Rose Hep, Apothecary Rose, Cherokee Rose, Dog Rose

Scientific name: Rosa canina (Rose family)

Habitat: Wild in North America, USDA zone 3-9.

Uses:
Rosehips contain more vitamin C than any herb and many times more than citrus, even when measured gram for gram.
They also contain compounds promoting good health for the skin and eye. Native Americans also used rosehips for their anti-inflammatory and pain-relieving properties. Adding rosehips into your diet help decrease inflammation and oxidative stress in the body. In addition, rosehip seeds help protect your skin against UV rays, pollution, and cigarette smoke and promote skin moisture and elasticity. Oil pressed from rosehip seeds has anti-aging and wound healing effects. Taking by mouth has been effective in relieving pain for people with osteoarthritis.
Use rosehips to make vitamin-rich jam or syrup. Rosehips make a flavorful, mild-flavored tea, perfect on a chilly night. Or try infusing the leaves, stems, and flowers for a fuller repowering tea. You can also use rose leaves, which are rejuvenating and astringent. Beautiful fragrant flowers are used in love, heart potions, and various flower essence formulas.

Caution:
Consuming large doses of rosehips might cause kidney stones. Excess vitamin C in rosehips may cause upset stomach, nausea, constipation, and heartburn. Large quantities may be harmful to people with iron disorders or sickle cell anemia. Consult with your doctor before starting taking rose hips by mouth. There is not enough research on whether it is safe to take rosehips while pregnant or breastfeeding.

Sage

Common names: Sage, Common Sage, Culinary Dage, Garden Sage

Scientific name: Salvia officinalis (Mint family)

Habitat: Sage grows in hot. Gather the leaves in dry, sunny weather in May or June shortly before or just when the flowering season begins, and then dry them in the shade. In USDA zones 5–8, sage will be perennial. In USDA zones 9 and above, sage will be annual.

Grow and Harvest:
The plant is not picky about soil types but requires well-drained soil. Sage does not do well in areas of high summer humidity but does well in dry heat areas.

Seeds are slow to germinate, and the plant grows better from seedlings or cuttings. Water once or twice per week for the first few weeks so that the soil is moist but not saturated. Once the plant has a well-developed root system, it can be watered every week or two, be sure not to overwater.

The plant flowers in mid-summer but should not be harvested in the first year while the plant becomes established. The medicinal part of sage is the leaves, which can be collected throughout the year. To maintain the plant, remove buds before flowers form.

Harvest stems by cutting from the main stem and hanging upside down to dry.

Uses:
Sage has astringent, antispasmodic, estrogenic, antimicrobial, anti-inflammatory, antibacterial, antihistamine, carminative, spasmolytic, antiseptic, and anhidrotic properties.

Use sage as a spice and in culinary preparations. Sage is one of the most sacred herbs and has powerful purification properties. It is a very effective remedy for abdominal cramps, spasms, colds, and flu when taken internally. Externally, use sage preparations for cuts.

Typical uses for sage involve problems with the stomach, colon, kidneys, liver, lungs, and skin. Sage infusions help to reduce the severity of colds and flu and are a laxative. Sage increases mental and cognitive function.

Use internal preparations as a digestive and appetite stimulant and for gas. Sage tea works wIf you have ell against flatulence, abdominal cramps, bloating, spasms of the digestive tract, diarrhea, and stomachache. It can reduce sweating, and as a mouthwash, it helps reduce inflammations of the mouth, throat, and tonsils. Use a sage lozenge for soothing sore throats and a gargle to help soothe mucous membranes.

For women's complaints, sage is excellent for regulating menstruation, easing menstrual cramps, and breast milk production. When drunk hot, sage tea will promote breast milk production, and if drunk cold, it will reduce breast milk production.

It also helps during menopause; an infusion of sage drunk cold will help to reduce sweating and stop hot flashes. A douche of sage is an effective remedy for vaginal infections.

The antiviral properties and antibacterial properties have proven effective in inhibiting the growth of herpes viruses, E. coli, staph infections, streptococcus, and dysentery.

Use external preparations for insect bites and snakebites.

Sage is the most commonly used herb during the smudging ceremony because it protects against bad spirits, helping to draw them out of the body or out of the soul.

Caution:

Sage can be toxic in large quantities. Do not use it internally if epileptic or pregnant. Possible side effects of sage include a feeling of warmth, rapid heartbeat, dizziness, and convulsions.

Saint John's Wort

Common names: St. John's wort, Hypericum, Goatweed, Klamath weed, Tipton weed

Scientific name: Hypericum perforatum (Hypericaceae - St. John's Wort family)

Habitat: USDA zone 6–10.

Grow and Harvest:

Sandy soil, disturbed areas, and compost peat should be added yearly. Soil should be well-drained. The plant requires full to partial sunlight. The area should receive at least 4 hours of direct sunlight per day. The plant does not like to be kept soggy.

Plant seeds in early spring, water them frequently until they are established, and then cut back watering two times per week.

The flowers will be at their best and most fragrant from midsummer through early fall. Harvest flowers individually when they are fresh, and leaves may be harvested at any time.

Dry the flowers and leaves in a cool and dry area, lying flat until thoroughly dried.

Uses:

Since ancient times, St. John's wort flowers have been used for medicinal purposes for their antiviral, antidepressant, wound healing, nervine, and anti-inflammatory properties. Its chemical compounds, hypericin and hyperforin, help treat mild depression symptoms and relieve anxiety and mood disorders.

St. John's wort works as a nervine tonic, calms down nerves, and supports the central nervous system. Its properties also speed up enzymes which can support natural liver function but, on the other hand, affects the metabolism of drugs.

That's why it is dangerous to combine this herb with other medications. You must speak with your doctor before taking St. John's wort.

Native Americans used to treat sores, fever, gastrointestinal issues, ulcers, tumors, and insomnia with this herb. A decoction of herb and flower was used to help vomiting and bleeding after snakebites.

After you harvest fresh flowers, you may prepare St. John's wort-infused oil, perfect for healing balms and salves. If you crush St. John's wort flowers between your fingers, they release dark red liquid, which is a powerful antioxidant that will turn your oil red during infusion. The best way is to leave your jar in sunlight for 2 weeks to help it infuse properly and prevent rotting the fresh material.

Also, dry some of your harvests for tea as a mood booster during the dark winter months.

Caution:

Interacts with many drugs and might cause serious interactions with some medications (in some cases could be life-threatening interactions). Consult with your doctor first before using St. John's wort.

Using St. John's wort might cause severe skin irritation after sun exposure. Avoid it during pregnancy and breastfeeding as it might cause defects to the infants. Avoid if you have Alzheimer's disease, schizophrenia, bipolar disorders, and major depression. If you have a surgery scheduled, stop taking it at least two weeks before and inform your doctor about that. For children, you must consult with their health practitioner first.

Saw Palmetto

Common names: Saw Palmetto Berry, American Dwarf Palm Tree, Cabbage Palm

Scientific name: Serenoa repens (Arecaceae family – Palm tree family)

Habitat: Native to southeastern parts of North America (mainly Florida, Georgia, Cuba, and the Bahamas), USDA zone 7–11.

Grow and Harvest:

Can tolerate slightly salty soil and prefer sandy areas. Fertilizer should be added yearly. It tolerates full sun but grows best in partial sun and shade. You can keep the plants indoors as long as there is enough light. The seeds germinate very slowly and may take up to a month to sprout. Once the seed sprouts, it should be grown in a container for 2–3 years before transplanting it outdoors. Water about once per week, but don't overwater. Saturated soil will stunt growth. The plant will be drought tolerant when established. To maintain the plant well, remove brown leaves and stems as they appear.

Fruit is a medicinal part and will appear when the plant is between 3 and 6 years old. The berries are ripe when they turn dark or black.

The fruit will only stay fresh for a few days and must be thoroughly dried if it is to be used for medicinal preparations. The best way to dry them is to wash them and then spread them in a single layer in the oven at the lowest temperature for a few hours. Alternatively, you can use a food dehydrator.

Uses:

Native Americans used saw palmetto fruit for its nutritional, diuretic, sedative, aphrodisiac, and cough-reducing properties. The berries were eaten whole or dried and used to make tea.

Nowadays, dried and ground saw palmetto in capsules or tablets is widely available or oily extracts of the dried berries.

Saw palmetto is commonly known for treating enlarged prostate (BPH) and other prostate problems.

Saw palmetto is also used to balance hormone levels and prevent hair loss, especially male-pattern hair loss.

Caution:

Mild side effects can include dizziness, headache, nausea, fatigue, upset stomach, and diarrhea.

Don't use while pregnant or breastfeeding. Don't use it for children. Don't use it if you are undergoing surgery, as it might slow blood clotting and cause bleeding.

Valerian Herb

Common names: Valerian, All-heal, Amantilla, Baldrian, Garden Heliotrope, Tagar, Setwall

Scientific name: Valeriana officinalis (Honeysuckle family)

Habitat: Widely diffused in North America, Canada, USDA zone 4-9.

Medicinal parts: Root.

Uses:

The first European settlers sent valerian with all their possessions to start a new life in the area. Since this herb is an easy-to-grow natural strain, I consider it one of my favorite nerve tonics and muscle relaxers. It is also called "food for the brain." It works well for many people; a small proportion of people find it annoying and overly stimulating.

It is helpful for insomnia, pain, irritability, headaches, digestive problems due to nerves, and muscle aches.

Due to its content of volatile oils, valerian root is aromatic with a strong taste and smell. Depending on the person, the scent is enjoyed or considered offensive, but I adore the scent of its flowers, as it reminds me of violets or rich and sweet earth. Valerian root is often dried or vaporized rather than taken as tea due to its smell, although it does taste pleasant. One of my favorite preparations is valerian salve, a gentle relaxant I use on my feet before sleep.
Herbalists debate whether fresh or dried herb works better, and I find it a matter of personal taste. It smells and tastes better when fresh, but the dried root works better than the fresh root.
Cats love valerian roots more than catnip. Sprinkle some on your bed or the floor for fun.

Caution:
Mild side effects can include dizziness, drowsiness, headache, upset stomach, fatigue, and vivid dreams. Avoid it while pregnant or breastfeeding and for children. Don't use it if you are undergoing surgery as it slows down the nervous system and, in combination with anesthesia, is very dangerous. It also interacts with certain drugs. Consult your doctor before using valerian, as the herb is not safe for everyone.

Water Birch

Common names: Water Birch, Red Birch

Scientific name: Betula occidentalis (Birch family)

Habitat: Widely diffused in the inland regions of the Western United States and Canada, up to the east part of Alaska. USDA zone 2-4.

Characteristics:
This small tree can grow up to 35 feet tall, with many trunks from the single rootstalk. From the trunks (covered by a red-brown and smooth bark) depart many branches populated by opposite, ovate leaves with serrated margins. Flowers are catkins: the male ones drooping down, the female erect. Seeds have horizontal "leaflets" such as a helicopter (samara). It helps them fly for long distances when they detach from the tree.

Medicinal parts: Leaves and bark.

Preferred solvent: Alcohol, water.

Main effect: Anti-inflammation, febrifuge.

Uses:
Native Americans used the water birch febrifuge properties by preparing a strong tea from leaves and barks. This infusion could also be used to wash for mild skin ailments, such as pimples.

Caution:
Do not use during pregnancy or breastfeeding. Do not use it for children. Pollen might cause allergic reactions in some people. It might interact with certain drugs.

Watercress

Common names: Watercress, Yellowcress

Scientific name: Nasturtium officinale (Mustard family)

Habitat: This wild plant thrives in watery environments such as marshes and bogs all over the United States and Canada.

Characteristics:
This plant grows in floating mats with roots immersed in the water. It spreads in width rather than grows in height, and it can reach 20 inches at its best. The plant grows in an intricate entanglement of stems with alternate, ovate, three-lobed leaves. From May to July, small groups of three to five white flowers bloom at the top of the stems.

Medicinal parts: The whole plant is edible. Mainly used are stems and leaves.

Preferred solvents: Water.

Effects: Detoxifying, carminative.

Uses:
The most documented use of this plant by Native Americans is the use of leaves to spice their dishes due to their spicy and acrid taste.
The medical use is less known and indicates the raw consumption of the plant to treat cough, colds, and indigestion due to its strong expectorant qualities. The astringent and expectorant properties of the plant will facilitate the removal of phlegm and excessive mucus in no time.
The plant also has strong diuretic characteristics and was indicated for cleansing and detoxifying.
Watercress is a popular vegetable, and you can easily grow it in your kitchen and add it to your diet as a culinary spice. I like adding watercress into my salad or sprinkling it on the top of my egg sandwich.

Caution:
There is insufficient research and evidence that watercress is safe for children and pregnant or breastfeeding women. Excessive use of watercress might cause stomach damage. People with kidney disease, stomach ulcers, or intestinal ulcers must avoid it.

Wild Carrot

Common names: Wild Carrot, Bird's Nest Root, Queen Anne's Lace, Bishop's Lace, Devil's Plague

Scientific name: Daucus carota (Apiaceae family)

Habitat: Widely diffused in meadows and fields all over the North American Continent, both in the United States and Canada. USDA zone 4-8.

Characteristics:
It is also called Queen Anne's Lace or Devil's Plague. This biennial plant is native to Europe, but it has been naturalized on the American continent. The root of this plant is white-yellowish and slightly scented. Leaves are pinnately compound and concentrated at the base of the plant. It is a umbelliferon, so flowers are concentrated in umbrella-like clusters at the top of the plant. The center flower is typically purple, while the others are white or pink. Seeds are brown and flat on one side. It flowers between June and August, and its seeds are ripe between August and September.

Medicinal parts: The whole plant.

Preferred solvents: Water.

Effects: Diuretic, deobstruent, vermifuge.

Uses:
Native Americans used tea obtained from the flowers as a treatment for dropsy. Other remedies prepared by natives include the powder obtained by pounding seeds and dried roots to treat many diseases, from intestinal disorders to intestinal worms to urinary tract infections. The powder also has emmenagogue effects, increasing menstrual flow in case of hypo-menorrhea or amenorrhea.
The poultice of the fresh root was used topically on abscesses and infected wounds. The oil obtained from wild carrot seeds is used as a medicine.

Caution:
Be very cautious while handling the plant. Touching the leaves or sap can cause phytophotodermatitis.

Using wild carrots increases the risk of sunburn, and do not take it if you are being exposed to sun or UV light. Because wild carrot irritates kidneys, do not use it if you have any kidney problems. Also, high doses of wild carrots might cause kidney damage and nerve problems. There is insufficient research and evidence if a wild carrot is safe for children and pregnant or breastfeeding women.

Willow

Common names: White Willow

Scientific name: Salix alba (Salicaceae – Willow family)

Habitat: Widely diffused in wet environments all over the North American Continent, both in the United States and Canada. USDA zone 2-8.

Characteristics:
Willow tree grows up to 80 feet tall. From the wide central trunk, depart many drooping branches widely populated by narrow and lance-shaped leaves with finely serrated margins. The drooping shape of its branches gives the tree its characteristic shape. Both male and female, Flowers are in the shape of catkins: yellow for males and green for females.

Medicinal parts: Bark.

Preferred solvents: Boiling water.

Effects: Diuretic, febrifuge, analgesic.

Uses:
Salix bark is known to be rich in salicin, which is the natural molecule from which aspirin is derived. In fact, natives and other ancient populations used salix bark to treat colds, rheumatism, and headaches, using the febrifuge and analgesic properties of this plant.
Salix bark decoction was effective for pain relief in cases of tendinitis, arthritis, and bursitis. Its anti-inflammatory properties helped reduce the swelling and the pain associated with those ailments.

Caution:
There is insufficient research and evidence if willow is safe for children and pregnant or breastfeeding women. The mild side effect might occur as diarrhea, vomiting, or heartburn. If you are allergic to aspirin, do not use willow as it might cause an allergic reaction, itching, or rash.

Witch Hazel

Common names: Witch-hazel, Common Witch-hazel, American Witch-hazel

Scientific name: Hamamelis virginiana (Hamamelidaceae – Witch-hazel family)

Habitat: Widely diffused in forests and woods all over the Eastern and Mid-Eastern part of the United States, from the Atlantic shore to the Mississippi River and the Great Lakes region. USDA zone 4-8.

Characteristics:
This bushy tree can grow up to 30 feet tall. The bark is peculiar: brown on the outside, bright red on the inside. Many twisted trunks depart from the ground rootstalk, widely populated by alternate leaves with serrated margins. At the bottom of the leaves, the flowers emerge in groups typically of seven. The petals of these are narrow, oblong, twisted, and yellow.

Medicinal parts: Bark, leaves, twigs.

Preferred solvents: Boiling water, alcohol.

Effects: Expectorant, diuretic, analgesic, antiseptic.

Uses:
Native Americans used the tea from fresh or dried leaves as a wash for wounds, burns, and eyes and in the treatment of hemorrhoids and other anal disorders from scratching, inflammation, pain, and burning. It was effective in skin conditions such as athlete's foot (due to its antifungal properties) and eczemas. If drunk, the tea helped with phlegm expulsion and is a powerful febrifuge. It also was used to treat sore throats and as an astringent to cure dysentery.
The inner bark is where the healing properties concentrate the most, so decoctions and teas prepared with it may result in more effectiveness.
The application of witch hazel bark, herb, or water to the skin eliminates moderate bleeding.
Native Americans harvested young buds in spring to prepare a decoction, considered a powerful tonic.
Witch hazel is a popular plant. You can often see it in first aid kits, usually as an addition to rubbing alcohol. The leaves and twigs of the tree are used in herbal medicine, and witch hazel is known for its astringency. It's used in wound healing since it helps to reduce inflammation. Witch hazel contains chemicals called tannins. Witch hazel can help minimize bleeding, help heal damaged skin, and kill bacteria when added directly to the skin. Use it for bites, stings, varicose veins, cysts, and rashes. These examples show that it is used externally only. Don't use witch hazel internally unless you are under professional supervision.
You will see a substance (Hamamelis water, purified witch hazel extract) called witch hazel water. It is a solvent distilled from witch hazel's dried stems, bark, and partly dormant twigs and has an astringent effect on tightening the skin.

Caution:
It is possibly safe for only topical application for children (not younger than 2 years).
Always perform a patch test for possible skin reactions before topical application.
Taking witch hazel by mouth only under medical supervision, and if taken in large
doses, might cause liver problems. There is insufficient research and evidence if witch
hazel is safe for pregnant and breastfeeding women.

Common Wormwood

Common names: Absinthium, Absinthe, Absinth, Absinthia Herbal, Absinthe Suisse,
Wermut.

Scientific name: Artemisia absinthium (Asteraceae family)

Habitat: Diffused in Canada and the northern United States, USDA zone 4-9.

Medicinal Parts: The parts above ground and oil.

Uses:
It is used for numerous digestion disorders, such as lack of appetite, gastrointestinal
upset, intestinal spasms, and gall bladder disease. It is also used to treat the liver's
illness, depression, body pain, memory loss, worm infections, and fever, improve
sexual desire, induce sweating, and as a tonic. It's also helpful for Crohn's disease and
a kidney dysfunction termed IgA nephropathy (Berger's disease).
Wormwood oil is often used to enhance imagination, improve sexual desire, and for
digestive disorders.
For osteoarthritis and curing wounds and bug bites, certain people apply it directly to
the body. The oil is a counterirritant and helps relieve pain.
Wormwood contains thujone, which is a potentially poisonous chemical compound.
When consumed by mouth, wormwood is harmless in the concentrations typically
used in food and drinks, including vermouth and bitters, as long as these items are
thujone-free.

Dose:
The required dosage of wormwood depends on several variables, such as age, fitness,
and some other user factors. There is not adequate clinical evidence at this point to
establish the optimal doses range for wormwood.

Caution:
Taking wormwood oil can induce failure of the kidneys.
Wormwood includes thujone, which may induce seizures. There is fear that
wormwood may make seizures more probable in people who are vulnerable to them.
Medications used to stop anticonvulsants (seizures) interact with wormwood.

Wormwood is possibly unhealthy in concentrations greater than typically present in food when ingested by mouth during pregnancy. Avoid topical use during pregnancy. There is not enough information about its safety during breastfeeding, so avoid using it.
Wormwood can cause an allergic reaction and if you are allergic to plants from the Asteraceae family, avoid use.

Field Wormwood

Common names: Field Sagewort, Filed Southernwood, Canadian Wormwood.

Scientific name: Artemisia campestris (Asteraceae family)

Habitat: Widely diffused in dry environments all over the North American Continent, both in the United States and Canada. USDA zone 4-8.

Characteristics:
The Artemisia Campestris has a two-year life cycle. It appears as a rosette of deeply divided, almost linear, gray-greenish leaves in its first year. In the second year, many reddish stems grow from the bottom. These are covered with smaller and more deeply cut leaves. Stems are covered with hair and have small, yellow flowers at the top.

Medicinal parts: Leaves and flowers.

Preferred solvents: Diluted alcohol.

Effects: Vermifuge, febrifuge, sedative, carminative, emmenagogue.

Uses:
The medical uses of the Artemisia Campestris are many and well known. Natives used to chew and swallow the juice of leaves to help with intestinal gas, using its anticonvulsant and carminative properties.
The decoction of leaves was a potent, sweat-inducing, fever-reducing drink. This decoction was also helpful for killing intestinal worms and other parasites and increasing blood flow in case of poor menstruation.
A bundle of fresh herbs was set to dry and then used as a stick to smudge the participants in the smudging ceremony.
The fresh herb was also used during the sweat lodge ceremonies.

Caution: Do not use if you are already taking anticonvulsants. Skin contact might cause allergic reactions or dermatitis for some people. If you are allergic to plants of the Asteraceae family, do not use this plant. For this species, there are no reports of its toxicity. Be cautious not to mislead other species of Artemisia absinthium.

Yarrow

Common names: Common Yarrow

Scientific Name: Achillea millefolium (Asteraceae family)

Habitat: Temperate regions of North America, USDA zone 3-9.

Characteristics:
The plant consists of the flowering tops of Achillea millefolium, a perennial herbaceous, rhizomatous plant, 30-50 centimeters high. It is cosmopolitan: it grows from the plains to the mountain areas, where it is common to find it in wet meadows, along ditches and hedges, and in uncultivated places.
The flowering tops are collected from June to September and dried in the shade below 40 degrees. After collecting the inflorescences in clusters, they are preserved in paper or canvas bags.

Uses:
Yarrow has emmenagogue properties (stimulates or increases menstrual flow); hemostatic (prevents and stops bleeding); spasmolytic (relieves spasm of smooth muscle). Indications are, therefore, amenorrhea (absence of menstruation) and dysmenorrhea (menstrual cramps); metrorrhagia (irregular periods); anorexia and gastrointestinal dyspepsia (indigestion); spasms of the digestive and uterine tract; venous conditions (varicose veins, phlebitis, hemorrhoids).
Yarrow has been used for centuries to facilitate menstruation.

Caution:
The use of yarrow is discouraged during pregnancy and lactation and in children: some of its components may have a neurotoxic action.
As for possible interactions, attention should be paid to its activity on blood clotting, especially in the case of people taking anticoagulant drugs, whose action could alter.
Since yarrow belongs to the Asteraceae family, it may cause allergic dermatitis in people particularly sensitive or allergic to plants of this family.
Due to a possible interaction with medications, always speak to your doctor before taking yarrow if you regularly take any medication or have a history of any chronic diseases.

Yellow Dock

Common names: Curled Dock, Curly Dock, Narrow Dock, Rumex, Sour Dock, Acedera, Broad-Leaved Dock

Scientific name: Rumex crispus (Polygonaceae – Buckwheat family)

Habitat: Widely naturalized in North America. USDA zone 4-7.

Medicinal parts: Roots and rhizomes.

Uses:
This crazy abundant weed of gardens, areas, and roadsides is possibly one of the best herbs for the whole digestive tract, including the liver.
The huge taproot is packed with anthraquinones, which have laxative activity. Although yellow dock root does not contain much iron, it helps assimilate and distribute iron in our body, making it especially useful for anyone with low iron levels. It is one of the best herbs for nausea and fatigue caused by low iron levels. The root is an excellent aid for slow digestion and constipation. Chemical components are easily extracted using a decoction of water and alcohol. The yellow dock creates a somewhat bitter decoction; therefore, it is best formulated with more delicious herbs. The tincture is excellent for the liver, liver, and digestion. It can be added to formulations due to its analgesic properties. Create an iron-rich syrup, incorporating other iron-rich herbs like nettle, chickweed, dandelion leaves, and root.

Caution:
Avoid yellow dock during pregnancy and breastfeeding. It might cause skin irritation or other allergic reaction if you are allergic to ragweed.
Raw and uncooked yellow dock is not safe due to its high oxalic acid content and can cause severe side effects, including vomiting, heart problems, or breathing difficulty. Cooking reduces oxalic acid, but excessive doses taken by mouth are possibly unsafe. They can cause mineral deficiencies in the blood, such as calcium and potassium, and other side effects such as diarrhea, stomach cramps, nausea, and excessive urination. Avoid yellow dock if you have a clotting disorder, as it might speed up the blood clotting. Also, avoid it if you have a blocked digestive tract, stomach or intestinal ulcers, kidney stones or have ever had kidney stones.

Conclusion

Native Americans have played a significant role in making us realize the importance of herbalism. The medicinal and herbal wisdom of Native Americans has long been ignored by history. This book aims to bring their medicinal expertise and deep knowledge of natural supplements to light.

With this book, you hold in your hands a proud tradition of herbal craftsmanship and culture. We have covered all the little details on how to grow herbs in your backyard. In addition, the use of the most important herbs, natural remedies, and herbal supplements in the local market are also part of the book.

Take it along on your nature walks: this book will guide you through the method of identifying, collecting wild herbs, and even transplanting herbs found in your backyard but often overlooked.

This handy encyclopedia will guide you from soil to table on your way to becoming a conscientious, compassionate, and skilled herbalist. Enjoy reading this book and learn all about this beautiful gift of nature known as herbs.

As you build your library, you can take the next baby step of growing your herbs. It can be a small herb garden in your home. The choice is yours, depending on your comfort level with the idea. If you already grow them, then you are already a budding herbalist.

What you decide to grow will depend on a few factors. If you're thinking about an outdoor garden, you need to figure out what will thrive in your climate.

Once you know what herbs to grow, you need to increase your chances of success by seeking advice on soil, sunlight, and other growing requirements.

You may not have the same luxury. But don't despair. Even if you don't have a mentor, this part of the book will guide you through the essentials of becoming your herbalist.

However, the key to any good journey is not to expect to arrive at your destination overnight. As you learn more about this topic, you'll keep asking yourself, "Am I there yet?" The answer is that you never really get there. Herbalism is a lifelong education in itself. There is always more to learn. There is always another path to take on the journey. As in life itself, the pleasure and satisfaction are in the journey and not the destination.

If using healing herbs is new to you, you must take baby steps. I know it may be difficult initially, but in doing so, you will be gaining a solid foundation and knowledge from which to build.

Then you may be surprised to learn that you've already started. Yes. By starting to read this book, you have taken the first step. And don't let this be the only volume you read on herbs. There are many out there.

Introduction

Herbs are part of the natural world, and they are grounded in the earth, so they strongly connect to Mother Earth. Native American Herbalism is deeply rooted in the belief that everything that grows acts as a teacher, healer, and life force. Plant consciousness is alive with meaning—each plant has its spirit and aura, which you can sense if you learn to ask for their presence. The plant has its journey of self-healing, which it shares with us simply by sharing space on our plate or shelf or garden bed. As we consume their energy (in food), we feed our bodies and souls more of their vital essence.

In Native American herbalism, the entire culture is based on this understanding. In our approach to natural medicine, we honor the plant spirit and all that it offers us. We honor the plant's journey of nourishing itself with its life force so that we may consume its life force in food. When we practice a diet including a wide variety of fresh fruits and vegetables, beans, corn, nuts, and seeds, alongside grass-fed meats and dairy products from animals raised on pasture—we naturally absorb more of these healing energies from Mother Earth. These forms of healing are connected to the earth on which they grow. There is no hierarchy of authority, knowledge, or power in Indian herbalism, and there are no rulers, priests, elders, or shamans. It is a culture that honors all people equally.

Native American herbalism uses traditional methods of preparing herbal medicines that retain their freshness and vibrancy. Those are not the methods of preparation perfected by "old medicine" over 500 years ago in Europe. We are still learning new methods and applying them to different plants each year. We learn to use herbs as medicine and as nourishment—but we also bring our tribal wisdom and cultural knowledge to this relationship with plants so that the plants teach us how to use them for healing purposes. We recognize that it is not the herb healing us but our relationship with the plant spirit.

Native American herbalism emphasizes the importance of quickly preparing herbal remedies, which means making them fresh. It means simply cooking with herbs in traditional methods of preparing herbs for use in food and medicine. We always experiment with new ways of making medicines - drying, grinding, freeze-drying, sifting, steeping, etc. - but Native American herbalism is based on using fresh herbs, so we always taste and evaluate our medicines by cooking them in dishes or putting them in herbal sachets to preserve their life force so we can use them again the next day.

Our approach to herbal medicine is a way of preparing food as a form of medicine— we call it "APOTHECARY KITCHEN COOKING." Native American healers have been preparing medicines in traditional ways for thousands of years. We prepare herbal medicines from fresh herbs and use Native herbal medicine recipes as a guide. We use these traditional herbal recipes as a form of a recipe book - we say: "Always start with herbs and use them the way a good cook does. Use them to make good meals." In this way, we can provide safe and effective preparations for later health care. Our medicines contain no synthetic chemicals or petroleum products.

The Power of Herbs

Many people view Native American herbalists as doctors or healers who know the use of plants, roots, and leaves to cure diseases and other ailments.

There are differing ideas about how Native American herbalism is used. Some traditional Native American practitioners believe that diseases are caused by a spirit that needs to be eliminated from the body, and the herbs only catalyze this process. Many Western-educated doctors believe that diseases can be cured with herbs, but they do not consider it possible to determine which herb will cure which disease without experimentation.

Native American herbalists believe that there are different herbal traditions within the Native American culture. The methods used by each tribe vary depending on their rituals, beliefs, and location. For example, the Ojibwa of Canada uses black hawthorn to treat tuberculosis.

There is a common belief among Western-educated doctors that many Native American remedies cause less harm than the disease they are prescribed to ward off. For example, they believe that unless a family has an ancestor or connection to an illness, they will not be able to cure it just by taking medicine and expecting it to work.

Native American herbalists are very important in maintaining wellness and physical and emotional health. They use various methods to heal the body of ailments, and this book is a great resource for learning more about some of their remedies.

The herbs that Native Americans use to heal the body are known by many different names. For example, tonic, medicine, herb, and sacred plant. Many of these plants were used by all Indian tribes because they are part of their customs and rituals.

In traditional Native American culture, herbs had been used for hundreds of years before European settlers came to North America. More advanced materials with them, such as gun powder and metal tools for farming and hunting, made life much easier. Native Americans had to use herbs for healing.

For example, the tribe I am from uses a plant called wild indigo root to remedy fever and colds. The wild indigo root is very bitter and has no taste, but it has magical powers that help you heal sickness and detoxify your body. When you eat the wild indigo root, you will feel better and warmer. It also tastes like carrageenan (gelatin) or applesauce, making it easy to swallow if eaten dry, without water. Wild indigo can be used externally on cuts and bruises and internally for sore throats, problems with your immune system such as yeast infections, or coughs.

Balance Whole Body Health

Herbs are a great way to balance your whole-body health and treat simple general ailments. They can be used externally or internally, showing quick results.
You can also use herbs to help support your existing medical conditions without side effects.

Below you will find a list of some of the most valuable herbs and what they do.

Yarrow

It helps with fever and infection and can be applied externally to wounds, and is great for supporting your immune system.

Red Clover

It supports the heart and mind and has been used for centuries as a tonic to stimulate hair growth.

Cinnamon, Cloves, Cardamom, Cayenne (all):

It helps with indigestion such as gas, bloating, or constipation. You can use it for tea, cooking, or extract in capsules.

Licorice

It supports your adrenal system, helps with stress, and feels especially effective on sore throats.

It's best to use herbs in combination with other natural treatments such as acupuncture, massage, and a healthy diet, primarily since herbs work with your entire system, not one specific part of your body. But if you feel like something isn't right and want to try something safe that won't harm you or make you feel worse, herbs are a great way to go.
Herbal remedies are potent, and when they are used correctly, they can have miraculous effects on your health. Some of the herbs that I frequently use are Stinging nettle, Dandelion, Red clover, Yarrow, Valerian root, Catnip, and Skullcap. I use them all the time to balance my hormones and keep my body healthy. My favorite is Stinging nettle tea because it helps with allergies and sensitivities to things like chemicals in skincare products; it also helps reduce muscle pain and relax muscles that tend to be tense.

What Can Herbalism Teach You?

In the Western world, there is a commonly accepted idea that you may not be able to control everything. In contrast, Eastern thinking does not focus on this concept of accepting the things you cannot control but goes deeper into what is happening in your life and how it is affecting your health and wellbeing.

Eastern philosophy believes that our health is connected to harmony in all aspects of our lives—mental, emotional, spiritual, and physical. When we are internally whole and healthy, we have a natural ability to find balance externally by working efficiently with those around us to achieve desired outcomes without undue struggle or struggle at all. This spirit of overall wholeness encourages taking ownership of our power to create effective change.

Herbal medicine works to support this overall philosophy of peace and harmony by addressing imbalances in the body's systems, with both intended and helpful side effects. Western medicine identifies problems, isolates them, and treats them directly. Its focus is on reducing symptoms rather than the eradication of the disease. This approach often leaves room for more problems to arise as a cascade effect of unaddressed underlying issues.

Herbs are tools that support you in your quest for internal harmony by helping to create balance in body systems that may be out of whack and create an environment where there is less energy available to disharmonious factors like viruses or disease-causing germs. Herbalism, considered a stand-alone therapy, is not a quick fix or a substitute for medical services. It is an effective way of healing, but it may be less accessible in our modern society.

The herbs used in this book reflect the traditions and knowledge passed down from generations of herbalists and nurses. They have been selected not just for their medicinal properties but also for their beauty and usefulness to human beings in general. An experienced nurse or herbalist will know how best to use each herb safely and effectively, following traditional practices and local guidelines. The information in the following pages is to help stimulate your knowledge and introduce you to herbal healing that I hope will encourage you to choose alternative methods of treatment for yourself, friends, and family.

Important To Know Before Getting Started with Herbal Healing

Know Before You Make a Decision

Native American medicines have been used for years. Even though its effects are not as significant as thousands of years ago, people are convinced of its power. However, before taking any indigenous medicine, you must first educate yourself.

Get a Diagnosis

You want to know everything as much as you can, and this is why you have to work very closely with your doctor so that there will be some monitoring as you embark on this journey into healing by nature. Once you understand what you're dealing with, you can move into the next stage.

Understand Your Ailment and Healing Options

Most people who seek native medicine have in mind that it is far better than orthodox medicine because it is natural. While this may be true for some medical issues, it may not be suitable for all. For example, there are situations or health problems that will undoubtedly require medical surgery, and there are no alternatives. Understanding your ailment also ensures that errors are limited or cut down to zero. No matter how determined you think you are, the nature of your condition will always be the primary determinant to knowing if it is something you should wholly subject to treatment through herbs.

Do Research

It is even more critical for people who have been dealing with specific ailments for a very long time. You should research your ailment's causes, triggers, and prevention options. If your doctor thinks you should try conventional medicine first, you can go on with it as long as you can afford it. If not, you still need to discuss with your doctor about herbals—and how you are going to use them the right way.

Who Should Consider Native American Medicine?

Some groups of people should consider Native American medicines more. Of course, it is available for all, but these people should take it even more seriously as it could be a very lasting solution to their problems.

You've Tried Conventional Medicine Without Changes

Evidence has shown that some people suffering from seemingly minor ailments had struggled with it for years without any good results.

For example, many people have reported dealing with insomnia, migraine, or headaches for years without finding a solution after taking plenty of pills. If you fall into this category, you must consider alternative medicine like Native American medicine. You need to discuss with your doctor about options before moving on to the alternative way.

You're Tired of Taking Pills

Some people have taken pills so much that it has become a mental burden. Yes, if you find reliable information about natural remedies, it is normal to feel that you want to get rid of the chemicals. Native medicine offers you the opportunity to try out nature in its unprocessed form. Our body contains similar elements that are available in nature, making it safe and acceptable for our internal organs.

You Hate Drug Side Effects

Many conventional medicines have side effects that might even be worse than the ailment itself. Some people have endured sleepless nights, skin rash, stomach upset, headaches, nausea, vomiting, itching, etc., just because they want to get a cure. Most herbs can have serious side effects unless you take them in moderation. Some herbs can help you overcome some of the side effects caused by the use of conventional medicine.

You Want a Combination

Sometimes your prescriptions may be working perfectly, but you still want to include natural herbs. You need to talk to your doctor and see how this works out. Self-medication in any form is dangerous, not to mention herbs and plants that you have no idea what they contain. Your doctor will guide you in the kind of herbs you can take. Many people had experienced faster recovery, fewer drug side effects, and better drug assimilation when they did it right.

You Want to Save Money

Conventional medicine is expensive. Understandably, alternative medicine is cheaper because it is made from nature, and the raw materials are derived from plants, trees, leaves, and roots that cost little to nothing to get. The manufacturing and process are also straightforward, and most times, the herbs come with their natural preservatives so that they don't get spoiled for a very long time. Alternative medicine can save you a lot of money and, at the same time, give you even more relief compared to what conventional medicine can do for you.

You Want to Try Out New Things

If you have been using pills for minor ailments like headaches, pain, sore throat, and cold, it is excellent for anyone to try out. You'll be doing some exciting experiments with your body and will be able to measure the difference between both methods.

Trying out alternative medicine will also help you discover new things about your body. The new stuff you find out about yourself, the healthier you'll live—no doubt about that.

Ingredients and Tools for Creating Herbal Preparations

Surprisingly, only a few tools are required to begin your home apothecary. The most important things you'll need are boil water, glass canning jars to store your products, and amber bottles to store herbal extracts. We will cover most of the essential tools you'll need to get started, many of which are not expensive. You can start small and upgrade your tools as you gain experience.

Herbs for the Home Apothecary

To begin, you'll need some herbs! I believe there are two ways to select useful herbs for beginners. One approach is to start with your passions. Start with a couple of herbs you've been reading about and believe might be a good fit for your requirements. You can start working with your herbs once you've purchased or planted them and then progressively spread them out to more herbs.

The other option is to follow a recipe, as we would describe in this book. So, as we would highlight two or three herbal recipes that you'd like to attempt, simply make a list of all of the ingredients and begin there. You'll have stocked your home apothecary with various herbs if you order more than you'll need for the recipes. Because most herbs have multiple applications, you can devote some time to learning about each one.

When it comes to Native American herbalism, one of the most important points to remember is that you must follow the rules. Avoid being inventive because even minor adjustments can result in unintended changes in the herbal mix, which is not good.

How many herbs do you need to buy? Three to four ounces of an herb is usually enough to start a home apothecary. That's more than enough to create a couple of recipes and still have plenty left over for future occasions. Herbs lose potency over time, so get them on the conservative side until you understand how much you regularly use, which should be within six months to a year.

Essential Tools

To prepare high-quality herbal medicines, you don't need expensive equipment or rare, pricey components. Instead, most of what you'll require is likely already in your kitchen.

Mason Jars

They're also helpful for producing tinctures and keeping herbs, among other things. The most versatile jars are the quart and pint sizes, while bigger jars may be necessary for storing dried herbs. Many store-bought goods come in mason jars, so wash them by hand or in the dishwasher and dry properly to reuse them.

Wire Mesh Strainers

You'll need strainers of various sizes for straining the tea or pressing out tinctures. Begin with a couple of single-mug strainers for single brewing cups of tea and a larger, bowl-size strainer to filter more significant amounts of herb-infused liquids.

Cheesecloth

Use cheesecloth for straining and compressing herbs that have been infused into liquid and wrapping herbs in a poultice.

Cup, Tablespoon, and Teaspoon

Useful are these measuring cups and measuring spoons with spouts that allow you to measure up to a quarter ounce.

Funnels

Getting tinctures and other liquids into bottles with narrow apertures is a breeze with a set of small funnels.

Amber or Blue Glass Bottles

These are perfect for the long-term storage of tinctures. The "Boston round" shape is preferred for tinctures and other liquid treatments, but any form will suffice. Make it a habit to save and reuse any colored glass bottles you come across—many Kombucha brands, for example, come in amber glass. Dose bottles should be one or two fluid ounces, whereas storage bottles should be four to twelve fluid ounces. Use basic bottle caps for storage, but dropper tops are required for dosing bottles.

Labels

As soon as you finish making your cures, label them. In most cases, address labels will suffice; in a pinch, masking tape will also suffice.

Blender

A regular kitchen blender will blend lotions, break down bulky fresh plant stuff, and do other tasks.

Other Useful Tools

These tools make incorporating herbs into your life easier, especially if you have a hectic schedule, but they aren't as crucial as before.

French Press

Our preferred tool for creating herbal infusions is the French press. It is easy to clean and allows the herb material to float freely in the water, exposing a large surface area for extraction.

Thermos

A decent thermos is useful whether traveling or carrying your tea to work. There are models with a filter integrated right into the lid, allowing you to put the herbs and water in the thermos together right away.

A Press Pots

It is an insulated pot with a lever that you press to dispense the contents. It'll keep you warm all day, and you can pour it out by the cup.

Herb Grinder

We used a simple, little coffee grinder for years, but if you want to prepare many herb powders, you may want to invest in a larger, dedicated machine.

Ingredients

Many preparations can be made from herbs and water alone, but some preparations require additional ingredients.

Alcohol

Tinctures are made up of a combination of botanical extracts and alcohol. Typically, we use vodka or brandy 80-100 proof.

Apple-Cider Vinegar

For herb-infused oxymels and topical treatments, use apple cider vinegar rather than distilled white vinegar.

Honey

If you can find it, choose unprocessed/unfiltered local honey wherever feasible.

Some big honey brands are tainted or even contain high fructose corn syrup, so be cautious. Herbal honey infusions are easier to make using liquid honey, but thicker honey is better for first aid and wound care.

Glycerin

To create non-alcohol-based tinctures, we use vegetable glycerin as a solvent. Vegetable glycerin is a colorless, odorless liquid with a sweet taste produced from vegetable oils such as palm, soy, or coconut oil. If you can, choose an organic, sustainably harvested, non-GMO glycerin. These sweet non-alcohol tinctures are called glycerites and are still quite effective and could be a good alternative for children or individuals sensitive to alcohol.

Oils

Olive oil can be used for almost anything, although in some cases, lighter oil, such as grapeseed or almond oil, or heavier oil, such as shea butter or cocoa butter, is preferable. Animal-derived fats, such as lard, tallow, or lanolin, can also be used.

Beeswax

Beeswax is used to thicken salves. Beeswax comes in rounds or pieces, which you can cut down for each usage. Beeswax pellets, which are easier to work with, are also available.

Witch Hazel Extract

Look for an alcohol-free witch hazel extract, as this is the most versatile—especially for first aid and wound treatment. You can find this in a local pharmacy or drugstore.

Rose Water

It is traditionally used for skin treatment, but it's also utilized in cooking. Rosewater from the grocery store's "ethnic foods" department is as excellent as the more expensive health and beauty area items.

Sea Salt and Epsom Salts

Adding a pinch of salt to baths, soaks, nasal sprays, and gargles improve the treatment.

Gelatin Capsules

These are the most commonly used when working with herbal powders to manufacture handmade herb capsules.

Begin with Herbs

I understand that not anyone has access to a forest or a meadow near their home, so I decided to write this part to guide the conscious purchase of herbs.

Although you may find the herbs you need for your preparations in the grocery store or herbal shop, my advice is to rely on local producers. They may be more expensive, but the quality is higher and generally worth the price.

When purchasing herbs, you must look at three key factors to determine the quality:

Soil

Ask where the herbs have been cultivated, and research that country's regulations regarding pollution. This task may seem complicated, but many big retailers already offer this certification of conformity in their products. If you are interested in urban farms, ask them if they use clean soil and if they have water filtration systems

Growing Practices

The aspects you have to take care of when inquiring about growing practices are Fertilizers, insects management, outdoor/greenhouse/hydroponic cultivation.

My go-to advice, in this case, is to trust your senses. If the herbs have vivid color and give off a fragrant aroma, their quality is almost certainly good.

Drying

The drying temperature is critical, and it will burn the leaves if too high, and you will lose all the precious substances. Look at the color of the leaves and discard them if it is brown-black.

Being someone who wildcrafts and dries her herbs, I have found the sweet spot is a temperature between 77°F and 86°F in a dark environment with the plants widely spaced or hung upside down from the ceiling. I found that leaves and flowers are completely dry in roughly one week and roots in one month using these low temperatures. The actual drying time depends on the plant itself, its water content, and size, so I always recommend checking that the leaves and flowers are 'crunchy' and that the roots are dry inside by cutting a sample.

Wildcrafting

The satisfaction of getting up early in the morning, hiking in the woods, and collecting your herbs is undeniable.

Always be aware of what you are going to do. Sometimes this is not your best choice: nowadays, a big problem is overharvesting endangered plants or destroying plants' habitats. You can quickly check the list of endangered species on www.unitedplantsavers.org.

The best solution is to grow your herbs or buy them from trusted producers who operate in the fair-trade circuit.

That is crucial because the use of some plants can cause damage to their growers (strangled by large companies) or populations that have been using them "quietly" for centuries and which have been damaged by a price spike followed by a random increase in popularity due to a trend.

It is the case of the Lepidium meyenii, a plant grown by Andeans for food purposes under the name of maca. This plant has aphrodisiac and testosterone-boosting properties. Not many years ago, big companies discovered this plant and its reputation. They started offering the producers more money than the locals to make money out of it. The latter could not afford it anymore and suffered severe famine problems.

Types of Preparations

Herbal remedies can be made at home in the form of teas, tinctures, washcloths, oils, and others. Some preparations also use external ways of application, for example, baths. This chapter will explain the basic types of preparations for your herbal creations.

Teas

Tea is well known and probably the most consumed beverage in the world. This herb for medicinal purposes is well known and has a strong research background. Black tea requires the essential and partial fermentation process of the tea leaves. However, green tea doesn't need this fermentation and can be produced by steaming the leaves. This process reduces the oxidation capacities of enzymes present in tea leaves, and the preservation of polyphenol is achieved through this process. Interestingly, Polyphenols belong to a family of flavonoids present 30-40 percent of the total weight in dried green tea leaves.

Teas are made from the specific plants of the tea family (Camellia Sinensis), and the top leaves of tea plants are primarily used in this process.

However, other herbs and leaves and their parts can also be used, such as flowers and fruits. It can be made from dried or fresh parts of tea-making plants, and the servings per day can vary from 2-6 doses depending upon personal needs and tolerance. Prepare tea by steeping dried or fresh herbs in hot water for 5-10 minutes. Then strain and consume. Tea has a pleasant flavor and can help with minor ailments or relax and calm your mind and body.

The dosing of tea depends upon different factors and situations. The current complaint guides the dosage when used in acute disorders and illnesses. Acute conditions may require multiple doses per day compared to chronic ones, which require fewer doses for a prolonged time. Herbal medicine incorporates dosage according to individual needs rather than treating symptoms with predetermined dosing strategies. It is not essential to stick with a specific dosing pattern, and it can vary according to personal needs and interests, which is not a practice in Western allopathic medicine.

Usually, you can find appropriate dosing with a recipe. If tea is prepared for acute or chronic conditions, better check proper dosing with an experienced herbalist or your health practitioner.

Infusions

An infusion is prepared by mixing the herbs with water or oil and waiting for the chemical compounds to mix with the solvent. This process is known as steeping. Infusion is used when the plant materials' active ingredients dissolve when put in the solvent. Many materials used are leaves, flowers, berries, and seeds, either whole or dried and pounded or ground. The liquid is boiled, and the herbs are added and allowed to steep for some time, usually 15-30 minutes. The herbs can be removed, or the liquid is strained and drunk immediately or later.

You can also inhale the vapors, depending on which herb you use and what symptoms you are relieving. Use infusions externally to form a poultice applied to the skin, as a rinse for hair, or added to bathwater as a skin soother.

Hot infusions are more potent than teas and have a bolder flavor. Because they are steeped longer, at least 20 minutes, they have more nutritional and medicinal value.

You can also prepare a cold infusion by steeping dried herbs in cool water for 6 to 12 hours before straining and serving.

Creating oil infusions takes time because well-dried herbs are infused in the preferred base oil for at least 6 to 8 weeks in a cool and dark place as some herbs could be destroyed by heat and are delicate aromatics. After this time, strain the herbs and bottle your infused oil into glass jars. It is an excellent method for creating great massage oils or bases for other remedies.

Decoctions

Decoctions are widely used sources of herbal medicine in herbalism. When roots or barks of plants contain medicinal benefits, it is hard to obtain extracts from these hard parts of plants, such as willow bark.

Decoctions are great ways when the extraction of herbal medicine is required from these hard parts of plants. To obtain this, simmer the herb in a hot water pan for at least twelve to thirty minutes on low flame. 1:32 ratio is essential to get decoctions from the herbs. A commonly used recipe involves 30 grams of herb and 1000ml of water.

Decoctions are prepared from combinations of dried or fresh herbs, fresh bark, dried roots, or stems simmered in pure filtered water. Use two tablespoons of dried herbs or one to two tablespoons of bark, roots, or stems for every two cups of cold water. Place the material into cold water in a pan or pot (use a non-reactive enamel pan), place the lid, bring it to a gentle boil, and let it simmer gently.

After 30 minutes, take off the heat, allow to cool to a drinking temperature and then strain out the plant material. Like teas, these will keep refrigerated for up to 48 hours. When ingested, decoctions can have strong effects, including dizziness and nausea, so use them carefully. Dilute to prepare as a drink since they are much more potent than infusions.

They make excellent compresses, applied externally to bruises, sprains, and strained muscles.

Decoctions are one of the primary therapies in Traditional Chinese Medicine. Many formulas have been created to treat various conditions, and some of these are still in use today.

Fomentation

Fomentation is a fantastic source of herbal delivery, and they are straightforward to administer. You apply warm wet coverings on the parts of the body to ease pain or inflammation. It can be made from teas and decoctions as well.

Liquid herbal preparation can also be frozen for cold fomentations. It also contains pain-relieving benefits, which are very specific for cold therapy to reduce the body's rising temperature. It is beneficial for treating wounds and injuries.

If we add sticks inside ice cubes, they can easily be turned into homemade sweet popsicles. This form of administration is highly famous among children. The ice bags and trays should be labeled accordingly to avoid issues.

Topical Wash

Washcloths are indeed a great source to get bathed on the bed. They can be used on a critically ill patient who cannot survive an active bath. In this comfortable way, medicine can easily be applied to the skin, and thus it can be transferred to a deeper area of the body through diffusion.

Washcloths can be warm by using hot infusions of medicine when specific heating impacts are needed, or they can be cold when benefits of cold are required. It all depends upon personal choice as well as symptoms of illnesses.

For acute injuries, such as brushing and treating sports fights, cold washcloths with specific benefits of ice and anti-inflammatory medicine can be wise to limit swelling and bruising and impede bleeding from fresh wounds.

Cold compresses also have anesthetic properties, making them a natural pain killer.

Tinctures

Tinctures are drops of herbs in liquid form, which are combined in 80-95% of the alcohol base. The most crucial benefit of this administration type is the long preservation period of medicine achieved by adding alcohol to it. It is such a diluted form of treatment that hardly any side effects occur. That is the sole reason why homeopaths have used these types of tinctures for centuries to administer drugs to human bodies. The tincture can be prepared by mixing herbs into wine, vodka, or rum.

A more diluted media such as apple cider vinegar or glycerin can also achieve these benefits. Alcohol-free media can also make tinctures of very diluted quality for those who don't like to ingest alcohol. Tinctures can be prepared in homes and can also be available in markets. However, the best practice is to make it at home because it doesn't require any special treatment to prepare all these effective tinctures. Lay herbalists are famous for making their tinctures.

Raw alcohol is best to make tinctures rather than flavored vodka or rum to preserve the maximum benefits of herbs. Flavoring is also rich in dirty surfers, which are not the right choice for medicinal purposes. Grain alcohol is the most popular alcohol used by herbalists to prepare the highest quality tinctures. Vodka and grain are very different because they are made from different sources. Twenty percent net alcohol should be used when the dried herb is made, and 40% of alcohol can be mixed with the fresh herb to ensure proper mixture and administration without side effects.

Willow bark is known to have high tannin concentration, and thus adding a few amounts of glycerin can be a bright idea for extracting maximum herb concentration. A tincture is nothing when inferior ingredients are used. Alcohol is just a base for it; however, the medicinal benefits of a tincture can only be achieved by using proper herbs. A perfect ratio is 1:5, which is 1 part alcohol with five parts of herbs to ensure more herb concentration in a tincture. This guide is critical and accepted in herbalist societies all over the world.

In the case of yarrow, we make an alcohol-based tincture. Yarrow or other types of tannin-containing herbs can be mixed with glycerin and alcohol to extract the medicinal benefits from them properly. The next stage is to put the solution in a dark room while keeping the solution in a tight jar for more than three weeks. A proper shaking of the jar every week can also promote proper extraction of the herbal medicinal benefits.

Bath

Skin is the body's largest organ and has a complex structure characterized by various properties and colors. Skin is porous and can allow transmission of medicine into deep structures when suitable media is used. Teas and decoctions are also used to enhance medicine delivery, such as in sauna bathing. Hands and feet can be bathed alone in pots filled with herbal water, or the entire body can be soaked in a bathtub to achieve the medicinal benefits of herbal medicine. A damp cloth with therapeutic fluid in bedridden patients is an intelligent way of medicinal bed bathing.

Hot baths are necessary because they can cause the skin to become porous, allowing more medication to enter the body. Be cautious when using a hot water bath to avoid burns and bruises. To prepare the bath, place the dried herbs in a bath or in steeping bags to release the maximum healing effects. Even loofa made from herbs can be rubbed on the skin directly to maximize the absorption of the medicine. It may happen that the bathtub will be a little dirty, but it should not be difficult to clean it afterward.

Herbal Ointments

Is it an ointment, a salve, or a balm? These can all be described under the heading of ointments, but there are slight differences between them, mainly inconsistency and designated use. All are mixtures of herbal-infused oils and essential oil designed for external use. The wax helps create a protective layer on the skin and the stiffness or consistency of the product.

Balms are stiffest since many are used in twist-up dispensers—think of lip balm or deodorants. There is a higher ratio of wax to oil in balms, and usually, the essential oil is added for its stronger aroma and healing properties.

Salves are mainly made with herbal-infused oils and beeswax and do not usually contain essential oils. They are softer than balms and easy to spread over a bruise or injury.

Ointments are almost identical to salves, with an oilier texture and essential oil content for healing. Due to the higher oil content, the skin easily absorbs the healing components.

Vegetable oils are the best choice, specifically coconut oil. Other choices are olive oil, almond oil, or avocado oil. Choose organic oil.

Begin making a salve by creating an oil infusion. Place your chosen herbs and oil in a glass or enamel pot, and place that over a larger pot with water—an improvised double boiler. Bring the water to a boil. Reduce to a simmer, and allow the oil and herbs to infuse for up to an hour.

Take the infused oil from the heat and strain it through cheesecloth layers, squeezing out as much oil from the herbs as possible. Measure so you know how much wax is required, and you need an ounce of beeswax for each cup of oil.
Place the wax in a clean pot over low heat; pour in the infused oil, and allow them to combine as the wax melts. Pour the final mixture into sterile jars and cover.

Herbal Syrups

Syrups are made similarly to decoctions, using herbs and water. Boil the mix of herbs and water gently until the liquid reduces by half. Strain out the herbs, add one to two tablespoons of unpasteurized organic honey for every two cups of liquid, and store the syrup in the refrigerator.

A simple thyme cough syrup can be made using 1/4 cup dried thyme or 1/2 cup fresh thyme leaves in one and a quarter cups of water.

Simmer the thyme and water for 20 minutes, or until the water is reduced to half. Remove from the heat and strain the thyme out through cheesecloth, squeezing it to get as much liquid as possible.
Add two tablespoons of unpasteurized, unfiltered honey and the juice of half a lemon.

Other herbs that work well for making syrups to fight colds and flu are sage, ginger, horehound, and peppermint.

Poultice

Poultice or Mahram is a type of herbal medicine applied to skin sores and wounds to achieve healing at maximum pace and unlock bactericidal and anti-inflammatory benefits. It is an excellent source of delivering treatment from the skin to other, more profound body layers. Again, it is a popular form of medicine in traditional Chinese, Indian, and Muslim herbalism. It is so easy to apply the poultices that they can be used on gums in the mouth and lips to treat herpes and other STDs symptoms.

Any type of fresh, damp, or dried herbs can be used to make poultices. Another effective way to apply them is to keep them on wounds for extended periods to achieve maximum absorption. It is a widely used method of administration in herbal dentistry because it is by far the safest method to be used in the oral cavity. A poultice can be left overnight or longer in the mouth to avoid bruising and sores in the mouth. It will also help improve the freshness of the mouth and thus promote a better odor in breath. It is essential to know the dosage of the herb in a poultice. A poultice is a damp or less wet medication, more like a paste made by mixing water, tea, or decoction in a dried herb paste. A mixture of different herbs can also make a poultice to unlock many benefits hidden in these other herbs. It is a fantastic strategy that many herbalists use. For example, an analgesic herb containing pain killer properties can be mixed with antioxidant, anti-inflammatory, or any type of bactericidal herb to achieve all these impacts by a single use of poultice. A great recipe involves using herbal tea with blueberry and willow to unlock the actions of all these three herbs in a single poultice.

In many countries, herbal remedies are still widespread—often the only treatment available. They are becoming more mainstream in North America and Europe as well.

Herbal remedies can treat many common ailments, such as infusions, decoctions, syrups, compresses, poultices, and ointments. Each of these is prepared in a certain way and is appropriate for only certain herbs.
Recipes will always vary, depending on the herbs used and the symptoms being treated. For this reason, no specific individual recipes are included, simply a general preparation description of how to prepare them.
If you're new to using and making herbal remedies, consult a qualified, reputable herbalist or a health professional for detailed information on properties and preparations.
Herbal treatments can be dangerous if you don't know the properties of the herb and its consequences.

Herbal Plasters

Plasters are similar to poultices, but there is one big difference. They aren't applied to the skin directly. Because they don't contact the skin, you can use spicier or hotter herbs with greater antiseptic and healing abilities. Ginger and mustard are often used for plasters.
With plasters, the plant materials are often dried or powdered and mixed with a carrier like oatmeal, ground flax, or honey to make a paste when mixed with hot water.
The resulting paste is spread onto a piece of cloth, set in place, and then bound to the area with a strip of cloth. Test to make sure the plaster is not too hot before applying it. Allow up to four hours for the plaster to set.

Compresses

Compresses are cloths soaked in a liquid and applied externally to an aching muscle or a bruised and swollen area. Use a tincture or a decoction of an herb recommended for the specific ailment to help treat aches, sore throats, and skin conditions. Compresses can be used either cold or hot. Hot compresses ease muscle pain, while cold compresses can ease headaches and reduce swelling.
Begin by making a strong tea or tincture. Take a small towel, a washcloth, or a piece of clean, dry gauze, depending on which part of the body you're treating, and dip it into the tea. Apply it to the affected area. Once it begins to cool, re-soak it in the warmed tea and reapply as often as needed.

Cream

Creating a homemade herbal cream is a great way to incorporate herbal healing properties into your skin and body care. You can choose if you make your cream thick or more liquid as a lotion. I recommend not making too much at a time as it doesn't have a very long shelf life. If you do not use any preservatives, you should use your cream within one week and keep it refrigerated between uses.
To create a homemade cream, you will need an herbal-infused oil. You will learn how to make that one in the other part of the book with recipes.
The other two ingredients you will need are beeswax and distilled water (or you can use rosewater).
For every ¾ or infused oil, use ½ to 1 oz. of beeswax, depending on your preferred consistency (if you use more beeswax, your cream will be thicker).
The first step is to put the herbal oil and beeswax in a double boiler, heat gently until the beeswax melts, and stir well to combine the two ingredients. Transfer the mixture to a blender and allow it to cool, as the blender would get too hot while blending.
The next step is to start mixing the oil and beeswax mixture in a blender on high speed and slowly start adding a steady, thin stream of water to the center of the vortex.
After some blending time, the mixture emulsifies into a thick consistency and turns white. Once you reach the desired consistency, stop adding water. You can now add 1-2 drops of preferred essential oil if you like.
Use a spatula to transfer the ready cream into a sterilized glass container—store with a lid and label in the refrigerator.
Always perform a patch test for possible skin reactions before starting use.

Important Knowledge About Right Dosages

For herbal medicine to be safe and effective, it is essential to follow these procedures. Know the difference between internal and external medicine. Herbal medicines have precise uses, and you need to know whether the medicine you want to use is for internal or external use. Oral use of medicines for external use can cause many problems. For example, comfrey, which is an excellent herb for wound healing, can cause catastrophic liver damage when taken internally. Be sure to follow the exact directions for the use of the medicine.

Know how and when to use essential oils:

Essential oils are oils taken directly from the plant, and as such, they are very aromatic and powerful, and they should be used with care. If you're going to use them externally, you should use them with a carrier oil. If you want to massage your partner's shoulders with essential oil, use only a few drops with a greater amount of coconut, olive, or sunflower oil, basically 1-part essential oil to 20 parts carrier oil. Never take an essential oil internally unless you are under the supervision of a doctor. Use caution when using essential oils for herbal remedies.

Know the parts of the plant you're using:

Different parts of plants can have different effects. For example, consider the herb pokeweed. Its berries are toxic, but its leaves have been used for herbal remedies in the past. So, it's important to know which parts of the plant must be used. Aerial parts include leaves, stems, and flowers. Roots are, well, roots. Know which part you should use for the safest effects.

When chopping or crushing any herb, make sure you are sitting upwind of it. The oil can irritate your nose. You should also be careful not to touch your eyes while chopping the herbs.
Be sure to wash your hands thoroughly with soap and warm water after handling any herb, either fresh or dried.

Know what the plant looks like:

Mistaken identity can be a very costly error. You should know what each herb looks like before using it. You don't want to use a different herb that looks similar. It is just the case when foraging for mushrooms. Another example is how St. John's wort is similar to ragweed, which is toxic. Knowing how to identify the herbs correctly can help ensure that you choose the right one. This book doesn't talk about identifying herbs, but you can find many resources online for recognizing herbs properly.

Know your prescriptions and how they may be affected by herbal remedies:

While most herbal remedies are helpful when you are already taking medications, some of them can lessen the effectiveness of your prescriptions. If you take a drug, talk to your doctor or herbalist about possible reactions between herbal remedies and your medication.

Safety Tips

Prepare every remedy in the proper size. Do not prepare too much of them, or you will risk wasting it because they went spoiled.

Check the substances before using. Look for signs of mold and always check the integrity of the packages before using a specific remedy.

Dosage

Following the correct dosage for each remedy is crucial to help you get better. For the adult doses, follow their measurements and times precisely. Don't double remedies, just like you wouldn't double heart medication. Finally, don't take more than two herbal remedies at once, as they could interact with each other or cause more negative effects.

Some of the remedies mentioned here are suitable for children or the elderly, but the dosage needs to be changed accordingly:

- For babies, don't give any herbal remedies if they're under the age of 6 months old.
- For a 6-month-old to a 1-year-old, give 1/10 of the adult dose, measured by weight.
- For a 1-year-old to a 6-year-old, give 1/3 of the adult dose, measured by weight.
- For a 7-year-old to a 12-year-old, give ½ of the adult dose, measured by weight.
- For elderly adults, give ¾ of the adult dose, measured by weight.
- For pregnant women, try not to take any herbal remedies unless prescribed by a doctor.

After taking the herbal remedy for 2-3 weeks, see a doctor if you still don't see any improvement. If you notice any negative effects, see a doctor. And if you are seriously ill or wounded, you must see a doctor immediately.

Storing Herbal Remedies

Use a glass jar with a tight seal for storing your herbal remedies. Dangers of some glass jar seals exist, so you must research which seal is best suited for the particular herbs you are storing.

Glass jars should be stored away from products that can dissolve them. If your products are particularly sensitive to heat, you should keep them in a freezer.

In general, it is best not to use plastic containers for storing herbal remedies because they can often melt as a result of the sunlight as well as extreme heat as the weather gets warmer. Plastic is not designed for such prolonged exposure to excessive heat, nor should you leave products in plastic containers overnight without proper ventilation, or they will fill with gas and eventually explode. This can pose a serious danger when trying to transport these products from one place to another. Furthermore, if you are going on a trip and carrying a lot of plastic containers, they can melt in extreme temperature situations.

Glass jars are excellent for storing herbal remedies because they allow you the flexibility of adequately absorbing the sun's rays during sunlight hours. Put a good quality lid on your container because some tops will actually absorb or radiate heat back onto your products. It can result in overheating, which may destroy the product or cause it to lose potency.

If you don't have a good quality lid on your jar, you may have a very runny product that could melt in extreme temperature conditions. Use glass rather than plastic because it won't melt in the sunlight. As long as your product is sealed tight within the jar, you can store it without worrying too much about it melting.

Remember to keep your jars in a cool, dark spot such as a kitchen closet or pantry. You don't want light or heat to keep melting the contents inside the jars. If you use a plastic container and get exposed to too much heat, it could melt and explode, and it can pose a serious danger and should be avoided at all costs.

Some people use plastic bottles and water bath canning them, but you risk the bottle exploding and ruining your herbs inside. Other people who use water bath canning try to avoid it because it is not fire-safe.

Storing Tips

The storage of herbs is essential. I recommend storing your herbs in a dark, cool, dry place because it can help preserve their potency. Store the herbs in glass containers with good lids to keep moisture out and prevent them from absorbing excess heat or light. You might want to store them in the refrigerator if they are sensitive to heat. Using glass jars for storing herbal remedies is by far the safest way to keep them. Using mason jars instead of plastic bottles is better because the lids on mason jars are meant for heat and cold, protecting your herbs from absorbing too much heat.

Herbal Remedies and Recipes

Abscess

That is what is regarded as the accumulation of pus. It can be excruciating, and it often leads to fever, swelling of the region affected, and redness. It usually occurs on the skin and around the tooth gums. The best treatment is to use your herbs as it is highly effective and doesn't present any side effects (if used appropriately) like some modern drugs. However, if things get worse, seek medical help immediately.

Fresh Yarrow Poultice

Ingredients:

- 2 tsp. fresh yarrow leaves

Tools Needed:

- Clean cotton cloth

- Knife

Instructions:

1. Get the chopped yarrow leaves, apply them to the abscess, use a cloth to cover, and leave for 15-20 minutes.

2. Do it twice a day, and let it be for the time frame.

3. Stop only when the abscess has healed.

Advice:

- If you notice any reaction or unusual changes in your body, stop the use immediately. Avoid this herbal medicine while pregnant or breastfeeding.

Echinacea and Goldenseal Tincture

Ingredients:

- 10 oz. dried echinacea root

- 6 oz. dried goldenseal root

- 4 C. 40% unflavored vodka (80 proof)

Tools Needed:

- 2-pint jars

- strainer

- Cheesecloth

- Funnel

- Dark-colored glass bottle

Instructions:

1. Put Echinacea, and Goldenseal chopped dried roots into a well-sterilized pint jar, add the vodka to cover the herbs and other 2-3 inches of alcohol above that, and cover the jar with a lid.

2. Put a label with the date you made the tincture, herbs used, and solvent. Let your tincture mixture extract for 4-6 weeks and shake every day.

3. Put the cheesecloth over the strainer and pour the mixture into an entirely new pint jar through the funnel. Squeeze all the liquid from the herbs out of the cheesecloth.

4. Bottle your tincture in a dark brown or blue bottle and store it out of the sunlight.

5. When fully prepared, take just 12 drops 3-4 times daily for 10-12 days. Drink in a cup of water or tea as alcoholic tinctures are a strong taste.

Advice:

- Diabetic patients should stay away from this herbal remedy. One of its contents, goldenseal, reduces blood sugar levels.

- Pregnant women mustn't use this remedy.

Note:

To make a non-alcoholic tincture, use apple cider vinegar as a solvent. You can also make this tincture from other parts of Echinacea.

Acne

It happens when the sebaceous glands get infected and, as a result, shoot out painful bumps—what we all call "pimples." Acne affects all age groups and can appear on any part of the body.

Witch Hazel Toner

Ingredients:

- 3 tbsps. fresh rosemary

- 1 C. water

- 1/4 C. witch hazel (alcohol-free)

Tools Needed:

- Colored glass bottle (dark)

Instructions:

1. Bring water and rosemary to boil, lower the heat and let it simmer until it reduces in half. Allow the mixture to cool down and strain through the wet cheesecloth into a measuring glass.

2. Put rosemary water and witch hazel into a dark-colored glass bottle and shake.

3. Prepare a cotton pad, dip this in the mixture, and apply it on the surface affected every morning and evening until the acne disappears from your skin.

4. Use within 1 week stored at room temperature or up to 3 weeks stored in the refrigerator.

Sage-Chamomile Gel

Ingredients:

- 3 tsp. powdered sage leaf

- 1 C. water

- 3 tsp. chamomile

- 1/8 C. aloe vera gel

Tools Needed:

- Saucepan

- Cheesecloth

- Glass jar

- Cotton

Instructions:

1. Put the saucepan on medium heat, and add the sage leaf powder, chamomile, and water. Let it simmer, then remove from heat when it reduces by half.

2. Let it cool for 3 minutes.

3. Prepare a cheesecloth, cover the edge of the funnel, then pour all the mixture to the last drop into a bowl through the funnel.

4. Add the aloe vera gel to the mixture, and mix to blend.

5. Pour into the jar and store in a fridge.

6. Dip the cotton into the mixture and apply it to the affected skin every morning and evening.

Advice:

- Anyone allergic to any plant type that falls under the same family as sage leaf and chamomile should avoid using this remedy.

Allergic Reactions

That is an abnormal reaction of the immune system to the effect of some substances. These substances are found in many things, including drinks, foods, and even the environment we live in.

Cattail Tincture

Ingredients:

- 4 oz. 40% unflavored vodka

- 4 oz. dried cattail

Tools Needed:

- Sterilized pint jar

- Cheesecloth

Instructions:

1. Put the cattail in the sterilized pint jar and add vodka. Make sure it slightly covers the top of the cattail.

2. Place the jar cap, make sure it tightly covers the jar, then shake gently to mix. Label your mixture.

3. Store for about 8-12 weeks and shake to mix twice daily.

4. Dampen the cheesecloth at the mouth of the funnel, pour the tincture into another sterilized jar and drain till all the water comes out. Dispose of the herbs and sieve into a clean glass bottle (preferably dark-colored).

5. Take 8 drops daily for a few days until the reaction stops. If it's too strong, add some water or juice to dilute.

Advice:

- If you're allergic to anything that falls under the same plant family as cattail, do not use this remedy.

- It's also not suitable for use by pregnant women and nursing mothers.

- If the reaction doesn't stop or worsen, seek medical help immediately.

Garlic-Ginkgo Syrup

Ingredients:

- 3 oz. fresh or freeze-dried garlic, chopped

- 3 oz. Ginkgo Biloba, crushed or chopped

- 2 ½ C. water

- 2 C. local honey

Tools Needed:

- 1 saucepan

- Measuring cups (glass)

- Sterilized jar

- Cheesecloth

- Funnel

Instructions:

1. Put the garlic and Ginkgo Biloba in a saucepan with water, bring them to a boil and leave them to simmer over low heat for 30 minutes. Next, turn off the heat and let it steep and cool down another 1 hour.

2. Put the few layers of cheesecloth over the funnel and pour the mixture through the funnel into a sterilized glass measuring cup. Squeeze all the liquid from the herbs out of the cheesecloth. Ensure the mixture is cold enough, so you don't burn your hands or use gloves.

3. Measure the amount of created liquid and let it cool to almost room temperature. Measuring honey needs to be at least half of the final liquid. (For example, you strained 2 cups of liquid, which means you will add 1 cup of honey at least, more honey more preservation).

4. Pour honey and your created liquid into the sterilized glass jar and mix well together to create sirup texture.

5. Label your syrup with the date and the ingredients used, and store it in the refrigerator.

Advice:

- If you're on antidepressants, you're strongly advised not to use this herbal remedy.

- Children under the age of ten should only take ½-1 tsp. of this remedy 3 times per day.

- Anything that contains honey is not recommended for children under 1-year-old as it can cause rare health conditions infantile botulism.

- Pregnant women, people with diabetes, and blood disorders should not take ginkgo.

Asthma

It is when there is a blockage in the bronchial tubes in the lungs, thereby resulting in breathing shortage and difficulty when anything offensive is inhaled.

Ginkgo-Thyme Tea

Ingredients:

- 2 C. boiling water

- 1 ½ tsp. dried Ginkgo Biloba

- 2 tsp. dried thyme

Tools Needed:

- Large mug

Instructions:

1. Boil water. Pour it into a big mug, add the dried herbs, and allow the tea to steep for 13 minutes.

2. Serve and take your time to enjoy the tea.

Advice:

- Not to be used when on antidepressants.

Mint-Rosemary Vapor Treatment

Ingredients:

- 8 C. steaming-hot water (not boiling)

- 2 C. crushed fresh mint leaves

- 1 C. finely chopped fresh rosemary leaves

Tools Needed:

- 1 large shallow bowl

- 1 large towel

Instructions:

1. Get a big bowl and put the fresh mint and rosemary leaves in it. Add steaming hot water, place it on a table, and sit facing the mixture.

2. Get a big towel to cover your head and the bowl and inhale the steam coming from the herb.

3. Stop after the water stops steaming.

4. Do this regularly until you notice some significant changes.

Advice:

- People with epilepsy are strongly advised not to undergo this procedure.

Athlete's Foot

A fungus infection affects the toe's warm, moist, and dark parts. If not treated as an urgent matter, it can spread to the toenails and cause discoloration and foot disfigurement later on.

Fresh Garlic Poultice

Ingredients:

- 2 garlic pressed cloves

- 2 tsp. raw honey

Tools Needed:

- 1 small bowl

- Cotton-cloth

- A pair of socks

Instructions:

1. Mix garlic and honey in a small bowl. Use cotton to touch the mixture and apply it to affected areas.

2. Afterward, get yourself the fresh, clean socks pair and rest your feet in them.

3. Let the poultice be on for some time, for about 30-60 minutes.

4. Wash your feet afterward.

5. You can repeat this twice every day until your foot heals up.

Advice:

- If you have skin that reacts easily, you should stay away from this remedy as it could cause skin reactions like rashes, etc.

Goldenseal Ointment

Ingredients:

- 2 C. light olive oil

- 4 oz. diced dried goldenseal root

- 2 oz. beeswax

Tools Needed:

- Medium-sized cooker

- Cheesecloth

- Cotton cosmetic pad

- Jar

Instructions:

1. Set your cooker on low heat. Add olive oil and goldenseal, and leave for 1 hour.

2. Set aside to cool.

3. Once cool, pour infused oil through the cheesecloth into the clean pot. Squeeze all the oil out of the cheesecloth. Dispose of the used herbs and the cheesecloth.

4. Add beeswax to the infused oil and let it warm for some time on low heat.

5. When the beeswax has melted completely, put it into a very clean jar and allow it to cool. Label the jar.

6. Use a cotton pad to apply to the affected area 3 times a day until healed.

Advice:

- Avoid while pregnant or breastfeeding.

- Do not use it if you have high blood pressure.

Backache

Backache is a pretty common condition in older people. However, most young people also suffer from it, especially those stressed or overworked. Besides, inactivity, injury, and inflammation can also cause backaches.

Devil's Claw Tea

Ingredients:

- 2 C. boiling water

- 3 ½ tsp. dried Devil's Claw leaves

Tools Needed:

- Mug

Instructions:

1. Boil some water and put the dried herbs into a mug.

2. Add the boiled water into the mug and allow it to steep for like 8 minutes.

3. Take the tea 2-3 times every day until you feel relieved.

Advice:

- Not recommended for pregnant women and nursing mothers.

Ginger-Mint Salve

Ingredients:

- 2 C. light olive oil

- 1 ½ oz. chopped, dried ginger root

- 2 oz. crushed dried mint leaves

- 2 oz. beeswax

Tools Needed:

- Cooker, saucepan, jars

- Cheesecloth

- Stirring tools

Instructions:

1. Set the cooker on low heat. Add olive oil, mint, and ginger, gently simmer for 90 minutes, and stir occasionally. Don't boil the oil.

2. Take it from the heat and let it cool for some time or leave it overnight to infuse longer.

3. Use cheesecloth to strain the infused oil mixture into a jar—squeeze all the oil out of the cheesecloth. Dispose of herb material and cheesecloth.

4. Pour your infused oil into a saucepan and set the cooker on low heat to warm it up gently. Add beeswax and mix very well until melted. Or, if you are using a big piece of beeswax, you may melt it first before adding it into an infused oil and mix well.

5. To test your salve's consistency, take a little bit of the salve mixture with a clean spoon and put it into a freezer for a few minutes. If it is too soft, you may add more beeswax to reach thicker consistency.

6. Once mixed well, pour the still-warm salve into a new clean jar or smaller jars and allow it to cool before covering it. Label it with the date and ingredients used.

7. Apply the affected area 5-6 times daily until the pain goes away.

Advice:

- Store in a cool, dry place. It lasts up to a year.

- If trying anything new on your skin, do a patch test first.

- Do not use this remedy if you are suffering from any gallbladder disease.

Bee Sting

The area affected after bee bites often gets swollen and very painful. So, these remedies would reduce their effectiveness.

Slippery Elm Poultice

Ingredients:

- 3 tbsps. finely cut fresh slippery elm leaves

Instructions:

1. Apply the chopped slippery elm leaves to the affected area.

2. Leave for 12-15 minutes.

3. Use continually until the pain subsides.

Lavender-Aloe Gel

Ingredients:

- 3 tsp. dried lavender

- 1 C. water

- 2 ½ tbsps. Aloe Vera gel

Tools Needed:

- Saucepan

- Sterilized jar

- Cotton cloth

Instructions:

1. Put the lavender into a saucepan, add some water, and boil the mixture over medium heat.

2. After some minutes, reduce the heat to low. When the mixture has reduced its water content to half, remove it from heat. Let it cool for some time.

3. Drape the cheesecloth over the mouth of the funnel and pour the mixture into a jar.

4. Wring the cheesecloth till all water comes off.

5. Add aloe vera gel to the lavender decoction and stir to mix properly.

6. Transfer into a glass jar and cover it. Label it.

7. Store in your refrigerator.

8. Apply lavender-aloe gel to the affected area using a cotton cloth.

Bloating

The primary cause of this is overfeeding. Bloating also occurs in some women going through their menstrual periods.

Angelica-Mint Tea

Ingredients:

- 2 C. boiling water

- 1 ½ tsp. dried mint leaves

- 1/3 tsp. ground angelica root

Tools Needed:

- A big mug

Instructions:

1. Boil water.

2. Pour it into a big mug, add the ingredients and let it steep for about 15 minutes.

3. Drain the tea into a mug and serve.

4. Drink 1 cup a day for bloating relief. Or 1/3 cup half-hour before main meals.

Advice:

- Don't use it during pregnancy.

Dandelion Root Tincture

Ingredients:

- 10 oz. dandelion root, finely chopped

- 4 C. unflavored 80-proof vodka (40%)

Tools Needed:

- Pint jar

- Funnel

- Cheesecloth

Instructions:

1. Put the dandelion root into a sterilized pint jar. Pour vodka 2 inches on top of the dandelion root, cover the jar tightly, and shake to combine.

2. Keep it away from the sun in a cool and dry place and shake 5 times daily for 8-10 weeks.

3. Over the mouth of the funnel, place a cheesecloth and pour the mixture over it into the jar.

4. When done, wring till all the liquid comes off.

5. Take 1 teaspoon per day or 10-15 drops once or twice a day just for a few days. Always drink plenty of water while using tinctures to flush all the toxins out of your body.

Advice:

- Don't use dandelion for too long as it is a diuretic.

Dispersing Infusion

Preparation Time: 10 minutes.

Cooking Time: 20 minutes.

Servings: 3 to 3½ cups dried herb mix (enough for 18 to 24 quarts of tea).

It helps with bloating, no matter what kind. If you don't have all the herbs, it's still effective, or you can adjust the proportions to your taste. However, be forewarned: This will induce you to pass on some gas!

Ingredients:

- 1 cup dried calendula flower

- 1 cup dried self-heal leaf and flower

- ½ cup fennel seed

- ½ cup dried ginger

- ½ cup dried peppermint leaf (optional)

Instructions:

1. In a medium bowl, mix all the herbs by hand. Store in an airtight container. Label the container with a date and herbs used.

2. Make hot infusion: Prepare a pot of boiling water. For every 2 to 3 tablespoons of herbal mix, measure a quart of water. Put the herbal mixture in a mason jar or French press, pour in the boiling water, cover, and steep until sufficiently cool to drink or at least 20 minutes. Then strain the infusion.

3. Drink 1 to 3 teacups after meals to prevent or dispel bloating.

Intestinal Gas Tincture

Ingredients:

- 3 tablespoons fennel seed tincture

- 3 tablespoons ginger root tincture

- 3 tablespoons licorice root tincture

- 3 tablespoons peppermint tincture

- 3 tablespoons chamomile flowers tincture

Instructions:

1. Put the tinctures in an amber glass bottle with a dropper lid in the indicated proportions and shake to mix well. Label it. Take 5 drops after each meal.

Preventive Tincture

Ingredients:

- 3 tablespoons fennel seed tincture

- 3 tablespoons dandelion root tincture

- 3 tablespoons licorice root tincture

- 3 tablespoons sage leaves tincture

Instructions:

1. Put the tinctures in an amber glass bottle with a dropper lid in the indicated proportions and shake to mix well. Label it. Take 3 drops before each meal.

Dispersing Tincture

Preparation Time: 10 minutes

Servings: 4 fluid ounces (60 to 120 doses)

A few drops of this tincture mixture will disperse gas and fluid bloating.

Ingredients:

- 1 fluid ounce tincture of calendula

- 1 fluid ounce tincture of self-heal

- 1 fluid ounce tincture of fennel

- ½ fluid ounce tincture of ginger

- ½ fluid ounce tincture of angelica

Instructions:

1. In a small bottle, combine the tinctures and shake to mix well. Cap the bottle and label it.

2. Take 1 to 2 drops after a meal as needed.

Burns

Healing Honey

Preparation Time: 10 minutes and 1 month infusing

Servings: about 1-pint

Honey is one of the best healing agents for burns: If you have nothing to compare or get some other options, plain honey is still an excellent remedy on its own. It gets even better, though, when you try to infuse all these healing herbs into it ahead of time.

Ingredients:

- ½ cup fresh calendula flower

- ½ cup fresh rose petals

- 1-pint honey, gently warmed

Tools Needed:

- Pint-size mason jar

- Double boiler

Instructions:

1. Put fresh calendula flowers and fresh rose petals in a pint-size mason jar.

2. Fill the jar with warm honey. Seal the jar and place them into a warm area to infuse for 1 month.

3. Use a double boiler to gently warm the closed jar in water until the honey gets a liquid consistency. Next, strain all the infused honey into a new jar, pressing against the strainer to extract as much honey as possible.

4. After cleaning a burn site, apply a layer of the infused honey and then cover all lightly with a gauze bandage. Refresh all the applications at least twice a day.

Sunburn Spray

Preparation Time: 20 minutes

Cooking Time: 20 minutes

Servings: Eight fluids ounces

A few spritzes cool off the skin and begin to reduce inflammation.

Ingredients:

- 1 tablespoon dried peppermint leaf

- 1 tablespoon dried plantain leaf

- 1 tablespoon dried self-heal leaf and flower

- 1 tablespoon dried linden leaf and flower

- 1-quart boiling water

- 4 fluid ounces of rose water

Tools Needed:

- Mason jar

- 8-ounce bottle with a fine-mist sprayer top

Instructions:

1. Create a hot infusion: Combine all dry herbs in a mason jar.

2. Pour in the boiling water, cover, then steep for 20 minutes.

3. Move the jar to the refrigerator when it's cold.

4. Strain the infusion and fill half of an 8-ounce bottle with a fine-mist sprayer top. The remaining infusion can be used for compresses or as a cooling drink. Keep it refrigerated for 3 days.

5. Add all the rose water to the spray bottle and mix with the infusion. Cap the bottle and label it.

6. Apply copiously. When not in use, keep it refrigerated.

Chickweed-Mullein Compress

Ingredients:

- 3 tbsps. finely chopped fresh chickweed

- 1 ½ tsp. finely chopped fresh mullein leaf

Instructions:

1. Mix the finely chopped plants, run the compress on the burn and its surroundings, and protect it with a soft, clean cloth.

2. Let it stay for about 15-20 minutes.

3. Do it every 3-4 hours until the pain subsides.

Fresh Aloe Vera Gel

Eases sunburn pain, mild burns, and psoriasis.

Aloe is a very common ingredient in sunburn ointments. In its natural state, it helps heal and moisturize the skin. It helps with any skin issue involving redness and itchiness.

Ingredients:

- Aloe Vera plant

Tools Needed:

- Knife

- Cotton

Instructions:

1. Cut 2 inches from the aloe vera leaf.

2. Use a sharp knife to cut out the tip, use cotton to take some gel, and apply generously on the burn.

3. Do this 3-4 times daily.

Bronchitis

Allergies and infections mainly cause this condition. The area infected gets bloated and becomes painful, which often leads to constant coughing.

Rosemary-Licorice Root Vapor Treatment

Ingredients:

- 8 C. water

- 2 C. chopped dried licorice root

- 1 C. finely chopped fresh rosemary leaves

Tools Needed:

- Saucepan

- Bowl

- Big size bowl

Instructions:

1. In a saucepan, pour some water, add the dried licorice root and boil over medium heat.

2. Then, simmer for 15 minutes.

3. Next, pour it into a bowl and add the rosemary leaves.

4. Put the bowl on a table, sit in front and get a big towel. Cover your head with this towel. Make sure your head faces the bowl directly.

5. Close your eyes during this procedure and inhale the steam from the mixture.

6. Do this again and again until you feel a significant improvement.

Advice:

- Not to be used by people having any of the following: high blood pressure, epilepsy, kidney-related issues, heart diseases, and diabetes.

Goldenseal Syrup

Ingredients:

- 1 oz. dried goldenseal root, chopped

- 2 oz. dried hyssop

- 2 ½ C. water

- 2 C. honey

Tools Needed:

- Saucepan

- Glass measuring cup

- Jar

Instructions:

1. Add the goldenseal, hyssop, and water to a saucepan on low heat. Heat until you notice the water has been reduced by half.

2. Pour the content of the saucepan into a glass cup and sieve through a dampened cheesecloth back into the saucepan.

3. Let it boil again for about 2-5 minutes. Add some honey, and stir continuously till thoroughly mixed.

Advice:

- Avoid while pregnant or breastfeeding.

- Not to be used by anyone who has epilepsy and high blood pressure.

- It should not be given to children under 13 years of age.

Bruises

It is a common injury we have on regular days. It could even be a domestic cause, like one scratching our leg over a piece of furniture at home. However, if left unattended, it could lead to more severe conditions. If you find yourself at any point sustaining different bruises, use any of the herbal remedies below or contact your doctor.

Evening Primrose- Arnica Salve

Ingredients:

- 2 C. light olive oil

- ½ cup dried Evening Primrose flowers

- ½ cup dried Arnica flowers

- ½ cup beeswax

Tools Needed:

- Pot

- Cheesecloth

- Cotton cosmetic pad

Instructions:

1. Set the pot on low heat. Put the olive oil, evening primrose, and arnica flowers in it and let them heat together for 4-5 hours. Afterward, switch the cooker off to allow the infused mixture to cool off.

2. Strain the infused oil through a few layers of cheesecloth, squeeze all the oil from the cheesecloth and dispose of the herbal material.

3. Put your infused oil into a clean pot and add some beeswax into the infused oil and warm gently. When it completely melts and mixes well together. To test the consistency, dip a clean spoon into the salve and put it in the freezer for a few minutes. If it is too soft and you desire a thicker consistency, add more beeswax.

4. Remove it from heat and pour it into a clean jar to cool.

5. Label your jars with a date, product name, and ingredients used. Store in a cool, dry place. It lasts up to a year.

6. When cool, use your clean finger or cotton cloth to apply this mixture to the bruised area. Use three times per day until the bruises are healed.

Advice:

- It can cause skin irritation, so do not apply it to broken skin.

Fresh Sage Poultice

Ingredients:

- 3 tbsps. finely chopped fresh sage leaves

Instructions:

1. Put the chopped leaves on the affected area. Cover with a clean, soft cloth, and leave for about 15-20 minutes.

2. Do this 3-4 times daily until you are healed.

Advice:

- Not to be used by pregnant women.

Chickweed Tincture

This tincture can be applied to irritated skin, acne, scrapes, bumps, bruises, and any other area where you need skin healing. A standard dose (20–75 drops) can also be added to tea for digestive issues like constipation.

Ingredients:

- ¾ cup chickweed, fresh, chopped

- 1 cup 80/100 proof alcohol (like vodka)

Instructions:

1. Put chopped chickweed in a clean jar and pour vodka over the herbs to be entirely covered. Seal and label the jar. Let it infuse for 4-6weeks in a cool, dark place and shake it at least once a day.

2. Next, strain the tincture through a cheesecloth over a funnel into a dark-colored glass dropper bottle and label it. Store the tincture at room temperature, out of direct sunlight, and it will last up to five years.

3.   Apply topically on the affected several times a day until healed.

Canker Sore

They are small opened ulcers in the mouth, making your eating difficult as they are painful.

Sage poultice

Ingredients:

- 3 tbsps. finely chopped fresh sage leaves

Instructions:

1.   Put the chopped leaves on the affected area, cover with a clean, soft cloth, and leave for about 15-20 minutes.

2.   Do this 3-4 times daily until you are healed.

Advice:

- Not to be used by pregnant women.

Goldenseal and Sumac

This treatment helps significantly with pains and helps heal internal and external wounds faster.

Ingredients:

- 1 tsp. dried goldenseal leaves

- 1 tsp. dried sumac leaves

- 3 tbsps. hot water

Tools Needed:

- Mortar and pestle/grinder

- Infuser spice bags

Instructions:

1. Grind dried goldenseal and sumac leaves in a grinder to a fine powder, then enclose them in a small, thick infuser pack.

2. Boil pack in some water for not more than 5 minutes. Remove from water and let it cool a bit to don't burn yourself.

3. Put a very light cloth on the sore. Place the packet over the sore and leave for about 20 minutes.

4. Repeat this 2-3 times daily.

Goldenseal Tincture

Ingredients:

- 8 oz. dried goldenseal root, finely chopped

- 2 C. unflavored 80-proof vodka

Tools Needed:

- 2-pint jars

- Cotton cloth

Instructions:

1. Get a sterilized jar, put the goldenseal, and cover the herb with vodka.

2. Cover the jar and shake gently. Label the mixture.

3. Afterward, store for about 7-9 weeks in a cool, dry place while shaking 2-3 times daily.

4. Then, cover the mouth of the second jar with a clean cotton cloth and pour the mixture into a new sterilized jar.

5. Make sure to squeeze the cloth well so all liquid will drain.

6. Pour your tincture into a bottle, preferably a dark bottle, and store it in a cool, dry place. Put a label on the bottle.

7. To use, get some cotton, dip it into the mixture and apply on the affected areas, about 3-4 drops at once.

8. Do 3-4 times daily until healed.

Advice:

- Avoid this herbal remedy if you are pregnant or breastfeeding.

- You can mix a few drops with warm water and use them as a mouthwash to help heal canker sores in the mouth.

Echinacea Remedy

This remedy is perfect for canker sores.

Ingredients:

- 2 tablespoons sage tincture

- 2 tablespoons echinacea tincture

- 2 tablespoons lemon balm tincture

Instructions:

1. Mix well all three tinctures in a dropper bottle. Use one dropper full of the mixture to swish around your mouth 2–3 times daily.

Chest Congestion

Chest tightness occurs when you experience some difficulty breathing well. These remedies would do a lot to clear all that mucus in the lungs and its pathways.

Mint and Sage Infusion

Ingredients:

- 6 C. boiling water

- 6 tsp. dried mint leaves

- 5 tsp. dried sage leaves

Tools Needed:

- Teapot

- 1 cup

Instructions:

1. Put your dried herbs in a teapot. Cover with boiling water and let it simmer for 15 minutes.

2. Strain and serve to drink on the spot.

3. You can refrigerate and heat it again whenever you want to use it again. Use within 2 days.

Advice:

- Not for asthmatic, epileptic patients, pregnant women, or nursing mothers.

Angelica-Goldenseal Syrup

Ingredients:

- 2 oz. angelica, finely chopped

- 2 oz. dried goldenseal root, finely chopped

- 3 C. water

- 1 ½ C. honey

Tools Needed:

- Saucepan

- Glass cup

- Jar (sterilized)

Instructions:

1. Get your saucepan on low heat and add water and herbs. Let it boil for some minutes, then shift the cover aside.

2. Let it simmer until the water in the mixture reduces by half. Then turn the heat off.

3. Pour all the mixture into a cup first and strain through the cheesecloth into a new saucepan.

4. Add honey, and put the mixture back on to the low heat. Stir continuously without stopping until well mixed.

5. Pour into a sterilized jar, label it and store it in your fridge.

6. Take just 2 tablespoons 3 times daily until the symptoms stop.

Advice:

- Not to be taken by pregnant women.

- If you're on anticoagulant medications, do not take this herb.

- Avoid this herb as goldenseal increases blood pressure if you have high blood pressure.

Chickenpox

Chickenpox is caused by a virus called "varicella-zoster." It is highly contagious and spreads uncontrollably if left unchecked. Chickenpox is not curable, but it can be managed with herbs until it's successfully suppressed (along with the pain that comes with it).

Pitcher Plant and Licorice Bath

Ingredients:

- 6 C. organic unfiltered apple cider vinegar

- 1 tsp. pitcher plant tincture

- 1 tsp. licorice root tincture

Tools Needed:

- Jar

Instructions:

1. Put apple cider vinegar and tinctures into a dry jar.

2. Ensure it tightens every well. Keep it in a cool dark place till there is a need for it.

3. Soak the mixture in a bucket with lukewarm water and have your bath.

4. Do this twice daily.

Advice:

- Anyone with high blood pressure, kidney disorders, heart diseases, and diabetes should refrain from taking this herbal remedy.

Aloe and Goldenseal Gel

Ingredients:

- 3 oz. dried goldenseal root, chopped

- 3 C. water

- 3 C. aloe vera gel

Tools Needed:

- Saucepan

- Cheesecloth

- Cotton-cloth

Instructions:

1. Add water and the goldenseal to a saucepan and boil over medium heat for a few minutes. Lower the heat to simmer till the water reduces by half.

2. Remove from the heat and let it cool.

3. Cover the funnel mouth with clean cheesecloth and drain the mixture from the saucepan into a bowl. Squeeze all water out of the cheesecloth.

4. Add aloe vera gel to the goldenseal decoction and stir to mix properly.

5. Transfer mixture into a new clean glass jar and cover tightly. Label the jar.

6. Apply at least 3 times daily using your cotton cloth.

7. Store in a cool, dry place when not in use.

Advice:

- Avoid this remedy while pregnant women or breastfeeding.

Cold and Immunity Boost

The symptoms of this include catarrh, shivering, and cough, among others. It is usually caused by certain infections or too much exposure to cold.

Rosemary Tea

Ingredients:

- 2 C. boiling water

- 3 tsp. dried rosemary

Tools Needed:

- Mug

Instructions:

1. Boil about 1-2 cups of water.

2. Next, pour it into a large mug. Add the dried rosemary and cover.

3. Steep for 15 minutes before drinking the tea.

4. Don't gulp down the tea immediately. Just take your time with it.

Fire Cider

It is a great recipe to boost your immune system to prevent and fight colds during the cold season.

Preparation Time: 30 minutes and 2 weeks maceration

Servings: about 1-quart

Ingredients:

- 1 whole head of garlic, cloves peeled and chopped

- 1 (2-inch) piece fresh ginger, chopped

- ¼ cup dried pine needles

- ¼ cup dried sage leaf

- ¼ cup dried thyme leaf

- ¼ cup dried elderberry

- ¼ cup dried rosehips

- 2 tablespoons dried elecampane root

- 2 tablespoons dried angelica root

- 1-quart apple cider-vinegar

- Honey and water for sweetening or diluting (optional)

Instructions:

1. Fill a jar with herbs, mix them well, and pour vinegar over them. Cover with a plastic lid and put a label on it. (Metal lid can corrode due to vinegar.)

2. Macerate all the herbs in the vinegar for 2 weeks or longer in a warm place, and give it a gentle shake daily.

3. Strain into a small bottle and label the finished fire cider. If the vinegar is too hot, to be comfortable on your stomach and avoid any effects, add more honey (up to one-fourth of the total volume), or dilute your dose with lukewarm water.

4. Take a shot (about ½ fluid ounce) at the first sign of mucus buildup in the lungs and every couple of hours until symptoms resolve.

Antioxidant Tea

Preparation Time: 10 minutes

Cooking Time: 20 minutes

Servings: About 3 cups dried herb mix (enough for 12 to 16 quarts of tea)

Gentle linden helps soften and direct to other herbs in this blend, focusing on their side effects to take all the blood vessels to improve integrity and reduce inflammation. Drink 1-2 cups of this tea daily.

Ingredients:

- 1 cup dried linden leaf and flower

- ½ cup dried rose petals, rosehips, or a combination

- ¼ cup dried cinnamon bark

- ¼ cup dried yarrow leaf and flower

- 1 tablespoon dried ginger

- Boiling water

Instructions:

1. In a medium or small bowl, mix all the herbs. Store in an airtight container.

2. Use 2 to 3 tablespoons of herb mix for each quart of water. Add herbs in a mason jar or French press, pour in the boiling water, cover, and steep for 20 minutes or until sufficiently cool to drink.

Rose Hip Quick Jam

Preparation Time: 20 minutes

Cooking Time: 1 hour

Servings: About three ounces (two servings)

This easy and tasty jam is a source of vitamin C, bioflavonoids, and antioxidants. Stir it into your porridge or other hot cereals, or simply eat it with a spoon!

Ingredients:

- 2 tablespoons dried rosehips

- 2 fluid ounces of water

- 1 teaspoon honey

- 1 teaspoon powdered cinnamon

Instructions:

1. Stir together the rosehips and water in a small pot on low heat and bring it to simmer for 5-10 minutes. Mash the rosehips with a fork; they'll get into a jam-like substance.

2. When the mixture has cooled to almost room temperature, stir in the honey and cinnamon.

3. Prepare fresh each day for maximum potency. If stored in the fridge will last up to 1 week.

Elderberry Syrup

Elderberry has an excellent specific ability to prevent influenza viruses from entering the body and multiplying; it also fights colds and other viruses. Take all this syrup in addition to remedies for your specific symptoms: 1 to 3 tablespoons three to five times per day whenever you suspect a cold or flu is present.

Preparation Time: 20 minutes

Cooking Time: 2 hours 20 minutes

Servings: About 1-quart (twenty to sixty doses)

Ingredients:

- 3 cups fresh elderberries

- 6 cups of water

- 1 teaspoon powdered cinnamon (you can use 1 whole cinnamon stick instead)

- 1 teaspoon dried chamomile flower

- 1 teaspoon fennel seed

- 1 teaspoon powdered ginger

- 2 cups honey, plus more as needed

Instructions:

1. Combine the berries, water, and herbs in a medium pot and bring to a boil on high heat. Once boiling, reduce the heat to simmer them uncovered for 1 to 2 hours or until the mixture reduces by half.

2. Get a spoon to mash all the berries in the pot into small sizes. Stir and simmer for 15 or 30 minutes more. Remover from the heat and cool down almost to room temperature.

3. Next, strain the mixture through a cheesecloth into a new pan. Squeeze the leftover berries well to get out every last bit of liquid.

4. Place the pan with the elderberry decoction over low heat. Add an equal amount of honey, warming it gently as you stir to mix thoroughly with the elderberry decoction.

5. Bottle and label the syrup. It will stay in the refrigerator for several months.

Tip:

- Some recipes use sugar, as this creates a small shelf-stable product. However, we try to avoid sugar, so we use honey. Another alternative is to add 2 cups of tincture (in addition to the decoction and honey) to your syrup; the alcohol content will preserve it. Tinctures of ginger, garlic, pine, yarrow, and many more thyme are excellent options.

Vitamin C Pills

Vitamin C tablets boost the immune system and fight colds and flu-like symptoms.

Ingredients:

- 1 tablespoon rosehip powder (the fruit of a rose plant, which has a high Vitamin C content)

- 1 tablespoon amla powder (an Indian gooseberry that has strong antibacterial properties)

- 1 tablespoon acerola powder (a Barbados cherry, which is excellent for stomach discomfort)

- Honey

- Orange peel powder (optional) (orange is a citrus fruit, and its peel is often used for flavor)

Instructions:

1. Blend the powdered herbs, smoothing out any clumped powder. Pour a few droplets of slightly warmed honey into the powdered mix.

2. Stir, add a few more droplets, and stir again. Mix until the combination holds together without being too sticky or moist.

3. Shape the mix into pea-size balls. Roll these around in the orange powder if you've selected to use it. The mixture should make 45 balls. Store these in an air-tight container to give them an extended shelf life. Take 1–3 daily.

Hyssop Oxymel

It is excellent for colds, flu, and bronchitis.

Ingredients:

- Hyssop, fresh or dried (an herbaceous plant with antiseptic and expectorant properties)

- Honey

- Apple Cider Vinegar (vinegar made from cider that is great for weight loss and heart health)

Instructions:

1. Fill a jar lightly with chopped fresh hyssop. (Only half fill it if you're using dried hyssop).

2. Then, fill the jar with honey just 1/3 of the way and top it off with the apple cider vinegar. Put the plastic lid on the jar (metal lid can corrode due to vinegar).

3. Let it sit for 2–4 weeks in the sealed jar before straining.

4. You can take 1–2 teaspoons of this remedy for a congested cough every hour. Keep the hyssop oxymel in the fridge for better preservation. It will last a winter season.

Advice:

- Avoid during pregnancy.

Cold Sore

It is an infection that affects the mouth and lips, caused by a virus called "herpes."

Garlic Poultice

Ingredients:

- 1 garlic clove, cut in half

Instructions:

1. Make sure the affected parts are clean.

2. After cutting the garlic into 2, use one part to rub the affected area for about 15 minutes. It should be done 4-7 times every day.

Advice:

- If you notice any strange reaction at the earliest stage, halt the usage of this herbal remedy.

Echinacea-Sage Toner

Ingredients:

- 1 oz. dried Echinacea root, chopped

- 1 oz. dried sage, crumbled

- 3 tbsps. jojoba or light olive oil

- 3 tbsps. aloe vera gel

- 1/8 C. witch hazel

Tools Needed:

- Saucepan

- Cheesecloth

- Bottle

- Cotton

Instructions:

1. Put all the herbs and oil in a small-sized saucepan over low heat and cook for about 4-6 hours.

2. Strain the mixture into a bowl over a cheesecloth and wring it out until there is no more oil.

3. Dispose of the cheesecloth and herbs.

4. Next, drain the mixture from the bowl into a dark bottle, add aloe vera gel and witch hazel, and shake well to mix thoroughly.

5. Using a cotton swab, apply around the affected area. Use 3-5 times daily.

6. Store in a refrigerator.

Advice:

- Do not take this herb if you're allergic to any ragweed plant family.

Colic

This condition is common in infants between 3 weeks to 5 months old. Common symptoms include sleeplessness and crying. The herbal remedies below should help reduce the pain. If they don't, revisit your doctor.

Chamomile Infusion

Ingredients:

- 2 tsp. dried chamomile
- 2 C. boiling water

Tools Needed:

- Teapot
- Sterilized bottle

Instructions:

1. Boil 2 cups of water.
2. Combine the hot water with the chamomile in a teapot and let it steep for 15 minutes.
3. Strain the infusion and leave to cool for 5 minutes.
4. Once cool, administer only 2 tablespoons to the baby twice daily.

Advice:

- If you're on any blood thinners medication, do not use this herb.

Herbal Gripe Water with Catnip, Fennel, and Ginger

Ingredients:

- 1 tsp. crushed fennel seeds

- 1 tsp. chopped fresh ginger root

- 2 tsp. Catnip chopped

- 1 C. boiling water

Tools Needed:

- Teapot or mug

- Jar

Instructions:

1. Put all the herbs in a mug. Add water and cover for the herbs to soak for 15 minutes.

2. Strain the gripe water into the jar.

3. Leave it to cool down completely; then take 1 teaspoon of the mixture and drop it gently into the baby's mouth or add to his milk.

4. Do it once daily.

Advice:

- Avoid it if your kid has any bleeding disorder.

- You can prepare without ginger if you prefer so.

Cough

Ginger and Mint Tea

Ingredients:

- 2 C. boiling water

- 2 tsp. diced fresh ginger root

- 1 ½ tsp. dried peppermint

Tools Needed:

- Boiler

- Mug

Instruction

1. Pour the 2 C. boiled water into a medium-sized mug.

2. Add the herbs and cover the mug for some time.

3. Let it steep for 15 minutes, then take the tea slowly while inhaling the steam.

4. You can add honey as it naturally reduces mucus production and makes your tea taste sweeter.

5. Do this three times a day.

Advice:

- Do not use it for pregnant women and patients with epilepsy.

Licorice–Thyme Cough Syrup

Ingredients:

- 2 oz. licorice root, chopped
- 2 oz. thyme
- 4 C. water
- 2 C. honey

Tools Needed:

- Saucepan
- Measuring cups (glass)
- Sterilized jar

Instructions:

1. Set your saucepan over low heat, add the licorice root, some water, and thyme, and boil with the lids partially open for some minutes.

2. Let it simmer until it's reduced by half, then pour the mixture into a measuring cup and sieve the mixture into another saucepan using a cheesecloth.

3. Add honey to this mixture and let it warm for some time.

4. Put the syrup into the bottle or sterilized jar, label it and store it in a cool place, preferably inside a refrigerator.

5. Take 2 tbsps. 4 times a day until symptoms stop. Dosage for children under 13 should not be more than twice daily. Don't administer to children under 1-year-old.

Advice:

- Do not take licorice if you are suffering from internal diseases like high blood pressure, kidney-related problems, or heart disease.

Dandruff

Echinacea Spray

Ingredients:

- 2 C. witch hazel

- 2 tbsps. Echinacea tincture

Tools Needed:

- Glass bottle

Instructions:

1. Pour witch hazel into a dark bottle with a spray top and add Echinacea tincture. Shake it well to mix.

2. Apply spritzes to the affected parts 2–4 times at once. Then, use your hand or brush to comb your hair and let it blend well. Leave for 1–3 hours.

3. Then use shampoo or any other hair soap to clean the hair.

Advice:

- If you, at one point or the other, experience any reaction to Echinacea, a family of ragweed plants, stop using this remedy immediately.

Rosemary Conditioner

Ingredients:

- 2 C. natural, unscented herbal conditioner like Stonybrook Botanicals

- 55 drops of rosemary essential oil

Tools Needed:

- Large bowl; plastic bottle

- Whisk or fork

Instructions:

1. Get a big bowl, mix the conditioner with the essential oil, and use a fork or whisk to mix it. Transfer the mixture into a Biphenyl-free plastic bottle with a very tight lid. Alternatively, you can use a glass jar with a tight lid.

2. After applying shampoo, add a small amount of conditioner to the scalp and wait for 3–5 minutes before rinsing with cool water.

Advice:

- Do not use it if you have epilepsy.

Diarrhea

Cherokee Tea

Ingredients:

- 2 C. boiling water

- 3 tsp. dried Cherokee herb

Tools Needed:

- Mug

Instructions:

1. Boil 2 C. water, pour it into a big mug and add Cherokee herb.

2. Leave the tea to steep for about 15 minutes.

3. Drink slowly.

4. Take about 2–3 times daily.

Catnip–Raspberry Leaf Decoction

Ingredients:

- 10 C. water

- 4 tbsps. dried catnip

- 4 tbsps. dried raspberry leaf

Tools Needed:

- Saucepan

Instructions:

1. Set your saucepan over medium-high heat, add all the herbs and water, and boil for 5 minutes.

2. Simmer for a further 10 minutes on a lower heat until the water reduces by half.

3. Let the concoction cool before you take it.

4. Strain it into a mug and take it gently. Store in the refrigerator.

Advice:

- Do not use raspberry leaves if it's not well dried. Badly processed raspberry leaves can cause nausea.

Oily Skin

It results from the excess of sebum, an exocrine secretion that helps moisturize the skin.

Rosemary Toner

Ingredients:

- 1 ½ C. witch hazel

- 2 ½ tbsps. rosemary tincture

Tools Needed:

- Glass bottle

- Cotton

Instructions:

1. Combine all the ingredients into a dark-colored bottle and shake gently to mix well.

2. Using the cotton cosmetic pad, apply ¼ tsp. of the mixture on your face 2 to 3 times daily.

Advice:

- Epileptic people are strongly advised not to use this remedy.

Mint Scrub

Ingredients:

- 2 C. dried mint leaves, packed

- 1 C. baking soda

Tools Needed:

- Food processor or blender

- Container

Instructions:

1. Blend the mint leaves and baking soda in a food processor until the mixture turns fine powder.

2. Transfer the blended powder into a clean container and cover it with a lid.

3. Then, clean your face with water, apply about 1 ½ tsp. of the powder and rub it on your skin.

4. Use a couple of times a week and ensure you clean your face properly after usage.

Advice:

- Don't overuse it as you can mechanically irritate your skin.

Dry Skin

Cattail and Aloe Gel

Ingredients:

- 1 C. water

- 1 C. dried cattail

- 1 C. aloe vera gel

Tools Needed:

- Saucepan

- Cheesecloth

Instructions:

1. Set your saucepan on medium-high heat, add water and cattail herb, and boil for 5 minutes.

2. Take the heat level down to low and simmer until the water decreases by half.

3. Remove from the heat and let it cool down. Strain through a cheesecloth into a bowl. Wring all water out of the cheesecloth.

4. Add Aloe Vera Gel to the bowl with your decoction.

5. Whisk the mixture together, then transfer it into a glass jar and cap tightly. Label it.

6. Store in a fridge to chill. Apply on the skin 1-2 times daily.

Alder–Lavender Body Butter

Ingredients:

- 1 C. cocoa butter
- 1 ½ C. coconut oil
- ½ C. jojoba oil
- 2 C. shea butter
- 2 oz. powdered alder leaves
- 3 oz. powdered lavender

Tools Needed:

- Cooker
- Cheesecloth
- Hand mixer or blender

Instructions:

1. Add all ingredients into a pot, and put them on the lowest heat.

2. Allow the herbs to steep for about 4–6 hours, then turn the heat and let the mixture cool few minutes.

3. Put the cheesecloth over a large bowl and pour the mixture into a bowl through it. Wring out any remaining liquid from the cheesecloth into a bowl.

4. Store the mixture in your refrigerator overnight. It will cool and harden.

5. Whip up the body butter mixture with a hand mixer for about 20 minutes until it's fluffy.

6. Transfer it into your storage glass or plastic jar and put a label on it.

7. Apply it daily to the affected areas with the tip of your finger.

8. Stop after you notice positive changes.

9. Store in a refrigerator or a cool and dark place. Use it within 3 months.

Earache

Garlic–Cherokee Infused Oil

Ingredients:

- 1 C. light olive oil

- 4 tsp. crushed or finely chopped dried or freeze-dried garlic

- 4 tsp. dried Cherokee flowers

Tools Needed:

- Boiler

- Glass jar, dropper

- Cheesecloth

- Small bowl

Instructions:

1. Put the garlic, Cherokee flowers, and olive oil into a pot and heat for 4-6 hours. Let it cool down, then.

2. Strain the oil through a cheesecloth over a funnel into a glass jar. Squeeze out all the oil from the cheesecloth and dispose of herbal material.

3. Before putting a lid, let it cool completely and label the jar.

4. When done, drop 4–5 times into your ear and cover with cotton to protect the drops from seeping out.

5. Leave for 20 minutes and repeat 3–4 times daily.

Advice:

- Garlic may have adverse reactions on some bodies, so stop using it if you notice anything unusual.

Fatigue

It is caused by stress and demanding jobs that drain your whole energy. The herbal remedies below would do the magic by helping you recover your lost energy so quickly.

Heal-All Tincture

Ingredients:

- 12 oz. heal-all leaves

- 6 C. 80% unflavored vodka

Tools Needed:

- Pint jar

- Cheesecloth

Instructions:

1. Put the heal-all leaves in a sterilized pint jar and add the vodka to cover the herbs. Close the jar and shake well. Label your mixture with a date and all ingredients used.

2. Store the mixture for 7–8 weeks in a cool and dark place.

3. During this period, shake 3 times daily to combine the herbal properties with the liquid contents.

4. Dampen the cheesecloth over the funnel and pour the mixture through it into another sterilized pint jar. Wring and drain the water from the heal-all herb.

5. Then, pour it into a sterilized bottle and mix 12 drops of tincture into a glass of water or juice.

6. Drink this 4–5 times daily until you notice some improvements.

Advice:

- Not to be used by pregnant women and anyone allergic to any ragweed plant.

Licorice–Rosemary Syrup

Ingredients:

- 2 oz. dried licorice root, chopped

- 2 oz. dried rosemary leaves, chopped

- 3 C. water

- ½ C. honey

Tools Needed:

- Saucepan

- Measuring cup

- Cheesecloth

Instructions:

1. Get your saucepan ready, place the herbs in and cover with some water. Boil this mixture over low heat until you notice the water has reduced by half.

2. Then, strain the mixture from a saucepan into the sterilized bottle through a cheesecloth. Wring all water out of the cheesecloth.

3. Add some honey to the mix and simmer over low heat, constantly stirring to ensure it doesn't burn.

4. When mixed thoroughly, remove from the heat and let it cool down. Then transfer the syrup into a sterilized bottle and keep it in a refrigerator. Put the label on.

5. Take 2 tbsps. 4 times daily until the symptoms stop.

Advice:

- If you have diabetes or have high blood pressure, do not take this herbal remedy or any other that contains licorice root.

Flatulence

An increment in dietary fiber causes it. It is often painful and uncomfortable.

Mint–Angelica Tea

Ingredients:

- 2 C. boiling water

- ½ tsp. dried angelica

- 1 ½ tsp. dried mint

Tools Needed:

- Large mug

Instructions:

1. Boil some water, add into a mug, add the dried herbs, cover the mug, and let it steep for 15 minutes.

2. Take tea slowly and inhale the steam as well.

3. Repeat up to 3 times daily until you feel much better.

Advice:

- Not recommended for pregnant women.

Fresh Ginger and Fennel Decoction

Ingredients:

- 10 C. water

- ½ tsp. crushed fennel seeds

- 1 ½ tbsp. minced fresh ginger

- 1 tbsps. honey or stevia (optional)

Tools Needed:

- Saucepan, pint jar

Instructions:

1. Add water, fennel, and ginger into a saucepan and place it on high heat.

2. Let it boil until the water reduces by half before taking off the heat.

3. After the decoction has cooled down, strain it into a pint jar.

4. Add some honey, then place in the refrigerator. Drink 2 C. each evening after dinner. Use the mixture within 3 days.

5. Continue to use remedy until flatulence subsides.

Advice:

- Do not take this herbal juice if you have any gallbladder problems.

Gingivitis

It occurs due to the constant brushing of teeth and then affects the gums.

Golden Alexander–Chamomile Mouth Rinse

Ingredients:

- ½ oz. dried calendula

- 1 oz. dried chamomile

- 5 C. water

Tools Needed:

- Saucepan

- Measuring cup

- Cheesecloth

Instructions:

1. Add herbs and water into a saucepan. Boil over low heat, with the lid partially open, until the water reduces by half.

2. Turn the contents of the saucepan into a glass measuring cup, then return the decoction through a dampened piece of cheesecloth into a new saucepan.

3. Wring the cheesecloth until no more water comes out, transfer the mouth rinse to a clean bottle and store it in the refrigerator.

4. Take 3 tbsps per day until this condition stops, but do not swallow this mixture. Children under the age of 13 should take only 1 tbsp of this mixture.

Advice:

- If you've reacted, at any point, to any ragweed plant, in general, avoid this mixture.

Goldenseal–Sage Oil

Ingredients:

- 2 oz. dried goldenseal root, chopped

- 1 oz. dried sage, crumbled

- 1 C. coconut oil

Tools Needed:

- Saucepan

- Cheesecloth

- Paper Towel

Instructions:

1. Combine the herbs and coconut oil in your saucepan, place over low heat setting, cover, and slow cook for 4–6 hours to steep the herbs in the oil.

2. Turn off the heat and allow the infused oil to cool.

3. Pour the infused oil through a cheesecloth into a bowl, and wring out the oil from the cheesecloth to the last drop.

4. Transfer the infused coconut oil to a clean, dry jar and allow it to cool completely before replacing the lid. Label it.

5. Take 1 tsp of this oil and let it melt in your mouth. Make sure it spreads to every part of your mouth and teeth, but do not swallow.

6. Keep the solution in your mouth for up to 25 minutes.

7. You can take more if you like.

Advice:

- Not for pregnant people and nursing mothers.

- Do not spit oil down the sink since this can clog your plumbing system.

Headache

Cooling Headache Tea

Preparation Time: 10 minutes.

Servings: 2

Ingredients:

- 2 tablespoons fresh mint leaves, roughly chopped

- 1 tablespoon fresh thyme leaves, finely chopped

- 1 teaspoon anise seeds, crush in a mortar, or zest from a lemon in a spice grinder

- 5 cups boiling water

Instructions:

1. Boil 5 cups of water, pour over the herbs and let steep for 5 minutes before straining into a jug.
2. Pour into mugs and drink while hot or let it cool down and add ice cubes for a refreshing cold version.

Warming Headache Tea

Preparation Time: 10 minutes.

Servings: 2

Ingredients:

- 1 tablespoon Cinnamon

- 2 Cloves

- 1 tablespoon Ginger

- 1 tablespoon Cayenne pepper flakes

- 2 Teabags

- Water (about 2 cups)

Directions:

1. Add about 4 tablespoons of water to a small pot and bring it to a boil.

2. Add the tea bags filled with spices and cayenne pepper flakes and allow boiling for about 5 minutes straight. Remove from heat just before the tea turns black or becomes bitter.

3. Allow the tea to cool slightly before drinking it. Add honey for sweetness if desired. Drink once a day until symptoms disappear or on an as-needed basis if pain persists after relieving symptoms.

Peppery Headache Tea

Preparation Time: 10 minutes.

Servings: 2

Ingredients:

- 1 tablespoon ginger

- 1 teaspoon dried pepper pods

- 1-liter water

Instructions:

1. Bring all the water to a boil. Turn the heat off, add ginger and pepper, and steep covered for 5 minutes. Strain and enjoy!

Valerian Root Capsules

They help with insomnia, headaches, and stomach aches.

Valerian is a powerful medicinal herb with its benefits found in the root. People who don't want to use sleeping pills turn to valerian root instead. It also eases headaches and stomach aches. However, it should not be used if you're on anti-anxiety medication.

Ingredients:

- 3000–6000 mg valerian root, dried

- 10 capsules

Instructions:

1. Grind the dried valerian root in a mortar and pestle or food processor. Once you get a sandy texture of the powder, fill the capsules with it.

2. If you're using a machine, you'll pour the powdered herb over the machine base into one-half of the capsules. Then, spread the powder over the capsules to fill them.

3. With the tamper, press the powder down to pack it into the capsules. Then, keep spreading with the card and tampering until the capsules are full.

4. Sweep off any extra powder. Go ahead and take off the bottom of the stand. Put the top of the capsule machine on the base and press down. The capsules should now be capped.

5. Over a container, press down on the back of the machine's top part to release the capsules. That's it!

6. Based on research for capsules, we saw that herbalists often recommend shaking a little bit of valerian powder around in the container, so you'll taste a little of the root when you take a capsule.

7. Tasting helps your body recognize what it's consuming, which can help it respond better to the powder.

Hangover Teas

Hangover Tea 1

Servings: 1

Ingredients:

- 1 teaspoon catnip dried leaves

- 1 teaspoon peppermint dried leaves

- 1 teaspoon barberry dried leaves

- 1 cup boiling water

Instructions:

1. Pour boiling water over the herbs mixture. Let it rest for 30 minutes. Strain and drink.

Hangover Tea 2

Servings: 1

Ingredients:

- 1 teaspoon barberry dried leaves

- 1 teaspoon heal-all dried leaves

- 1 teaspoon Oregon grape root

- 1 cup boiling water

Instructions:

1. Pour boiling water over the herbs mixture. Let it rest for half an hour—strain and drink throughout the day.

Hangover Tea 3

Servings: 1

Ingredients:

- 1 teaspoon barberry dried leaves

- 1 teaspoon goldenseal dried leaves

- 1 teaspoon Oregon grape root

- 1 cup boiling water

Instructions:

1. Pour boiling water over the herbs mixture. Let it rest for half an hour. Strain and drink throughout the day.

Hangover Tea 4

Servings: 1

Ingredients:

- 1 tablespoon plantain dried leaf

- 1 tablespoon calendula dried flower

- 1 tablespoon chamomile dried flower

- 1 tablespoon dried linden leaves

- 1 tablespoon licorice root

- 1 tablespoon dried ginger root

- 1 tablespoon dried St. john's wort leaves

Instructions:

1. Mix the herbs in a mason jar for easy storage. Put 1 tablespoon of the mixture in 1 cup of boiling water. Let it rest for half an hour—strain and drink throughout the day.

Fast-Acting Hangover Tea

Servings: 1

Ingredients:

- 1 green tea bag

- 1 cup of water

Instructions:

1. In a saucepan, boil water, turn the heat off, and let it cool down for a couple of minutes.

2. Then add the green tea bag to a mug and pour the hot water.

3. Lest it steep for five minutes, then enjoy!

Indigestion

It is characterized by bloating, belching, stomach ache, discomfort, etc. It often happens when your stomach reacts to something you take. The herbs below should offer you the quick relief you'd need for the symptoms.

Chamomile–Angelica Tea

Ingredients:

- 2 C. boiling water

- 2 tsp. dried angelica

- 1 ½ tsp. dried chamomile

Tools Needed:

- Large mug

Instructions:

1. Boil 2 C. water.

2. Add the dried herbs to a large mug and pour boiled water over them.

3. Let it steep for 15 minutes and strain. Serve and sip gently.

4. Take your time to enjoy the refreshing tastes.

5. Take this 5–6 times daily.

Advice:

- Not to be taken by pregnant women.

- If you're allergic to ragweed, please do not take it.

Ginger Syrup

Ingredients:

- 3 oz. fresh ginger root, chopped

- 3 C. water

- 1 ½ C. honey

Tools Needed:

- Saucepan

- Measuring cup

- Sterilized jar

Instructions:

1. Combine ginger and water in a saucepan, then boil over low heat until water is reduced to half.

2. Pour the content into a measuring cup and back to a new saucepan through the cheesecloth to sieve the liquid. Wringer the cheesecloth until no water is left.

3. Add honey to the mixture and heat it again on low heat. Mix thoroughly together

4. Then, pour the syrup into a bottle and refrigerate. Label it.

5. Shake well and take just 2 tbsps whenever you want to use it. 4 times a day. Younger children under the age of 13 should take just 2 times per day. Not for children under 1 year old.

Advice:

- If you're on any blood-thinning medication, try as much as possible to avoid this herbal medicine.

- Avoid this remedy if you have any internal disease like gallbladder disease or bleeding disorder.

Digestive Tea 1

Ingredients:

- 1 teaspoon licorice root dried, powder

- 1 teaspoon peppermint dried leaves

- 1 cup boiling water

Instructions:

1. Pour boiling water over the herbs. Let steep for 20 minutes. Strain and drink warm to help digestion.

Digestive Tea 2

Ingredients:

- 1 teaspoon ginger root dried

- 1 teaspoon angelica root dried

- 1 teaspoon chamomile dried flowers

- 1 teaspoon peppermint dried leaves

- 1 ½ cup boiling water

Instructions:

1. Pour boiling water over the herbs mixture. Let it steep for half an hour. Strain and drink.

Digestive Tea 3

Ingredients:

- 1 teaspoon black cohosh root dried

- 1 teaspoon angelica root dried

- 1 cup boiling water

Instructions:

1. Pour boiling water over the herbs mixture. Let it steep for 30 minutes—strain and drink throughout the day to help with persistent indigestion.

Insomnia

When a person has trouble sleeping at night, which can be caused by stress or anxiety, a caffeine overdose can also lead to insomnia.

Lavender and Hops

Ingredients:

- 2 C. boiling water

- 3 ½ tsp. chopped dried lavender

- 1 ½ tsp. crushed dried hops

Tools Needed:

- Large mug

Instructions:

1. Boil 2 C. water.

2. Pour the boiled water into a large mug, add the dried herbs, stir and cover the mug. Steep for about 15 minutes.

3. Find a spot to relax and take your tea quietly and slowly.

4. A great time to take this is some minutes before your bedtime.

Advice:

- Do not give to prepubescent children.

- Do not use it during pregnancy.

Chamomile–Catnip Syrup

Ingredients:

- 2 oz. dried chamomile

- 2 ½ oz. dried catnip

- 3 C. water

- 1 ½ C. honey

Tools Needed:

- Saucepan

- Measuring cup

- Sterilized jar

Instructions:

1. Add chamomile, catnip, and water into your saucepan, boil over low heat until the liquid content reduces by half, with a slightly opened lid.

2. Then, turn the mixture into your measuring cup and back into the saucepan using a clean cheesecloth as a sieve.

3. Add honey and heat the mixture over low heat while stirring occasionally. Ensure honey and decoction mix thoroughly.

4. Once the heat reaches about 110°F, turn it off, let the syrup cool down and transfer it into a sterilized bottle or jar. Put the label on.

5. Store in your fridge for a while before use.

6. Take 1 ½ tbsp 1 hour before sleep. Don't give to children unless consulted with a health practitioner.

Advice:

- Do not take it if you're pregnant.

- If you are allergic to any plant under the ragweed family, do not take this remedy.

Sleeping Formula

Ingredients:

- 2 fluid ounces tincture of wild lettuce

- 1 fluid ounce tincture of betony

- ½ fluid ounce tincture of chamomile

- ½ fluid ounce tincture of linden

Instructions:

1. In a small bottle, combine the tinctures. Cap the bottle and label it.

2. 2 hours before bedtime, take 1 to 2 drops.

3. 30 minutes before bedtime, take another 1 to 2 drops. At bedtime, take 1 to 2 drops.

Insomnia Relief Tea

Servings: 1-2

Ingredients:

- 1 teaspoon chamomile flowers
- 1 teaspoon hops
- 1 teaspoon valerian root
- 1 cup boiling water

Instructions:

1. Combined all the above herbs.
2. Cover 1 tablespoon of the mixture with boiling water, leave to infuse for 30 minutes, and strain.
3. Drink warm, as needed, half a cup at a time.

Sweet Dreams Tea

Servings: 2

Ingredients:

- 2 teaspoons catnip leaves
- 1 teaspoon hops
- 2 teaspoons chamomile flower
- 2 teaspoons passionflower
- 2 cups boiling water

Instructions:

1. Combine all the above herbs in a glass container and cover with boiling water. Steep for 30 minutes; cool and strain.
2. Take one hour before bedtime.

Sleepy Time Tea

Ingredients:

- 1 cup (235 ml) water

- 1 teaspoon passionflower

- 1 teaspoon chamomile

- 1 teaspoon lemon balm

Instructions:

1. Put water and herbs in a pot and bring to boil. Expel from the heat and let steep for 10 minutes.

2. Take one hour before bedtime.

Menopause

It is a regular change in the function of the female hormone due to maturity. But, while it is often considered normal, the pain and physical discomfort that comes with it can be pretty challenging to handle. But, with the herbs below, dealing with menopause symptoms should be a lot easier for you.

Red Clover – Sage Decoction

Ingredients:

- 3 C. water

- 1 ½ tsp. dried red clover herb

- 1 ½ tsp. sage

Tools Needed:

- Saucepan

Instructions:

1. Put red clover, sage, and water in a saucepan and boil over medium heat for 5 minutes.

2. Afterward, reduce the heat and let the water simmer for some minutes until it reduces by half.

3. Turn off your heat, strain the mixture and let it cool for 10–15 minutes before serving and drinking!

Black Cohosh Tincture

Ingredients:

- 10 oz. black cohosh, finely chopped

- 2 ½ C. unflavored 80-proof vodka

Tools Needed:

- Pint jar

- Cheesecloth

Instructions:

1. Put the black cohosh into a pint jar and cover the herb with vodka. Cover with a lid and store for up to 2 weeks out of the sunlight. Label your mixture. Shake daily 2-3 times.

2. After 2 weeks, strain your tincture through a cheesecloth and funnel it into a dark glass bottle. Label your tincture.

3. Take 2 tbsps thrice daily until you feel relieved.

Mental Wellness

Many things around can threaten one's peace of mind or mental health. It could be overwhelming career demands, relationship problems, tight schedules, and more, which often makes one depressed, and anxious, thus leading to the lack of energy to do anything more.

St John's Wort Tea

Ingredients:

- 1 ½ C. boiling water

- 1 ½ tsp. dried St. John's wort

Tools Needed:

- Large mug

Instructions:

1. Pour the boiled water into a large mug, add St. John's wort herb and cover the mug to steep for 15 minutes.

2. Strain and take tea slowly. Inhale the steam as you drink.

3. You can prepare this thrice to 4 times daily until you feel much better.

Advice:

- If you're on any MAOI (Monoamine oxidase inhibitor) or any selective serotonin reuptake inhibitor (SSRI), do not take this or any other remedy with the St John's Wort Plant.

Chamomile–Lemon Balm Decoction

Ingredients:

- 3 C. water

- ½ tsp. dried chamomile

- 1 ½ tsp. dried lemon balm leaves

Tools Needed:

- Saucepan

Instructions:

1. Add chamomile, lemon balm, and water into a saucepan, place over medium heat, and let it boil for 5 minutes. Reduce heat afterward and let the mixture simmer until the water reduces by half.

2. Strain, let it cool for 5 minutes and enjoy your tea.

Advice:

- If you're allergic to ragweed plants, do not take this remedy.

- Avoid use during pregnancy and when taking blood thinners.

Oat Straw Infusion

This oat straw infusion is excellent for its calming, stress-relieving effect.

Ingredients:

- 2 oz. of the oat straw herb (comes from Avenal Sativa, which has long-lasting energy effects)

- Boiling water

Instructions:

1. Put oat straw into a 1-quart jar, pour boiling water over the herb, and cap it with an air-tight lid.

2. Allow the mix to rest for 4–6 hours, which will infuse the minerals throughout the solution.

3. Strain it. You can add something extra to your mixture once it's made—for example, lavender, lemon verbena, rosemary, etc.

4. Enjoy Oat straw infusion as a base for juices, lemonades, and frozen concentrates. Make a tasty lemonade from it whenever you feel you want to stop, relax and calm down. You can also use it to create ice cubes or ice pops.

Nausea

It is caused by foodborne pathogens and is usually a precursor to conditions like flu and fever.

Mint Leaf Tea

Ingredients:

- 2 ½ tsp. mint leaves

- 2 ½ C. water

Tools Needed:

- Saucepan

Instructions:

1. Combine the mint leaf and water in a saucepan and boil over medium heat for not more than 15 minutes. Then, let the water simmer on lower heat until it reduces by half.

2. Take off the heat, strain, and let it cool for 10–15 minutes before consuming.

3. Take this remedy 4–5 times every day until you feel better.

Chamomile–Ginger Tea

Ingredients:

- 2 C. boiling water

- ½ tsp. dried chamomile

- 1 ½ tsp. chopped fresh ginger root

Tools Needed:

- Large mug

Instructions:

1. Get a large mug, pour the boiled water and add ginger and chamomile.

2. Cover the mug for 15 minutes tops, just for the tea to steep in the water.

3. Then strain, serve and enjoy your tea slowly.

4. Also, make sure to inhale the steam as it will benefit you.

5. Do this 4–5 times daily.

Advice:

- Do not use chamomile if you're allergic to ragweed plants.

- Do not take ginger if you have bleeding disorders or gallbladder problems.

- Also, if you're on any blood thinner medication, avoid using this mixture.

Detoxifying Teas

Liver-Kidney Cleansing Tea

Ingredients:

- 1 teaspoon dandelion root powder

- 1 teaspoon burdock root powder

- 1 cup of spring water

Instructions:

1. Place herb powders and water in a tea kettle or pot.

2. Boil for 10 minutes on medium heat. Then take it off and leave it covered for another 10 minutes.

3. Strain and serve.

Refreshing Kidney Cleansing tea

Ingredients:

- 1 teaspoon Prodigies powder

- 1 teaspoon burdock root powder

- 1 cup of spring water

Instructions:

1. Place herb powders and water in a tea kettle or pot.

2. Boil for 10 minutes on medium heat. Then take it off and leave it covered for another 10 minutes.

3. Strain and serve.

Mucus Liver Cleansing Tea

Ingredients:

- 1 teaspoon dandelion root powder

- 1 teaspoon Prodigies powder

- 1 cup of spring water

Instructions:

1. Place herb powders and water in a tea kettle or pot.

2. Boil for 10 minutes on medium heat. Then take it off and leave it covered for another 10 minutes.

3. Strain and serve.

Colon-Gallbladder Cleansing Tea

Ingredients:

- 1 teaspoon Cascara powder
- 1 teaspoon Rhubarb root powder
- 1 cup of spring water

Instructions:

1. Place herb powders and water in a tea kettle or pot.
2. Boil for 10 minutes on medium heat. Then take it off and leave it covered for another 10 minutes.
3. Strain and serve.

Colon-Gallbladder Tea

Ingredients:

- 1 teaspoon Cascara powder
- 1 teaspoon Chaparral
- 1 cup of spring water

Instructions:

1. Place herbs and water in a tea kettle or pot.
2. Boil for 10 minutes on medium heat. Then take it off and leave it covered for another 10 minutes.
3. Strain and serve.

Popsicles

They are excellent in hot summer and very popular among children. You will need a high-speed blender and popsicle molds with sticks to prepare popsicles.

Strawberry Basil Popsicle Recipe

Ingredients:

- 2 cups fresh or frozen strawberries

- ½ cup 100% unsweetened orange juice without vitamin A

- ¼ cup almond milk (or other non-dairy milk)

- 1 tablespoon finely chopped basil leaves

- 1 tablespoon honey (or pure maple syrup if vegan)

- 4 or 5 ice cubes

Instructions:

1. In a blender, purée all ingredients until smooth. Pour slowly into your popsicle molds and place the sticks.

2. Let it set in a freezer for a couple of hours or overnight.

Cherry Limeade Popsicle

Ingredients:

- 12 ounces of frozen organic cherries

- 6 ounces frozen limeade concentrate

- 6 ounces 100% white grape juice (or any other non-dairy juice you'd like)

- 2 tablespoons sugar (optional) or 1 tablespoon honey (or pure maple syrup if vegan)

Instructions:

1. In a blender, purée all ingredients until smooth. Pour slowly into your popsicle molds and place the sticks.

2. Let it set in a freezer for a couple of hours or overnight.

Mango Papaya Popsicle

Ingredients:

- 2 cups 100% orange or apple juice
- 1 cup mango or papaya chunks
- 1/2 lime, juiced
- 2 tablespoons shredded coconut

Instructions:

1. In a blender, purée all ingredients until smooth. Pour slowly into your popsicle molds and place the sticks.

2. Let it set in a freezer for a couple of hours or overnight.

Mint Lemonade Popsicle

Ingredients:

- 1/4 cup fresh mint leaves
- 1/2 cup fresh lemon juice
- 3 tablespoons cane sugar (or any other sweetener of your choice)

Instructions:

1. In a blender, purée all ingredients until smooth. Pour slowly into your popsicle molds and place the sticks.

2. Let it set in a freezer for a couple of hours or overnight.

Poultices

Garlic – Mullein Poultice for Earache

Ingredients:

- 2 cloves garlic

- 3 tbsp. fresh mullein leaves and flowers

- 3 tbsp. water

Instructions:

1. Crush garlic and mullein leaves and flower in a mortar and pestle with a bit of water.

2. Cover your hurting ear with a thin layer of gauze, put your poultice onto a clean cotton cloth and place it against the gauze over your hurting ear.

3. Leave it overnight or at least some time until you feel pain relief.

Plantain Leaf Poultice for Sore Joints

Use this poultice also for boils, blisters, and bug bites.

1. Mix 1 part plantain leaves and a few spoons of water in mortar and pestle until it forms a paste. If using dry plantain, blend it first to a powder texture, and by adding a little bit of water, make a paste.

2. After applying to the affected area, cover with a clean cloth or muslin. Then wrap with plastic wrap or a cloth to hold it in place.

3. When the poultice dries out, apply a new fresh layer.

For Sprains And Strains:

1. Mix 1 part yarrow, 1 part plantain leaves, and 1 part lavender flower petals in a mortar with a bit of water until the smooth texture of the poultice is formed.

2. After applying to the affected area, cover with a clean cloth or muslin and leave it overnight. If necessary, cover with another dry cloth or plastic film to hold them in place.

3. When the poultice dries out, apply a new fresh layer.

For Bruises:

1. In mortar and pestle, mix 1/2 cup dried nettle leaves with a few tablespoons of hot water until thick paste forms (use gloves while handling nettles - they can sting!).

2. After applying to the affected area, cover with a clean cloth or muslin and leave it overnight. If necessary, cover with another dry cloth or plastic film to hold them in place. Caution, don't let it get in your eyes!

3. When the poultice dries out, apply a new fresh layer.

For Aching Muscles:

1. In mortar and pestle, mix 1 part catnip, 1 part plantain leads, 1 part mullein leaves or flower petals (allowing them to dry slightly) with a few teaspoons of water until it forms a thick paste.

2. Mix in about 5 drops of lavender essential oil. Lavender oil contains analgesic compounds to relieve pain. (optional)

3. After applying to the affected area, cover with a clean cloth or muslin and leave it overnight. If necessary, cover with another dry cloth or plastic film to hold them in place.

4. When the poultice dries out, apply a new fresh layer.

For Swelling:

1. In mortar and pestle, mix 1 part yarrow and 1 part mullein leaves or flower petals and a few teaspoons of water to make a thick paste.

2. Add about 5 drops of lemongrass essential oil (optional).

3. After applying to the affected area, cover with a clean cloth or muslin and leave it overnight. If necessary, cover with another dry cloth or plastic film to hold them in place.

4. When the poultice dries out, apply a new fresh layer.

For Inflammation:

1. In mortar and pestle, mix 1 part yarrow and 1 part mullein leaves with a few teaspoons of water until it forms a thick paste.

2. Add about 5 drops of lavender essential oil. Lavender oil contains effective analgesic and anti-inflammatory compounds.

3. After applying to the affected area, cover with a clean cloth or muslin and leave it overnight. If necessary, cover with another dry cloth or plastic film to hold them in place.

Achy Bones

Peppermint Soak Off

It is a fantastic remedy for achy bones and tired feet.

Ingredients:

- ½ cup of olive oil

- 4 Drops of Peppermint essential oil

Instructions:

1. Combine the oils and pour them into a hot tub.

Roses Bath Soak

Roses are beautiful and relaxing, and the essential oil derived from them is full of goodness. Rose essential oil relieves anxiety and is a potent antioxidant. So take a load off with this when you are up to your shoulders in stress.

Ingredients:

- 1 cup of Epsom salts

- 6 Drops of Rose essential oil

- Rose petals

Instructions:

1. Mix the essential oil with the salts and place them in an airtight glass container. Sprinkle rose petals into a tub and add a large pinch of the salt and oil mixture.

2. You can save the rest of the mix for later, so keep some dried rose petals on hand.

Relaxing Bath

Lavender Luxury Soak

Sometimes we need some pampering time. Put on some relaxing music, turn off or dim the lights and light a candle. This soak is so glorious. The recipe allows for plenty of soaks because you will undoubtedly want more.

Ingredients:

- 1 cup of Epsom salts

- 1 cup of baking soda

- 5-10 Drops of Lavender essential oil

Instructions:

1. Mix the ingredients and place them in a glass container.

2. Place a heaping pinch in each bath for a magnificent soak that is so refreshing you will never want to get out of the tub.

Pep Me up Soak

While most bath soaks are designed to relax you and get you ready for a good night's slumber, this one is perfect for when you just want to relax before a night out. You will be revived and ready to roll when you immerge from this soak.

Ingredients:

- 1 cup of sea salt

- 5 Drops of Lime essential oil

- 3 Drops of Peppermint essential oil

Instructions:

1. Mix the sea salt with essential oils and place it in a glass container for later.

2. Place about a tablespoon in a hot to warm bath and enjoy!

Lemon Up Bath Oil

Add some zest to your bath with this surprisingly delightful twist. It's perfect for an evening spent pampering yourself with a bit of pick-me-up power.

Ingredients:

- ½ cup of jojoba oil

- 6 Drops of Lemon essential oil

Instructions:

1. Combine the oils and pour them into a tub of hot water. You can make extra to store in an airtight glass container to use later.

Breast Milk

Following recipes can help lactating mothers improve their milk supply. They are nutritious food and tea recipes.

Steamed Quinoa

Ingredients:

- 1 cup of quinoa (rinsed)
- 1-2 tablespoons of sesame seeds
- Salt to taste
- Water

Instructions:

1. Pour the quinoa, sesame seeds, and salt into a pan.
2. Add water so it covers the quinoa by about an inch. Cook covered over medium heat for about 10 minutes or until all liquid has evaporated.

Honey and Cinnamon Tea

Ingredients:

- Honey
- 1 cup of warm water
- Cinnamon powder

Instructions:

1. Steep the teaspoon of cinnamon powder in the cup of warm water for five minutes before adding honey to taste instead of sugar.
2. Stir together, then drink while it's warm.

Fenugreek Tea

Ingredients:

- 2 tablespoons of fenugreek seeds

- 2 cups of water

Instructions:

1. Steep the fenugreek seeds in the water for two hours. Then, strain and drink the tea up to three times a day.

Advice:

- If using fenugreek, don't use cinnamon at the same time as they can cause a drop in blood sugar.

Ginger Tea

Ingredients:

- 2 teaspoons of fresh ginger juice

- 2 cups of water

Instructions:

1. Stir 2 teaspoons of fresh ginger juice into 2 cups of boiling water. Strain. Allow to cool, then drink. If desired, sweeten with honey.

2. Heat the ginger juice first, and then add cold water if you want cold instead of hot ginger tea. Consume it 1-2 times a day during the postpartum period.

3. Consuming this daily amount can improve breast milk production by 30%. In addition, this herb helps with morning sickness and nausea at the beginning of pregnancy.

Warm Cinnamon Milk

Ingredients:

- 1 cinnamon stick

- 1 cup of milk

Instructions:

1. Warm up the milk in the pot with a cinnamon stick. You can add honey if you desire. Transfer into a mug and enjoy.

Fennel Tea

Ingredients:

- 1/2 teaspoon of fennel seed

- 1 cup of water

- Honey, to taste

Instructions:

1. Steep the fennels seeds in boiling water for about five minutes, strain, and add honey to taste. Drink once a day.

Premenstrual Syndrome (PMS)

It happens when the monthly menstrual cycle is about to take place. As a result, women often have mood swings, bloating, headaches, nausea, etc. It makes them uncomfortable both mentally and physically, but with the help of the following herbal remedies, they can have relief from the symptoms that come with PMS.

Dandelion and Ginger Tea

Ingredients:

- 1 ½ C. boiling water

- 2 tsp. chopped dandelion root

- 1 ½ tsp. chopped ginger root

Tools Needed:

- Boiler

- Large mug

Instructions:

1. Boil just 1 ½ C. water.

2. In a large mug, add the roots, pour over the boiling water, and cover for 12 minutes to steep.

3. Take tea slowly and inhale the steam as well. Do this 6 times daily until you feel much better.

Advice:

- Do not take ginger if you're on medications for gallbladder diseases, kidney-related issues, or blood thinners.

Black Cohosh Syrup

Ingredients:

- 3 oz. black cohosh

- 2 ½ C. water

- 2 C. honey

Tools Needed:

- Saucepan

- Measuring cups

- Jar or Bottle (Sterilized)

Instructions:

1. Put the black cohosh and water together into a saucepan. Boil the water over low heat with the lids slightly open.

2. Leave the water to simmer until the water in the saucepan reduces by half.

3. Then, pour the content of the saucepan into a measuring cup. Cover the measuring cup with a cheesecloth and pour the mixture back into the saucepan through the cheesecloth. Wring the cheesecloth dry and dispose of it.

4. Put the saucepan over low heat, add some honey, and stir gently to mix.

5. Keep in the low heat until the mixture becomes slightly hot.

6. Then pour the syrup into a glass jar, let it cool down, and store it in a refrigerator. Label it.

7. Take 2 spoons daily till the symptoms stop.

Steady Cycle Tea

These herbs provide substantial nourishment and gentle kidney, lymphatic, and endocrine stimulation.

Ingredients:

- 1 cup dried nettle leaf

- 1 cup dried dandelion leaf

- ½ cup dried goldenrod leaf and flower

- ½ cup dried self-heal leaf and flower

- ¼ cup dried Tulsa leaf

Instructions:

1. Mix well all the dried herbs together in a bowl. Store in an airtight container.

2. Make a long infusion: Prepare a kettle of boiling water. Get 2 to 3 tablespoons of herbs per quart of water, then place in a mason jar or French press. Pour in boiling water, then cover for 8 hours or overnight.

3. Serve a cup daily until used what you have prepared. Keep refrigerated and drink within 3 days.

4. Don't drink continuously. Always do a break 1-2 weeks in between.

Daily Soothing Menstrual Tea

Ingredients:

- 2 teaspoons black haw root or bark

- 2 teaspoons passionflower

- 2 cups cold water

Instructions:

1. Mix the above herbs in a pot, pour cold water over them, soak overnight and strain the next day.

2. Drink half a cup up to four times daily. You can warm it if preferred.

Ringworm

It is a fungal infection that forms circular patches over the affected spot. Blister edges and redness usually accompany it. Ringworm is highly contagious and itchy, and it can spread to others with physical contact.

Fresh Garlic Compress

Ingredients:

- 2 1/3 C. steaming-hot water

- 2 ½ garlic clove, cut in half

Tools Needed:

- Silk cloth

- Boiler

Instructions:

1. Boil 2 ½ C. water, soak a soft cloth, and place the garlic cloves cut in half.

2. Slightly squeeze the cloth and apply it onto the affected areas, press over the affected regions for 15–20 minutes, then dispose of the garlic.

3. Repeat this twice daily, with new garlic cloves and cloth.

Advice:

- If you have sensitive skin, minimize the use of garlic and if there is any effect while using this remedy, stop immediately and consult with a health practitioner.

Goldenseal Balm

Ingredients:

- 3 oz. dried goldenseal root

- 1 C. coconut oil

- 1 oz. beeswax

- 23 drops of tea tree essential oil (optional)

Tools Needed:

- Saucepan, boiler

- Cheesecloth, sterilized jars

Instructions:

1. Prepare your saucepan and place over low heat. Add the goldenseal and coconut oil into the cover slightly and heat for 4–6 hours.

2. Turn off the heat and allow the infused oil to cool.

3. Strain through a cheesecloth into a new saucepan, wring the oil out of the cheesecloth and dispose of it.

4. Add beeswax to the mixture in the pan and let it simmer over low heat until the beeswax melts.

5. Test the consistency of your balm by dipping a clean spoon and put into a freezer for a few minutes. If it is too soft and you desire a thicker consistency, add more beeswax. If it is too thick and you wish for a smoother texture, add some hot water into the mixture.

6. Then, put the tea tree essential oil into the boiler, quickly pour the mixture into clean, dry jars or tins, and let cool completely before covering. Label your final balm.

7. Apply over the affected areas 2–3 times daily.

Advice:

- Avoid during pregnancy and if you are breastfeeding.

Urinary Tract Infection (UTI)

It is a condition that affects the urinary tracts and causes patients great pains during urination.

Cranberry Tea

Ingredients:

- 2C. grated fresh cranberries

- 10 C. boiling water

Tools Needed:

- Saucepan

Instructions:

1. Put grated cranberries and water into a saucepan and bring to a boil. It shouldn't take more than 15 minutes.

2. Turn off the heat and wait for the mixture to cool to room temperature.

3. When cool, strain it into a glass and drink immediately.

4. Take one glass every 3 hours until you notice changes or the pain subsides.

Advice:

- Anyone with low thyroid function should not take this remedy.

Dandelion Tincture

Ingredients:

- 10 oz. dandelion root, finely chopped

- 2 C. unflavored 80-proof vodka (40%)

Tools Needed:

- Sterilized jar

Instructions:

1. Prepare a sterilized pint jar, add the dandelion root and cover with vodka.

2. Cover the jar well and shake to mix.

3. Label the jar and store it in a cool, dry place for 4-6 weeks. Give your mixture a good shake once daily.

4. Cover the funnel with cheesecloth and strain the mixture into another pint jar. Make sure to squeeze out the cheesecloth till all the liquid comes out.

5. Transfer water into a glass bottle and always take it from there.

6. Take 1 spoon 4–5 times daily for a few days.

Wrinkles

They are a sign of aging, and it is perfectly normal. However, these concoctions would help prevent it and would help you manage it well if it's already manifesting.

Calendula Toner

Ingredients:

- 1C. Witch hazel
- ½ tbsps. calendula oil

Tools Needed:

- Dark-colored bottle
- Cotton cosmetic pad

Instructions:

1. Put witch hazel and calendula oil into a dark-colored glass and shake gently.
2. Apply 6 drops to your already washed face using a cotton cosmetic pad.
3. Use twice daily.

Aloe Facial Gel

Ingredients:

- 2 tbsps. Aloe Vera gel
- 2 tsp. coconut oil

Instructions:

1. Clean your face with clean water.
2. Apply some Aloe Vera gel, wait for your skin to absorb, and spread coconut oil over it.
3. Dampen a soft cloth in the warm water and spread it over your face.
4. Let it rest for 5 minutes, then use warm water to remove excess coconut oil.

5.   Repeat for a minimum of 5 times every week.

Plantain Skin Care

Yield: 5 tablespoons (75 g)

Ingredients:

- 3 tablespoons (45 ml) plantain-mixed oil

- 1 tablespoon (14 g) cocoa butter

- 1 tablespoon (14 g) beeswax

Tools Needed:

- Boiler

- Pot

- Cosmetic glass jar (dark-colored) or tin

Instructions:

1.   Heat all the ingredients delicately over low heat until liquefied in a pot.

2.   Mix well and remove from the heat. Pour the balm into a sterilized jar or jars and let it cool down entirely before putting the lids.

3.   Test the consistency of your balm by dipping a clean spoon and put into a freezer for a few minutes. If it is too soft and you desire a thicker consistency, add more beeswax.

4.   Label your skin product and store it out of the sunlight.

Yeast Infection

Garlic Suppository

Ingredients:

- 8 garlic cloves, peeled

- 7 tbsps. plain yogurt with live, active cultures

Tools Needed:

- Food processor or blender

- Container

Instructions:

1. Combine garlic and yogurt into a food processor and blend until fine and smooth.

2. Pour it into an airtight, clean container and freeze in your refrigerator until you're ready to use.

3. Add about 1/7 of the remedy to an applicator-free tampon, then insert the tampon into your vagina.

4. Leave for 90 minutes. Then, remove the tampon after use and dispose of it.

5. Do this three times daily for 4 days.

Advice:

- Use this remedy carefully if your skin is sensitive, as it can cause severe skin irritation. Be sure you don't react to garlic before using this herbal medicine.

Chamomile–Calendula Douche with Echinacea

Ingredients:

- 6 C. water

- 2 tbsps. dried chamomile

- 2 tbsps. dried calendula

- 2 tbsps. chopped dried Echinacea root

Tools Needed:

- Saucepan

Instructions:

1. Put water, chamomile, calendula, and echinacea in a saucepan and boil the mixture over medium heat.

2. After some time, reduce the heat and leave it to simmer.

3. When the water reduces by half, remove the saucepan from the heat and leave it somewhere till it cools down.

4. Freeze until needed. You can use ice cubes form to freeze it.

5. Whenever you need, clean yourself with a cotton cloth and apply 2 C. the mixture in the vagina.

6. Repeat just once after 3 days, and you'll start to see some improvements.

7. If the condition persists, consult with your health practitioner.

Advice:

- Do not undertake this procedure if you're allergic to the ragweed family plants.

Heartburn

Cleansing Aloe Water

Aloe water is detoxing and provides constipation relief and heartburn relief. In addition, it can help with stomach issues like constipation.

People also drink aloe water to boost their energy and immunity. However, if you haven't eaten aloe before, we recommend talking to a health professional first.

Ingest only a tiny amount at a time as aloe can have laxative effects.

Ingredients:

- ½ teaspoon or 1 tablespoon aloe gel

- 1 cup water

Instructions:

1. Scrape the gel from a fresh-cut leaf into a blender or food processor. If you have never ingested aloe before, start with just ½ teaspoon.

2. Blend with water and drink!

3. To make the beverage tastier, you can add other ingredients like 100% fruit juice, cucumber, parsley, or raw honey.

Herbal Creations To Eat

Rose and Vanilla Elixir

Roses elevate the soul, quiet and focus the psyche, feed the heart, and support love and reproduction. In addition, they are astringent and tonic for the stomach-related issues and eliminative tract. Vanilla beans unwind and calm, warm the gut, bring us into our bodies, offer gentle love potion properties, and taste delectable.

Ingredients:

- 3 to 5 vanilla beans, cut the long way and finely hacked or squeezed

- 1–16 ounces (470 ml) container approximately loaded up with new flower petals

- 1 cup (235 ml) excellent, smooth-tasting liquor

- 1 cup (320 g) unadulterated crude honey

Instructions:

1. Add the vanilla to the container of roses. Mix liquor and honey, blend well and pour over the roses and vanilla.

2. Spread to the rim of the container and use a chopstick to ensure the herbal material is well distributed in the mixture.

3. Top the container and store it in a cool, dim spot for 4 days up to about a month and a half—next, strain and tap into a perfect jug.

4. Take a dropper of the mixture straight into your mouth, or add to some hot or cold water or tea whenever you need a touch of motivation, unwinding, or break. It's a phenomenal gut-warming stomach-related guide and is excellent over vanilla frozen yogurt!

Salvia Fritts

Here is a more muddled strategy for making seared sage leaves.

Yield: 16 to 24 sage leaves

Ingredients:

- 1 cup of coconut oil or olive oil (according to your preference)

- 1/4 cup (40 g) flour

- 1/4 cup (30 g) cornstarch

- 1/2 cup (120 ml) soft drink water

- 16 to 24 flawless sage leaves

- Sea salt

Instructions:

1. Heat the oil in a skillet. While it warms, mix the flour, cornstarch, and soft drink water in a bowl and whisk well.

2. Coat the sage leaves with the mix. When the oil is heated, add 4 or 5 of the coated leaves to the skillet, and fry until brilliant earthy colored (about 1 minute on each side).

3. Remove fried leaves from the oil and rest on paper towels to drain the oil.

4. Once done, sprinkle sea salt over them and serve them on their own as a snack or as a side with burgers or other favorite meals. Enjoy!

Sage Pesto

This formula utilizes garlic scapes, the empty cutting edges that develop in the spring only preceding a flower. The scapes must be snipped to forestall that sprout, keeping the plant's vitality concentrated on the bulb of garlic under the ground. Scrapes have gotten somewhat of a delicacy lately and are regularly found in ranchers' business sectors in the spring.

Yield: 3 cups (720 g)

Ingredients:

- 2/3 cup (160 ml) olive oil, or more varying, separated

- 1 cup slashed garlic scapes

- 1 cup sage leaves

- 1/4 cup (50 g) slashed pecans, toasted

- 1/4 cup (35 g) ground Parmesan cheese

Instructions:

1. In a blender, join 1/4 cup (80 ml) of the olive oil, the garlic scapes, the sage leaves, and pecan nuts—mix on high.

2. While the ingredients are mixing, including the remaining 1/4 cup (80 ml) olive oil in a stream. Then, blend in the Parmesan cheese with a spatula. Add salt if required.

3. Store in refrigerator and serve with pasta, crackers, or fish. Enjoy!

Herbal Healing Teas

Tullis-Chamomile Tea

It helps decrease cholesterol levels, eases stress, lowers blood sugar, and helps with cold symptoms.

Servings: 5 cups

Ingredients:

- 5 cups water

- A handful of holy basil leaves, fresh (or 1 ½ tablespoon holy basil, dried)

- 2 tablespoons fresh chamomile flowers (or 1 tablespoon chamomile flowers, dried)

- Raw honey to taste

Instructions:

1. Steep basil leaves and chamomile in hot water for 5–10 minutes. Strain and sweeten to taste. You can also serve this tea cold with ice.

2. Use less when using dried leaves and flowers, as dry herbs have a more intense flavor.

Parsley Tea

It helps with indigestion, kidney health, bladder health, and cramping.

Parsley is full of antioxidants and vitamins. It's anti-inflammatory and has been used to ease period cramps. If you have kidney disease, high blood pressure, or diabetes, talk to your doctor before drinking parsley tea. If you're pregnant, don't drink the tea. No one should drink it longer than two weeks in a row.

Ingredients: (makes 2 cups of tea):

- 4 tablespoons parsley, fresh, chopped (or 4 teaspoons parsley, dried)

- 2 cups hot water

- Raw honey to taste

Instructions:

1. Steep parsley in hot water for 5–7 minutes. You can use a tea strainer or steep the leaves in the water and strain them later.

2. Add raw honey for sweetness. Lemon juice is also tasty.

Peppermint Sun Tea

It is a unique and excellent recipe for a hot summer day.

Ingredients:

- Half cup or one cup dried or fresh peppermint leaves

- Half gallon of tap water

Instructions:

1. Put peppermint and water in half a gallon of a glass jar.

2. Put in a sunny area for two to eight hours.

3. Move to the fridge and let it cool. Enjoy it as a cold drink.

Tummy Tea

Ingredients:

- 1 part Chamomile flowers, dried

- 1 part Catnip leaf, dried

- 1 part Lemon balms leaf dried

Instructions:

1. Combine equal parts of lemon balm, chamomile, and catnip thoroughly in a jar. Then cap and label.

2. Then, to brew the tea, put one tablespoon of the tea blend into eight ounces of boiled water. Then allow it to steep for three to four minutes.

3.   You can add sweeteners as per your taste, or you may not. Finally enjoy.

4.   Remember that chamomile will get bitter if steeped for a long time.

Anti-Aging Tea

Preparation Time: 5 minutes.

Servings: 2

Ingredients:

- 1 teaspoon dandelion root

- 1 teaspoon burdock root

- 1 teaspoon Schisandra berries

- 1 tablespoon nettle leaves

- 1 teaspoon hibiscus flowers, dried

- 1 teaspoon chamomile-extract

- 2 cups of boiling water

Instructions:

1.   Combine all the herbs above, cover with boiling water, and steep for two to three minutes.

2.   Strain to a cup and enjoy.

Calm Down Tea

Servings: 2

Ingredients:

- 1 teaspoon powdered ginger
- 1 teaspoon powdered valerian root
- 1 teaspoon powdered pleurisy root
- 2 cups boiling water

Instructions:

1. Combine the above herbals in a nonmetallic container and cover with boiling water; steep for 30 minutes; cool and strain.

2. When needed, take one tablespoon at a time, up to two cups a day.

Shake-It-Off Tea

Servings: 1

Ingredients:

- 1 to 2 teaspoons peppermint leaves
- 1 teaspoon chopped dried valerian root
- 1 cup boiling water

Instructions:

1. Mix the above herbs in a mug and pour boiling water over them; allow to steep for 20 to 30 minutes; strain.

2. Drink up to 1 cup per day, as needed.

Conclusion

It was proven by various research that herbal plants are useful, helpful, valuable, and resourceful in aiding various conditions and diseases. They cover different aspects of the body's health. It focuses not only on a single problem but on other issues that it could do. Herbal medicines had been the real-life saviors of numerous native people or native tribes, as they were the only existing medicine in ancient times. Moreover, it got better when time passed, new technology, and new studies arose. Studies gave much knowledge needed when a person involves themselves with herbal medicine. Many visible improvements occurred with these researches as well, as they have been helping explore the maximum quality of each plant. Numerous experiments, approval, money, budgeting, and science had reached this moment of innovation. As a result, ignorance has been disregarded, and lesser harm occurs. Nonetheless, many studies are still needed to extend greater knowledge for more extensive queries. Some herbs are not still supported with facts, but they are indeed supported with real-life experiences.

Herbal plants are multi-functioning. May they be on trees or grounds; they exist to aid numerous conditions all at once. Plus, it is liberating to find medicines that can be as reachable as a person's garden. Their cost is also helpful for various people, as they are proven to be working but can be self-provided or even bought at an affordable price. They are famous when they are prepared as teas, pills, supplements, or creams. They are seldomly used freshly due to some circumstances like poisons.

Unfortunately, they are also limited based on their guidelines. Therefore, some factors must be considered before using a single herb plant.

Despite herbal plants' benefits, some possible side effects still could pose harmful results that can last a lifetime. It is best to follow protocol guidelines and even seek professional help to ensure everyone is safe. They might aid in almost similar conditions, but they are different in certain aspects. It may be their physical appearance, chemicals, compounds, habitat, or even season. Some are poisonous, and others have external factors that lead them to be harmful.

It is in great awe that up until this moment, herbal medicines are not fading, and they are still dominating a more significant part of the world. It is the best gift given by the native people or the ancient people to their race. Herbal plants or herbal medicine have been passed on from various generations, and they have never been a disappointment. It is crucial to be knowledgeable enough before engaging in any plants. Different plants must also be consumed with proper timelines and dosages, preventing harmful results. Therefore, it is essential to stay healthy and find the perfect medicine to fit a person's body.

The main mission of this book is the importance of educating yourself about the spiritual aspect of using natural medicines found in the mountains, forests, deserts, or plains all over North America. If you learn to listen to your heart and trust your intuition, you will be able to follow an authentic path toward physical healing and spiritual guidance.

This book was designed to catch the attention of Native Americans and anyone who loves herbal remedies but hasn't quite started on an herbal journey yet.

www.ingramcontent.com/pod-product-compliance
Lightning Source LLC
Chambersburg PA
CBHW051548030726
47592CB00001B/183